THE FUTURE
OF THE GLOBAL ECONOMY:
Towards a Long Boom?

ORGANISATION FOR ECONOMIC CO-OPERATION AND DEVELOPMENT

ORGANISATION FOR ECONOMIC CO-OPERATION AND DEVELOPMENT

Pursuant to Article 1 of the Convention signed in Paris on 14th December 1960, and which came into force on 30th September 1961, the Organisation for Economic Co-operation and Development (OECD) shall promote policies designed:

- to achieve the highest sustainable economic growth and employment and a rising standard of living in Member countries, while maintaining financial stability, and thus to contribute to the development of the world economy;

- to contribute to sound economic expansion in Member as well as non-member countries in the process of economic development; and

- to contribute to the expansion of world trade on a multilateral, non-discriminatory basis in accordance with international obligations.

The original Member countries of the OECD are Austria, Belgium, Canada, Denmark, France, Germany, Greece, Iceland, Ireland, Italy, Luxembourg, the Netherlands, Norway, Portugal, Spain, Sweden, Switzerland, Turkey, the United Kingdom and the United States. The following countries became Members subsequently through accession at the dates indicated hereafter: Japan (28th April 1964), Finland (28th January 1969), Australia (7th June 1971), New Zealand (29th May 1973), Mexico (18th May 1994), the Czech Republic (21st December 1995), Hungary (7th May 1996), Poland (22nd November 1996) and Korea (12th December 1996). The Commission of the European Communities takes part in the work of the OECD (Article 13 of the OECD Convention).

Publié en français sous le titre :

L'ÉCONOMIE MONDIALE DE DEMAIN :
Vers un essor durable ?

Foreword

As part of the preparations for EXPO 2000 – the World Exposition in Hanover, Germany – the OECD Forum for the Future is organising a series of four conferences to take place beforehand around the theme of "People, Nature and Technology: Sustainable Societies in the 21st Century". The series will consider four key areas of human activity: technology, economy, society and government. The conferences will explore possible evolutions of key variables and analyse different development paths in order to expose some of the main policy implications and options. Each conference will provide analysis of underlying trends and policy directions. However, the overall aim of the series is to build a comprehensive foundation for assessing the critical choices likely to face citizens and decision makers in the next century.

The entire series benefits from special sponsorship by EXPO 2000 and four German banks – Bankgesellschaft Berlin, DG Bank Deutsche Genossenschaftsbank AG, Nord LB/Norddeutsche Landesbank, and Westdeutsche Landesbank Girozentrale (WestLB). Additional financial support is provided by numerous Asian, European and North American partners of the OECD Forum for the Future.

This was the second conference in the series. It was hosted by the DG Bank Deutsche Genossenschaftsbank AG in Frankfurt, Germany, on 2-3 December 1998. The theme was "21st Century Economic Dynamics: Anatomy of a Long Boom".

After a day and a half of discussion, conference participants concluded that the world is on the threshold of a tantalising opportunity – the possibility of a sustained long boom over the first decades of the next millennium. A confluence of forces – particularly the transition to the knowledge society, the emergence of a global economy, and the pursuit of environmental stability – could come together to propel huge improvements in wealth-creating capacity and well-being worldwide. But for this to happen, major advances would have to be made on two policy fronts. First, exceptional efforts would be needed nationally and internationally to encourage continuous innovation and high levels of investment. And second, substantial leaps would be needed in levels of international co-operation on such matters as the diffusion of technology and knowledge, market integration and environmental transformation. The aim of this conference was to assess the prospects for a long boom in the next couple of decades and to explore the policy strategies that could help it become a reality.

The conference was organised into three sessions. The first looked at the generic factors likely to determine whether or not long-run economic dynamism will continue in the future. The second addressed specific driving forces likely to accompany economic dynamism in the next century and potentially spark the high growth rates of a long boom over the next twenty to thirty years. Finally, the third session considered the way policy choices are likely to influence the playing out of different scenarios for a 21st century long boom.

This publication brings together the papers presented at the meeting as well as an introductory contribution and summary of the main points of the discussions prepared by the Secretariat. The book is published on the responsibility of the Secretary-General of the OECD.

Table of Contents

Anatomy of a Long Boom

by

Wolfgang Michalski, Riel Miller and Barrie Stevens
OECD Secretariat, Advisory Unit to the Secretary-General

1. Introduction

One of the most promising and commonly evoked vistas of the future centres on the dazzling potential of new technologies. From that perspective many of today's profound problems, such as unemployment, malnutrition, disease and global warming could be solved through the clever application of breakthroughs in computer science, genetic engineering, nano-device construction and new materials creation. These hopes are not unlike those of a century ago, when the development and diffusion of technologies such as electricity, the radio and the internal combustion engine promised a new era of human well-being.

With the benefit of hindsight, however, it is clear that realising the potential of late 19th century new technologies required major economic and social transformations. Extending breakthroughs beyond the inventor's lab, imagining new applications, realising broad diffusion of initially unfamiliar technology and achieving deep integration of cutting-edge techniques – all of these processes were both protracted and difficult. In the end, many landmarks had to be changed, from where and how people lived to what and how firms produced. This in turn entailed the overthrow of old patterns, of entrenched expectations and accepted "common sense" notions – not to mention established management theories and hardened political realities.

What is striking is that similarly dramatic transformations, economy- and society-wide, seem once again to be a realistic prospect. Although there have certainly been other periods in recent history when the outlook for humankind was filled with promise, the current conjuncture constitutes one of those rare moments when a confluence of diverse and numerous developments generates new, potentially radical opportunities. These are not a forgone conclusion, for the necessary policies are highly ambitious and only just on the horizon for decision makers. But the fact remains that humanity could reap huge rewards if it is ready to undertake equally significant changes.

Two factors largely account for that unconventionally strong conclusion – one is methodological, the other conjunctural. First, the analytical method adopted here for exploring long-term possibilities is neither partial nor linear, characteristics common and justified for shorter-term forecasting. A systemic and interdisciplinary approach is what enables the identification of opportunities for more radical evolutionary and intentional transformations. Secondly, on the basis of this methodology, it becomes apparent that the current historical conjuncture – with its specific technological, economic and social developments – holds the seeds that could blossom into a period of above-average growth. Some may attribute the sense of exceptional opportunity to end-of-century jitters and obligatory optimism by governments at the launch of a new millennium. Such scepticism is only natural. However, the assessment offered over the following pages tends to confirm the view that the historical door is now open to both a dramatic wave of socio-technical dynamism and the rapid pace of expansion that characterises a long boom.

Looking to the past, no single cause accounts for either long upsurges of economic dynamism or historically specific phases of faster and slower growth. A bundle of factors made important contributions both to the creation of a prolonged period of dynamic possibilities and the succession of cyclical booms and busts. Certainly a crucial role was played by technological innovations – from the steam engine to the microprocessor – that improved productivity, gave rise to previously unimagined products, and opened up vast new sectors for economic and social activity. In addition to supportive demographic factors, powerful contributions to economic dynamism came from expanded and more open national and international flows of goods, services, finance and ideas. These trends were further encouraged by steady declines in transaction costs – facilitated by more efficient market rules, transportation systems and communication technologies – which in turn fuelled gains from trade and international economic specialisation. Other major forces nourishing long-run economic dynamism arose from significant improvements in social, educational and health status as well as the evolution of political institutions, in many but not all jurisdictions, towards greater democratic accountability and administrative effectiveness.

Few dispute the importance of these ingredients in creating the conditions that nurture long-run productivity growth and wealth creation. Less evident is the recipe(s) to ensure that such dynamism not only continues over the next few decades but is also accompanied by a phase of above-average expansion – a long boom where world GDP growth could be in the 4% per annum range and might lift world per capita GDP growth rates above the 3% mark. Then there is the open question of the extent to which overall economic dynamism, and the long boom that may go with it, actually correspond to people's aspirations.

Entering a new millennium, concerns are being raised not only about the sustainability but also about the desirability of this path. For some it is too turbulent and uncertain, bringing too many changes too quickly. For others the problem is change itself: the disruption of existing patterns, values and social structures is viewed as either unnecessary or inimical to human well-being. Certainly, long-run economic dynamism has, throughout its various phases, produced tremendous wealth, but it has also inflicted high costs. The last two centuries have seen massive disruptions to established patterns of work (from farm to factory) and everyday living (from rural to urban). The planet's ecosystem has been put under tremendous strain. Inequality within and between nations has, from a number of perspectives, increased. Even deeply entrenched values and cultural norms have been called into question. No wonder some see the dynamic past as a precedent to be avoided in the future.

The chapters in this book grapple with these issues. This first chapter provides an overview of prospects for both long-run economic dynamism and a long boom (Section 2) and a summary of the policies required to make them happen (Section 3). In Chapter 2, Richard Lipsey looks at the generic factors likely to determine whether or not long-run economic dynamism will continue into the future. The next three chapters turn to the specific driving forces likely to propel economic dynamism in the next century and potentially spark the high growth rates of a long boom over the next twenty to thirty years. Each chapter looks at a specific set of catalysts and constraints: Chapter 3, by Peter Schwartz, Eamonn Kelly and Nicole Boyer, deals with the transition to a knowledge economy and society; in Chapter 4, Horst Siebert and Henning Klodt look at the emergence of a global economy for goods, services, finance and technology; and Chapter 5, by Alain Lipietz, considers the challenge of environmental sustainability. Finally, in Chapter 6, DeAnne Julius assesses various policy options on the basis of three plausible scenarios for a 21st century long boom.

2. What is a long boom?

Long booms are exceptional events; there have been relatively few in the history of human economic development. For example, the two rapid growth periods of the last 130 years – one in the latter decades of the 19th century and the other after the Second World War – made major contributions to pushing the long-run historical average to a higher level. An anatomy of these past booms reveals two basic features. First, a boom's above-average pace of development is part of a longer, century-spanning flow. This powerful tide provided by long-run economic dynamism is a distinct phenomenon that should not be confused with the shorter cyclical expansions and contractions that fluctuate around the historical trend. Secondly, there is an interdependent constellation of diverse forces that work together in a specific historical conjuncture to spark the unusually fast rates of socio-economic change and productivity growth that characterise a long boom. Both of these features appear to be present in the current context.

Long-run economic dynamism: foundations for a long boom

For four centuries prior to 1820, the twelve countries that form the core of Western Europe experienced average growth in per capita income of 0.2% per annum. From 1820 to 1870 the pace increased considerably, reaching 0.6% per annum on a worldwide basis and then ratcheting up to twice the previous rate at 1.3% between 1870 and 1913. The next burst of world per capita income growth, three times that during the preceding war-torn period, occurred from 1950 to 1973 at the pace of 2.9% p.a. Since then, the world average has been closer to 1.2%. Viewed over the entire span from 1820 to 1996, these average per capita growth rates, in the face of very large population increases, are testimony to the tremendous wealth-creating capacity unleashed by economic dynamism. This was economic and social transformation on a par with the most significant – and much more protracted – leaps in the development of human civilisation.

Systemic chemistry

Certainly strong growth in investment, in the capabilities of the labour force and in trade is crucial for very long periods of sustained economic development. But the dynamic element that drives change forward is the systemic chemistry that either catalyses the process or stifles it. Recent events cast the role of system functionality or dysfunctionality into stark relief. The dire consequences of systems failure are evident, for instance, in the demise of Soviet command planning or the post-1970s plunge of many "debt crisis" countries into even deeper poverty. As for the immense benefits of system functionality, it can be seen in the postwar convergence of Europe and Japan to American income levels and the significant economic take-off of many Asian countries over the last two decades.

The historical record shows that long-run economic dynamism is orchestral. Like the single notes and chords of a melody that are then woven into a polyphony, a dynamic economy arises from a constellation of factors that together create a symphonic system. And, as with the multiple threads of polyphonic music, there can be harmony and dissonance as different melodies change, intertwine, catch-up and fall behind. Thus the current "Asian crisis", with its dissonant chords, confirms rather than denies the contention that economic dynamism arises from the combination of many distinct and diverse technological, institutional and cultural elements into a functioning system. Indeed, the ongoing development of an innovation-driven economy and society depends on a process of falling behind and catching up, a kind of disequilibrium among and between scientific breakthroughs, social structures, organisational models and value systems.

This systems perspective also reveals the basic attributes that are essential for sustaining economic dynamism over almost two centuries, through many short- to medium-term crises and into the future. The characteristics that combat stagnation and renew the capacity and desire to change over time can be grouped into three areas: the aspirations and imperatives that emerge from the co-evolution of democracy and a competitive market-place; the capacities to innovate and adapt that are allowed to flower when there is pluralism, transparency and openness; and the range of cultural values, such as a respect for both civil liberties and societal obligations, that facilitate a perpetual search for ways of balancing co-operation with competition and security with risk-taking. Succinctly, long-run economic dynamism is sustained by combining adaptability and innovation with good information based on clear and efficient incentives and signals. All of these traits are in turn shaped by the myriad institutions, explicit laws and tacit rules that set parameters for everyday behaviour.

Of course, systems that are hierarchical, closed and riddled with intolerance are capable of short bursts of development, particularly if the technological, organisational and social structures are imposed from above during wartime and/ or a period of forced industrialisation. But, as the record of this century shows, these are not dynamic systems capable of sustaining long-run economic development. Furthermore, as is gradually becoming apparent, the uniform and hierarchical formulas of the past are not only less desirable but also likely to be much less efficient in the future. Meeting a diversity of demand is breeding an ever greater diversity of supply, which in turn depends on the competitive encouragement of initiative, customisation and a relaxing of centralised controls. In fact, although the basic characteristics that sustain long-run economic dynamism remain fairly constant, the specific ways of realising these attributes change over time. For example, 19th century democracy and trading institutions offered tremendous scope in that era, as did the organisations of mass production, mass consumption and mass government that have dominated the 20th century. However, these institutional and organisational forms are unlikely to be adequate to the conditions and tasks of the 21st century. What, then, are the prospects for a continuation of long-run economic dynamism?

General determinants of long-run economic dynamism

Viewed from an aggregate perspective, the sources of economic dynamism in the 21st century are bound to share many characteristics with those of the century now drawing to a close. Continued expansion of the world's population, along with the unabated pressures of human needs and desires, will certainly drive economic activity. But beneath the surface of these basic demands, the general determinants of long-run economic dynamism can be divided into five categories. First, though not pre-eminent, are the tools or pervasive technologies that humans use to enhance their capacity to create value. Secondly, there are the institutional frameworks – economic (the firm), social (the household) and collective (government) – for managing risk, reducing uncertainty, enhancing flexibility and improving transparency. The third pillar of long-run economic dynamism is made up of the quantitative inputs (such as natural resources or fixed and human capital) that provide the ingredients for production. The fourth and fifth supports of a dynamic economy are the productivity-enhancing competitive forces and motivating aspirations that drive innovation, the reallocation of the full range of resources. Looking to the next few decades, the trends in each of these specific long-run factors will determine the course of economic dynamism.

- Technology

It emerged quite clearly in the previous book in this series, *21st Century Technologies: Promises and Perils of a Dynamic Future* (OECD, Paris, 1998), that there is a technological basis for a future wave of productivity-enhancing innovation in what, how and where economic value is produced. Humanity's technical genius has, on the eve of the next Millennium, opened up new territory in the basic fields of information technology, genetic engineering and materials science – leading to potentially powerful knock-on effects for other areas such as energy generation, transportation, medicine and agriculture. The possibilities are nothing short of astounding across almost the complete spectrum of human activity. New horizons are appearing for communications, the sharing of knowledge, the co-ordination of production, the execution of transactions and the inspiration of ideas through a sharing of culture and insight. Exciting and risky advances are being made in biology as the mechanics of nature's codes and building blocks begin to reveal the secrets of how to design and repair living organisms. Inanimate matter is also unlocking its mysteries as quantum theory and nano-level techniques begin to show the way towards new substances and methods for manipulating the atomic components of the universe.

Looking to the 21st century, the technological possibilities seem well within the same class of pervasive inventions as the steam engine, the railway, electricity, the telephone and the internal combustion engine. However, like the tools of the past, those of the future will be useful only to the extent that economic and social capacities keep pace. People choose to make use of tools to create and innovate. Thus, putting tomorrow's technologies to use will hinge on the desire and capacity to embrace socio-technical dynamism. Here, institutional factors will play a decisive role. As many schools of growth theory have made clear, economic take-off depends on the introduction of institutional innovations, from judicial due process and Taylorist management to universal compulsory schooling and economy-wide accounting standards. In the past, the institutional shells that structured the allocation of decision-making power have regularly been reconfigured, be it through the advent of universal suffrage or the shift in responsibility to professional managers from owners of the firm. Such upheaval has not vanished from the world stage – indeed, there is evidence that a new wave of institutional change will mark the outset of the next century.

- Institutions

Institutions, along with the rules and attitudes they sustain, are in motion throughout the world. At global, regional, national and local levels, in developed, developing and former centrally planned economies, public and private sector institutions are changing – in many cases radically. In the public sector governments are undertaking major reforms through privatisation, regulatory reform, programme redesign or devolution, and modernisation of state administrative methods. In the private sector, established managerial practices such as hierarchical command and control structures are being delayered, with radical implications for firms from New York to Vladivostok and from the leading-edge knowledge creator to the traditional artisanal niche producer. At the international level, governments are negotiating frameworks with respect to electronic commerce and climate change. Multinational corporations are reconfiguring global supply networks, value chains and organisational structure. Local firms are going global in an effort to find markets as the costs of discovering suppliers and buyers, sending goods or downloading information all fall. Significant efforts at regional integration are driving the search for flexibility and the redistribution of activities and factor inputs by both business and government. At the national level, public sector policy mixes are, in most places, shifting away from direct and frequently uniform service provision towards more decentralised, regulatory and individually managed approaches. Locally, there is a resurgence of activism and networking as people at work and at home assume greater responsibilities.

Overall, the closing years of the 20th century are witnessing what some have called a "paradigm shift" – a sweeping challenge to the one-way hierarchical division of labour and its power relationships. Such institutional discontinuity, in so far as it opens up the possibility of deploying new technologies and liberating innovation, may be a powerful stimulus to the continuation of economic dynamism. Making the right policy choices will clearly play a decisive role. So too will the availability and distribution of key inputs like fixed and human capital. Here there is good reason to expect continuity with past trends.

• Inputs

The availability of quantitative inputs, from tangible resources like energy and raw materials to intangible inputs like financial and intellectual capital, is not likely to hinder the continuation of long-run economic dynamism. Relaxing of certain important resource constraints of the past could be encouraged by trends, particularly in OECD countries, towards a growing share of intangibles in total output and the introduction of technologies, production methods and consumption patterns that are less resource-intensive. What is more difficult to anticipate in general terms is the extent to which cyclical forces and distributional problems could create bottlenecks and recessions, or open up new sources of supply and spark economic booms. In the past, mass migrations redistributed available labour, inadequate savings rates provoked credit crises, and postwar rebuilding generated sharp upturns. In the future there are likely to be many of these local and/or more widely diffused disequilibria, provoked by misguided or deliberate policy or even by chance events. Already on the horizon are a series of issues: large increases in the share of elderly in the total population in most OECD countries and China, the unequal geographical distribution of the supply of capital (savings) and demand (high-return investment opportunities), and the divergence in income levels between high and low contributors to climate change.

• Competition

Although these imbalances generate hardship and adjustment that in a world of perfect market information might not exist, in the real world such signals and responses generate the trends and allocative flows that are regular sources of improvements in the use and efficiency of resources as well as in institutions and policies. At the micro level, where resource allocation decisions are actually taken, such disequilibria are frequently provoked by confrontation with the constraint of competitive forces. In the private sector, the fact that companies come up with ways of being more productive and undercutting competitors on the basis of price, quality or both is usually a decisive reason to change resource allocation. In the public sector, the failure to meet voters' expectations often leads to either a change in policy or government – sometimes both.

The record of the past two centuries is fairly clear: competitive forces have been given ever greater scope to operate. Transparency and openness have improved as voters gain the right to know and consumers reap the benefits of freer intra- and international trade as well as antitrust and consumer protection laws. Once again, looking to the future, there are grounds for expecting that the competitive forces driving change will continue to operate and even gain greater hold on a wider range of activities. Supported by technological and institutional changes that facilitate information-sharing, the breadth and depth of comparative assessment appear set to grow. For example, developments such as the introduction of the euro and the spread of electronic commerce will simplify comparison shopping, while international efforts to eliminate bribery should reduce the secrecy that corruption demands.

- Aspirations

Increases in the transparency upon which the competition of ideas or items for sale depends also promise to spur the motivating aspirations that have driven considerable change in the past. From the most basic hopes for a life free of hunger and oppression to the pursuit of greater self-awareness and fulfilment, humanity's desires continue to create pressure for change. Long-run economic dynamism seems unlikely to falter on the demand-side limits of market saturation and excess material abundance, for several reasons. First of all, among the wealthy there is evidence of a shift to the pursuit of non-material and qualitative interests and pleasures. Secondly, the majority of humanity still has a long way to go to meet even minimum standards of material well-being. And thirdly, it seems likely that in the future the relationship between people's aspirations and the environment will be changing in ways that require rethinking what, where, and how people produce and consume. For the foreseeable future these processes should serve as driving forces for change in general and towards more democratic forms of political expression in particular.

Taken as an ensemble, the prospects for the diffusion of new pervasive technologies, efficiency-enhancing institutional change, continued availability of production inputs, the spread of competitive forces and the ongoing pressure of motivating aspirations lend credence to the view that a continuation of long-run economic dynamism is feasible. That does not necessarily imply that growth or change will be more rapid or profound than in the past. There is an open relationship between the general forces that set the stage for economic dynamism and the specific rates at which wealth-creating capacity increases. This ambiguity has not stopped some people, possessed of end-of-the-millennium sentiment and the recent euphoria over American economic growth, to declare the triumph of a single model of economic dynamism over all other approaches. Such a perspective overlooks the rich diversity of specific economic models and mistakes the common attributes of long-run economic dynamism with the particular historical conditions and policies that make it happen. A related error is to assume that creating the conditions conducive to long-run economic dynamism will necessarily give rise to the above-average growth rates of a long boom; the specific catalysts and constraints will determine actual outcomes.

Confident hopes that the economic dynamism of this century will continue into the first decades of the next are not as easily extended to the question of whether or not a new long boom is plausible. The prospects for tomorrow's long boom will be decided by the way humanity responds to three momentous opportunities, examined below.

Specific forces driving the next long boom: global catalysts and constraints

A confluence of historically specific technological, economic and social factors need to fall into place so that the global average rate of per capita income growth can be pushed over the 3% mark for the next few decades. Looking to the first quarter of the next century, there would appear to be three primary movers – or sets of catalysts and constraints – capable of launching a long boom: the development of a global knowledge economy and society; the emergence of a global economy based on international trade, investment and technology flows; and the pursuit of global environmental sustainability.

Each of these currents could make a major contribution not only to sustaining a dynamic economy but also to sparking a period of above-average growth – a twenty-year long boom to mark the start of the next century. Equally, the collapse of efforts to share ideas, open up markets and attain sustainability could seriously undermine overall economic prospects and dash the hopes for a long boom. With little disagreement about the positive implications should the catalysts win the day, or the negative implications should the constraints prevail, the main analytical and policy differences concern how to support the former rather than the latter. With this in mind, each of the subsections below touches, first on links between the prospects for a long boom and a particular set of catalysts and constraints, and then on the fairly marked differences of view regarding what to do.

The transition to a global knowledge economy and society

The full emergence of the knowledge economy and society, at first in a number of OECD countries, promises a shift from the abundance of uniformity in the mass-production, mass-consumption and mass-government era to the kaleidoscope of individual creativity in the "Internet era". This transition to the predominance of knowledge as input, output and structuring feature of the economy and society has been building for some time, particularly since the ascent of the service sector started to put a greater premium on closer contact between customers and producers. At the core of this transformation is the growing capacity to add the intangible and highly valued conceptual input of a personal design, a unique pattern or a customised form. Nothing better symbolises this take-off than the explosion of the Internet as an economic and social force. As much as the automobile, a tangible industrial product, came to symbolise the synergies of the mass-production and mass-consumption era, the future is likely to give the Internet with its intangible digital services the status of icon of the knowledge economy. The Internet is the facilitator of a much vaster system that spans all digital information, from biotech to nanotech, and all sectors of the economy, from agriculture to art. Like the automobile before it, the spread of this "network of networks" could be a primary force behind a long boom. The potential is there for a leap on a par with the dramatic changes that distinguish the living and working conditions of the average person of the 19th *versus* 20th centuries.

Yet the prospect of such major changes does not assure that the shift to a knowledge economy and society will provoke the above-average growth rates of a long boom. Indeed, the open question is whether or not the catalysts pushing a transition will be sufficiently strong, not only to overcome the constraints but also to drive change rapidly and broadly enough. Laboratory breakthroughs and product innovations offer no assurance of wide diffusion or of a profound reorganisation of the ways in which people work and live. Furthermore, as is well known, the spread of information technology has so far failed to produce a demonstrable productivity take-off. As with earlier transformations, like the move from craft to factory production in the previous century, there are likely to be very rocky phases as the requisite institutions, habits and cultural expectations are built up through a process of trial and error. Profound transitions in how and where people live and work as well as what they produce and consume do not come easily. Many habits and customs are called into question without obvious replacements for easing human interaction and reassuring people with the familiar. Introducing the points of reference and common language that will allow virtual reality to seem as normal as parking the car or grooming the horse will demand considerable effort and experimentation. As the pioneers of electronic commerce and biotechnology are beginning to recognise, the everyday trust taken for granted when conducting a transaction at the corner store for old fashioned, non-genetically engineered produce does not come as automatically when the order passes through a new medium for a new product.

There is still a long way to go to create the infrastructure for translating the potential for low-cost knowledge-based transactions into an economy and society capable of unique production and consumption. These are still the early days of deciding on the basic conventions or rules of the road, akin to the time before the now so familiar traffic light attribution of stop to red and go to green. On the Internet, for example, there is still no universally available, easy and efficient means of ensuring privacy, contract enforcement, consumer redress, payment for copying intellectual property, a predictable tax regime or universal access to what is rapidly becoming an essential service. Little has been done to address the social and economic implications of a major reshuffling of winners and losers – the ascendancy of the wired over the unwired.

With respect to access, the good news is that technological advances are reducing the cost of connecting and slowly chipping away at the elitist complexity of information technology. The bad news is that the majority of the world's population is still largely excluded from even basic telephony. Other, less directly related infrastructure will also need to emerge if the knowledge economy is to reach its potential. The proliferation of independent knowledge producers and consumers implies significant adaptation: of labour codes to new forms of work organisation; of regulatory safeguards able to manage new materials, genetic combinations and a proliferation of unique products; of educational suppliers and certifiers to the lifelong acquisition of knowledge; of social insurance and support systems to different patterns of earning over a day, a year and a lifetime.

How these challenges are overcome will largely determine the extent to which the emergence of the knowledge economy – on balance – ends up serving as a catalyst or constraint to a long boom. If there is a rapid, wide and deep diffusion of the new digitally-enabled economy, then there is a good chance that its creative potential will be realised through huge investments in: more efficient, intuitively accessible information technology; a vast range of new genetic permutations; the first quantum gizmos; a renewed learning infrastructure that goes beyond the mass-production school system; a huge range of diagnostic, preventative and non-invasive medical treatments and services; an across-the-board conversion of energy generation and conservation technologies; massive renewal of the housing stock as people change both the location and architecture of their homes; and more. A twenty-year boom arising from this surge in investment and productivity seems plausible. Alternatively, the transition to the knowledge economy could end up advancing slowly and failing to diffuse widely. Along this path the gap between information haves and have-nots might grow even wider, exacerbating the social costs of change. This would in all likelihood lead to investments that never pay off due to both lack of markets and the absence of multiplier effects that arise from synchronised, broad-based change.

In the end, the consequences for growth of a transition to the knowledge economy could end up being negative. An opportunity could be missed and the outset of the next century might instead be described as the long stagnation. The stark contrast between these two outcomes is partly what fuels the debate between those who advocate taking an activist approach to building the infrastructure of a global knowledge economy and those who believe it will emerge without making much extra effort. The activist versus non-activist positions are also distinguished by contrasting assessments of the scale of the changes implied by the shift to a world dominated by the production of knowledge. Finally, there is another schism that separates the two camps: their views regarding the interdependency of the transition to the knowledge economy with both the emergence of global markets and global environmental sustainability. Here again, as discussed in each of the following two subsections, there is a clear divide between those who do and those who do not advocate concerted action to make sure the catalysts rather than the constraints succeed in propelling tomorrow's long boom.

The emergence of a global economy for goods, services, finance and technology

The pace at which the world economy moves towards or away from open and transparent global markets for goods, services, capital and technology will be one of the decisive factors determining whether or not there is a long boom. At its most positive, the ambitious goal of creating fully global markets should allow consumers, producers, savers and investors to achieve greater efficiency and to be more innovative. The dividends generated by considerable improvements in allocative efficiency could then be devoted not only to meeting the investment demands of structural change, but also to dealing with regional inequalities and compensating those whose human and/or financial capital are devalued or destroyed in the process.

Alternatively, negative factors such as the potential for new forms or outbreaks of collusion, protectionism and financial volatility could end up undermining efficiency, imposing higher risk premiums and impeding change at the micro level. Here the downside risk is stagnation, as less transparency and reduced competition slow the development and diffusion of the knowledge economy, new institutional frameworks and the redeployment of a range of resources to more productive (and environmentally sustainable) uses. As a result, wealth-creating capacity, the foundation for the long boom, would be weakened. What then are the forces that are likely to encourage or discourage the emergence of fully functioning, efficient global markets for goods, services and capital?

One way of addressing this complex question is to consider the costs, benefits and often intricate negotiations that preceded the integration and opening up of markets within a nation or a region. The changes wrought in many OECD countries in the 19th century offer in microcosm a precedent for what it might take to really advance towards true global markets. First, integrating distinct or formerly closed markets is a protracted process that requires skilled and tenacious leadership in order to overcome myriad organisational and political, hidden and exposed barriers to transparency and open exchange. Even after a common political constitution and harmonised regulatory conditions prevail, there are the subtle complications such as effective implementation of antitrust laws and overcoming those regional inequalities (*e.g.* sufficient scale to support competing retailers) that can impede local competition. Second, there is rarely agreement on reducing the barriers that are identified without the introduction of adjustment mechanisms and compensation for the losers. Lastly, when opening the market also opens the door to serious instability and crisis, it is important to have the capacity to intervene in order to re-establish stability and avoid the even greater costs of complete collapse.

It is therefore important to be modest about what has been achieved so far in terms of creating operational global markets. Equally, it is very clear that to succeed fully, future efforts to integrate markets on a worldwide scale will have to meet the same conditions as previous, less geographically ambitious projects. Such an initiative will certainly build on past achievements and the important increases in trade of goods and services, capital flows and technology diffusion. These accomplishments, however, need to be kept in perspective. After all, most of the trade is intra-regional and intra-firm. The flows of capital investment have mostly been in the form of direct ownership, highly concentrated in a limited number of countries. Indirect portfolio investment has been less quantitatively significant until very recently, and remains very volatile. Technological leadership is highly concentrated in a few countries and regions within those countries. Diffusion is very uneven, for reasons ranging from insufficiently rich local markets to inadequate skill and transportation infrastructures. Simply put, there is still a long way to go before there is a fully global economy.

Yet, it could be argued that this underdevelopment is promising because it also implies that a large share of the gains from the emergence of a global economy are yet to be realised. Less heartening is the implication that there are still many formidable hurdles to be jumped. One of the obstacles already hindering progress is that assessments differ radically as to the problems likely to be encountered and the appropriate solutions. On one side are those who take recent experience with tariff reductions as the most pertinent precedent. From this viewpoint the problem is largely to overcome the resistance of countries to the dismantlement of customs barriers, tariffs, countervailing duties, regulatory controls and various ways of protecting domestic or national firms from external competition. The solution, according to this school of thought, is mostly to be found by exerting pressure either in multilateral/bilateral negotiations or through international sanctions such as refusing entry into the WTO. Eventually, it is contended, recalcitrant countries will see that the gains outweigh the costs and join the fold of world markets.

Another standpoint focuses on the forces that create popular opposition to the formation of world markets. Here one of the main concerns is the current asymmetry between national and global treatment of the distributional implications of market integration. From this perspective the economic and social frameworks devised to integrate markets should also be used to create a level playing field globally. As the proponents of this approach point out, it would be absurd in a national context to expect a failing region to be abandoned because its people and business are the losers from openness within the domestic economy. In these circumstances the winners usually compensate the losers, even if such pro-grammes are not always effective at rapidly putting the losing social group, area or sector back on track. Typically such partial compensation is seen as an acceptable price to pay for the net gains of integrated and transparent national markets. In a similar fashion, proponents of this approach argue that the large gains from forging an integrated world economy provide ample justification for developing frame-works that can take into account the ensuing costs and benefits of adjustment, locational competition, regional inequality, excesses in market volatility and dangers of regulatory races-to-the-bottom.

Realistically, as both schools of thought recognise, the contribution to the long boom made by major improvements in integrating the global economy will have to emerge from a world that is still mostly characterised by national-level mechanisms for guarding against noncompetitive practices, regulating financial and investment flows, and working out commercial, social and environmental dis-putes. Few would disagree that, scaled up to a global level, planet-wide markets will likely generate the same kinds of costs and spectacular benefits as the inte-gration of markets within national or regional space. But consensus about the gains vanishes into considerable disagreement about how to get there. As with the knowledge economy, there are those who advocate ambitious new initiatives as the most effective means of realising the gains of global markets and propelling the economic dynamism behind a long boom. On the other side are those who either consign the hope of forging more comprehensive global agreements and institutions to the realm of unrealistic ideas, or fail entirely to see the utility. Recently a new element has entered this debate, opening up new prospects for a more ambitious agenda. It is possible, as discussed next, that efforts to achieve global environmental sustainability could end up contributing considerably to the negotiation and introduction of both more globally integrated markets and the regulatory and institutional infrastructure to go with them.

Working towards global environmental sustainability

Recent years have seen the emergence of a ground swell of recognition that the world as a whole cannot follow the natural-resource and energy-intensive pat-terns of production and consumption taken by most OECD countries in the past. The current global energy system, predominantly based on fossil fuels, is inher-ently linked to the increase of atmospheric CO_2 concentrations and hence to accel-erating disruption of the global climate system. As industrialisation and urbanisation take hold in developing countries, and as the lifestyles, modes of consumption and high-energy-use patterns of the industrialised economies dif-fuse worldwide, the risk looms ever larger that over the next fifty years there will be a fourfold increase in energy demand in the developing countries. Gradual, marginal changes, though important, are increasingly perceived as likely to be insufficient to reach an environmentally sustainable trajectory within the next half-century. Changes will have to be much more fundamental, and they will have to be initiated in the very near future if sustainability is to be brought within reach. Energy infrastructures, urban settlements, the construction of dwellings, transport systems, the nature of the industrial capital stock, consumer technologies, values and attitudes – all these things that tend to lock societies into set patterns of energy-intensive production and consumption may take decades to change.

The potential to achieve such change and set the world economy on an environmentally more sustainable growth path is undeniable. A cluster of developments point in this direction: the gradual shift in economic structures away from manufacturing towards services; the considerable technological potential for major improvements in energy efficiency, for example in transport and in buildings; the emerging information society, with the prospect of telework, teletrade and the more energy-efficient reorganisation of work and production; and finally, the promise that rising global affluence will lead to higher demands (and willingness/ability to pay) for environmental quality. At a global institutional level, a succession of international agreements from Rio to Kyoto have created relatively favourable framework conditions for a new start.

However, it is becoming equally clear that the outcome of efforts to reduce the carrying costs of human activity will depend fundamentally on how such a goal is achieved. Some policies might accelerate the changes that propel a long boom, while others may seriously undermine robust wealth creation. For example, the pricing policies that bring about deep, enduring transformations to the energy intensity of the infrastructures underlying the economy (transport, urban, etc.) could trigger hugely beneficial waves of innovation and creativity in ecologically benign approaches to production, consumption, and lifestyles in general, and those in turn could provide an important stimulus for efficiency, long-run productivity growth and high, sustained economic performance. Alternatively, by imposing additional criteria on economic choices, environmental targets could hamper promising technological developments, generate extra costs for efficiency-enhancing changes, and stifle innovation. The question, then, is not if but how the world can take growing global environmental costs into account in order to shift to a more sustainable pattern of activity.

Starting where there is agreement, most solutions see the need for economic incentives to go to work changing the micro-level choices made by managers, investors, engineers and consumers, be they in the public or private sector. Confidence in market signals reflects the experience of most OECD countries that were able to change fairly dramatically the direction of growth rates in aggregate energy-to-output ratios after the oil price shocks. There is also fairly widespread optimism that the appropriate incentive structures will be met with sufficiently widespread innovation- and efficiency-enhancing resource reallocation to avoid undercutting productivity growth. Disagreement, however, sets in when it comes to what is meant by "appropriate incentive structures".

Fundamental schisms can be identified in three areas. First there is the question of the degree of social engagement – the incentives and disincentives of peer pressure or cultural norms – deemed necessary to reach sustainability objectives. On one side there are those who argue that market signals alone can do the job. On the other there are those who believe that a broader approach involving a rearticulation of values and a willingness to embrace collectively determined environmental objectives will be essential. Bridging this divide will be difficult because it reflects fundamentally distinct political philosophies. This gulf leads to a second schism, over the extent to which basic universal rights to the planet's ecological capacity should be made the cornerstone of the collective governance of the "appropriate incentive structures". Finally, there are many disagreements about how to share out the benefits and the burdens that go along with the taxes, permits and quotas that will be used to internalise the externalities. Here the devil is in the details and the distribution of power to resolve them.

All of these schisms are pertinent to the realisation of the long boom in so far as they might jeopardise the achievement of the requisite innovation and productivity growth. Furthermore, given the high stakes should efforts to redress growing global environmental hazards fail, there seems to be little justification for underestimating either the kinds of resources or the power over them that will have to be reapportioned in order to attain the goal of sustainability. A plausible case can be made that dithering and failing to make decisions or provide clear leadership could, one way or the other, blow the chances of making the transition to a more sustainable form of economic dynamism. The reasons for this are rooted in the nature of economic dynamism, its complex interplay of technological, institutional, resource, competitive and aspirational conditions. Even though this tapestry has been rewoven on numerous occasions as the world economy has moved through different phases, it has so far never been done without very high costs. As tempting as it might seem to believe that this time around it will be different, experience argues for prudence and concerted action to achieve such a difficult goal. Policy choices will be the key.

3. Policies for provoking a long boom

The preceding anatomy of the long boom shows that its prospects depend, first on the underlying "motor" systems that sustain long-run economic dynamism in general, and second on the historically specific possibilities that serve as fuel.

On both counts, the prospects for a long boom during the first decades of the next century would improve significantly if inter-systems harmony and convergence were to reign. Not because harmony is always superior to dissonance when it comes to moving systems forward or that convergence is possible without prior divergence, but because of the singular importance right now of the global diffusion of knowledge, of new institutions and of common objectives to realising a long boom. Viewed from a policy perspective, provoking rates of economic development well above the historical average will depend on making choices that, first, lead to an exceptionally strong and enduring period of systems harmony and convergence, and second, succeed – at a global level – in leveraging simultaneously rapid technological progress, deep market integration and a productivity-enhancing reorientation of microeconomic choices towards environmental sustainability.

Certainly there are no foregone conclusions. Future stagnation in the underlying technological, institutional, material, competitive and aspirational forces that drive improvements in efficiency and wealth-creating capacity cannot be ruled out. Nor can the possibility of a stalled transition to the knowledge economy, fragmentation of the world economy and a failure to shift the global environmental trajectory towards sustainability be excluded. Any or all of the five general determinants of overall long-run economic dynamism could fail either to develop or to be woven in with the others. Each of the three sets of catalysts and constraints of this historically specific long boom could be overwhelmed by the constraining rather than catalysing possibilities. Expansionary forces might be cancelled out by contractionary trends in another area; for example, successful globalisation could be undermined by the high costs of failed sustainability or strong knowledge diffusion through the Internet being undermined by the shredding of global markets due to sharp inter-regional conflicts. Finding policies that can navigate these varied and intricate problems will be a major challenge facing governments at the outset of the new millennium.

General policy criteria

One starting point for this task is to identify the types of policies that correspond best with the requirements for both economic dynamism and a long boom. At a general level progress along this path is likely to be most effectively encouraged by two categories of policy, one that fosters creativity and facilitates change, and the other that goes beyond simply reducing conflicts at a global level to creating a new, much higher degree of co-operative action.

Fostering creativity and change

The first group of policies involves initiatives that support people's capacity to experiment, innovate and take risks, both locally and globally. Traditionally the terrain for policies that improve incentives, information and insurance for people and enterprises has been the nation state. Within the national territory governments introduced the infrastructure of laws, common currency, regulations, universal education, shared language and a range of social insurance schemes – from unemployment and pension programmes to subsidies for restructuring. Many of these policies, at one time or another, played a part in reducing uncertainty, cutting transaction costs, facilitating the acceptance of often painful resource reallocation, fostering innovation and encouraging risk taking.

For the future, three fields could prove to be fertile ground for new policy initiatives, both in the public and private sectors. First, there are many rules, regulations, programmes and products that are stuck in the mass era. There is still a long way to go in reforming entrenched attitudes to such things as one-size-fits-all products, passive chain-of-command organisational structures and lack of responsiveness to customers' or citizens' needs. Second, there are the various antiquated incentive systems, from rigid seniority-based compensation packages and career ladders to risk-discouraging social insurance, taxation and regulatory schemes, that actively dissuade innovation and experimentation. Third and last are the more positive experimental initiatives that create new spaces where entrepreneurship and individual responsibility find a conducive framework for taking risks. In the future, as already discussed in 21st Century Technologies, the pay-off from the national-level policies that liberate creativity is likely to be very significant as people take advantage of the build-up in technological and intellectual capacity to develop the local foundations for a sustainable global knowledge economy.

Relative to domestic policies to foster change, international-level policies have one handicap and one advantage. The handicap is that so far the intensity of economic activity at the global level is much less developed than at a local level. As a consequence, the scope has been more limited for the kinds of experimentation, innovation, and forging of risk reduction schemes, common codes and the socio-economic lubricants that are typical of everyday transactions. The advantage at the international level is the relative absence of yesterday's institutional and regulatory infrastructure to act as a fetter on the future. In most areas of the global economy, apart from conventional trade in goods, the process of creating the institutional setting capable of delivering the trust, transparency and integration that characterises national space is still in its infancy. In the future, concerted efforts will be needed to provide global frameworks capable of establishing the fluidity and confidence that usually characterise national space in areas such as intellectual property rights, electronic commerce, foreign direct investment, capital markets and technology diffusion.

Fostering global co-operation

The pursuit of these frameworks at the global level leads to the second group of policies likely to be essential for realising a long boom – initiatives that enhance the capacity to resolve conflicts at a global level. Such efforts will be important for two reasons. The first is that, as past experience shows, conflicts could well develop between policies meant to nurture innovation and smooth the acceptance of open competition at the national level, and those that reach towards the integration of the world economy. Resolving this kind of friction, where the protection and encouragement of local interests come into conflict with the introduction of common standards, shared codes and the non-discrimination requirements of a sustainable global knowledge economy, will be crucial for making progress at the worldwide level. So far these contradictions have only been worked out at a deeper level in regional or federal contexts such as the European Union, where integration depends in part on the capacity to co-ordinate and develop the institutional and regulatory infrastructure that moves towards eliminating the distinction between domestic and cross-border risk taking.

The second reason why policies to enhance conflict resolution capabilities will be important for creating the conditions underlying a long boom is the critical role of global-level action. Ushering in a worldwide knowledge economy, the integration of international markets and environmental sustainability will demand a much higher degree of organisation and effective decision making. Perhaps the most positive precedent, decades of successful negotiation of trade liberalisation, actually demonstrates how hard it is to find both the institutional mechanisms and packages of trade-offs that can reconcile conflicting interests.

Indeed, as many current impasses at the international level demonstrate, existing institutional capacity is still inadequate to the task of introducing the risk-reducing frameworks and broader win-win trade-off schemes needed to forge an integrated global economy. Developing effective global mechanisms for making decisions that go beyond zero-sum games and actually organise integrated policy actions, such as the enforcement of antitrust or safe e-commerce, will be essential in creating the suppleness and inventiveness to power a long boom. The pursuit of environmental sustainability, for example, may pave the way for new institutional possibilities such as those entailed by the introduction of globally tradable CO_2 quotas.

Scenario-derived policies

One method for teasing out the elements and testing the feasibility of ambitious policy agendas required to provoke a long boom is to examine a number of scenarios where – with slightly different policy mixes – all of the various pieces might fall into place. For example, clear policy distinctions emerge from three plausible trajectories (elaborated in detail in the final chapter): "growth leader", where a booming United States drives the world forward; "growth shift", where the worldwide diffusion of economic dynamism promises a swift convergence of much of the developing world with the developed; and "growth clusters", where a densely connected network of innovative metropoles and regions spur far-reaching global change. Common to all the scenarios is the expectation that there will be little divergence from the prudent macroeconomic, fiscal and structural adjustment policies that are essential for creating a predictable and flexible investment context. Where the scenarios differ is in the driving forces and associated policies, both national and international, that set the long boom in motion.

Growth leader

In the first scenario, uncontested and invigorated American leadership pushes the technological frontier forward at a fast pace worldwide. Innovation is unleashed along with hyper-competitive pressures and the rapid creative-destruction of unconstrained economic flexibility. In policy terms, the primary focus is on national initiatives for facilitating radical changes in economic and social organisation in the pursuit of innovation-based productivity and profits, although global frameworks for protecting intellectual property rights and foreign direct investment play an important role. New international institutional arrangements are not, however, essential for success, leaving the negotiation of initiatives aimed at improving environmental sustainability on a slower track. There would nonetheless have to be a continuation of existing trends towards fiscal and monetary policies aimed at macroeconomic stabilisation as well as increased liberalisation of trade in goods, services and finance. The hard edges of economic imperatives and social inequality could become even sharper than they are today.

Growth shift

The second scenario sees the emerging economies of Asia, Latin America and perhaps Russia jumping on a rapid convergence track to the productivity and income levels of OECD countries. Here, the integration of world markets combines with the opportunity for developing countries to adopt global best practices. This in turn opens the door to a highly productive international division of labour. Most OECD economies prosper by focusing on intangibles and the adjustments to ageing, while the rest of the world leapfrogs along the industrial path to catch up with the most advanced productivity levels. The policy key is at the international level, where the free flow of goods, services, finance, technology and skills enables the kind of investment and knowledge transfer necessary for take-off in the developing world. At the same time, with the deep intertwining of interests, it could become much easier to get the co-operation needed to effectively pursue global financial stability and environmental sustainability, and to improve the chances of the world's poor and excluded.

Growth cluster

The third scenario envisions a long boom powered by the dynamism of net-worked growth clusters – world-spanning urban and regional hotspots of innovation and communication. Business and local governments work in tandem to develop the infrastructure and connections that catalyse a high-growth cluster. In this scenario, productivity growth explodes as the efficiency-enhancing impact of information technology finally pays off. Geographic advantages that arise from proximity, like in Silicon Valley, combine with the advantages of the virtual communities springing up on the Internet. Competition and innovation are fierce as knowledge-sharing and access to inexpensive technology lower start-up costs on the supply side and help inform consumers on the demand side. Facilitating electronic commerce in ways that lower both entry and transaction costs will entail policy breakthroughs in the areas of global antitrust, privacy, intellectual property and payment regulation and enforcement. Sustainability objectives could be served by the acceleration towards less resource-intensive economic activity, but modest requirements for international co-operation under this scenario may limit progress on issues like climate change and global inequality.

Clearly, pushing growth to the above-average rates of these long boom scenarios will call for more stringent requirements, and a degree of policy initiative that goes well beyond current thinking. Initially, the need for global systems harmony and convergence puts a premium on the policy makers' difficult task of articulating common goals and creating shared frameworks. The job will be made even more challenging because a long boom involves very high levels of experimentation and diversity that will, of necessity, generate gaps between the successful and failed projects. Bridging these divides will in all likelihood demand approaches towards encouraging risk-taking and change that go well beyond the traditional economic and social policy frameworks of the mass-production, mass-consumption and mass-government era.

Continuity and change – policies for provoking a long boom

Innovative policies at the local, national and global levels will be essential in order to spur creativity in all domains, from the emerging markets of the knowledge economy to the virtual enterprises and communities of a fully networked world. But, unlike the protracted process of introducing the property and labour laws that underpinned industrialisation, launching a long boom will require a rapid burst of enabling legislation covering everything from fine-tuning the protection of increasingly diverse forms of intellectual property to the economic incentives for introducing environmentally less harmful energy systems. Policies at the top of the agenda for encouraging a long boom will need to draw on the most promising opportunities that arise as real-world changes intermingle elements of the growth leader, growth shift and growth clusters scenarios. One way of coming to grips with the scope of a long boom policy agenda, at both the national and international levels, is to distinguish those areas where continuity might be sufficient from those where innovative breakthroughs are probably necessary.

Continuity

Considering the national level first, there are a number of existing policy priorities that will continue to be important. Efforts to maintain macroeconomic stability, based on government policies that aim for low inflation and solid public sector finances, will continue to help reduce uncertainty, while ongoing reforms meant to facilitate structural adjustment, including flexible labour markets, open and transparent capital markets, and competitive goods and services markets, promise continued improvements in the efficiency with which economic resources are allocated. Both of these traditional policy thrusts will help create the conditions conducive to the very high levels of investment and productivity.

Similarly, a continuation of the shift in government's role from direct provider of often uniform products and services towards a regulator of more diversified, decentralised and market-driven provision will help trigger and sustain a long boom by enhancing general economic efficiency and flexibility. Continued emphasis on reforms that help companies and governments to overcome the rigid, hierarchical methods of the past will also play an important part in spurring the introduction and invention of new products and services, new processes and technologies, and new ways of organising work and daily life. In addition, efforts will be needed at an international level to help extend and deepen the multilateral processes aimed at liberalising trade, investment and technology flows; improving corporate governance and financial transparency; and controlling various dangers such as infectious diseases and toxic chemicals. Persistence and vigour will be needed in applying current policies.

Breakthroughs

Above and beyond the difficulties of activating the catalysts and overcoming the constraints, the prospects for a long boom also hinge on the impact of systems harmony and dissonance, convergence and divergence. The implications for a long boom are difficult to untangle because, on the one hand, there are times when the sharp conflicts of dissonant systems (e.g. the United States versus the Soviet Union) or harmony (e.g. integration of the EU) can help to propel experimentation and above-average expansion. On the other hand, there are times when systems dissonance (*e.g.* civil war) or harmony (*e.g.* cartels) can cripple dynamism altogether. Similarly, alternate phases of convergence and divergence across and within systems can be an important mechanism for spurring dynamism by opening up learning, innovation and investment opportunities. Unfortunately divergence, as is evident from the unevenness of development and the growing inequality between rich and poor, is not always automatically self-correcting. Closing the gap requires active and effective responses. Here, as in other areas, the key to the realisation of the long boom will turn on making major policy breakthroughs.

For instance, fairly dramatic changes may be needed in areas such as social support systems, where the old ways of balancing risk-taking and security tend to stifle the much higher levels of adaptability, creativity and diversity that are essential to fuel the knowledge economy and society. In education, finally making the leap to lifelong learning will probably demand a breakthrough that pushes beyond the domination of existing educational institutions towards new ways of validating what people know regardless of how they have acquired that knowledge. In addition, developing new forms of risk-sharing and social solidarity will require major advances in the networks, work rules and incentives that facilitate co-operation, particularly at the local level. Perhaps the largest leaps for national-level policy will be those that occur in response to the challenge of reallocating responsibility. Such reallocation needs to occur not only between public and private organisations but also across local, regional and global levels.

At the international level the primary breakthrough may involve moving beyond reasoning from national considerations towards a logic that embraces the interests of the planet as a whole. A long boom will require accelerated and often more ambitious, planet-wide approaches to a number of key challenges. For instance, realising the full potential of information and communications technology, electronic commerce and the Internet will demand global solutions to such issues as consumer protection, safeguarding privacy, secure payment, verifying identities, attributing intellectual property rights and ensuring competitive market conditions.

Speeding up the intricate negotiations that pave the way to fuller market integration will push to the forefront debates over the most effective and acceptable solutions to the economic and social trade-offs. Without consideration of both efficiency and distributive issues, political success is probably unattainable. On the environmental front everything from global warming and bio-diversity to management of the world's fish stocks and oceans more generally will call for planet-wide perspectives and mechanisms capable of aiming at policy choices that are both efficient and politically acceptable. Finally, nations are being asked to leap past old modes of thinking when it comes to the global application of the rule of law in order to achieve goals like reducing corruption and drug trafficking, prosecuting crimes against humanity or evaluating the attainment of the environmental goals spelled out in international treaties.

4. Conclusion

Overall, this is not a modest policy agenda. The realisation of a long boom will depend on the continuing spread of the basic systemic attributes that have underpinned two centuries of long-run economic dynamism in OECD countries. Indeed this is likely to be the easy part, since the three sets of generic system attributes that played such a crucial role in the past do seem set to spread. More parts of the world are expected to grapple with the potent mixture of economic drivers and political expression that comes from combining democracy and competitive markets. The pluralism, transparency and openness that underpin the capacity to innovate and adapt are also spreading wider roots, albeit with considerable difficulty. Lastly, with respect to culture, there are signs that in the future people will not only accept but actively pursue and desire ways of creating a more densely networked world capable of achieving a workable balance between co-operation and competition, identity and integration. Civil society around the globe is on the path, albeit slowly and often at high cost, to improved ways of seeking diversity and combining security with risk-taking.

Provoking a long boom will undoubtedly necessitate combining as many of the available catalytic forces as possible. The most promising paths are probably those that encourage the openness and creativity of entrepreneurial exuberance; high degrees of international co-operation to facilitate the rapid development and diffusion of the know-how and technologies that underpin economic convergence; and dense global networks which both intensify competition and foster the joint undertakings of business, government and individuals. Such a vibrant development trajectory could make the best of the possibilities open to humanity on the eve of the 21st century. But possibilities are not always realised. The last few decades have also witnessed much deepening of inequality and exclusion. Reversing these trends could be one of the greatest benefits of a long boom and one of the main reasons for making the exceptional economic and social policy efforts required.

In the end, it is how decision makers – managers, investors, engineers, and consumers – respond (or not) to everyday challenges that will determine future outcomes. They will make their choices from where they are, in their homes, workplaces, boardrooms and parliaments. The final results may be surprising, may fail to correspond either to what policy makers intended or the values that people believe in. Such incongruity between intentions, desires and outcomes are endemic to human endeavour. For there are times when the low-power choices made by millions of individuals can have more impact than the solemn proclamations of high-powered governments. Nevertheless, it is human actions – whether they are just or right, by volition or inertia – that will make the difference between stagnation and dynamism, slump and boom over the next few decades. As a consequence, policy makers must accept a dual challenge, to find ways to encourage economic dynamism combined with a long boom and to do so in ways that are consistent with people's expressed values and aspirations. Such an ambition, often taken for granted, will probably be even more complex in the diverse and interconnected world of tomorrow. But it offers the chance of ushering in an unprecedented period of improvement in the human condition.

2

Sources of Continued Long-run Economic Dynamism in the 21st Century

by

Richard G. Lipsey
Simon Fraser University, Canada

1. Introduction

Observers of past and current trends have suggested many possible scenarios for growth and dynamism in the OECD countries in the first half of the 21st century. These range from secular stagnation at one extreme to accelerating technical change leading to periods of social and political unrest at the other. Where might the West perform between these extremes of stagnation and excessive dynamism?

To begin to come to grips with the issues, and the conjectures that must be an important part of any answers – for we are well outside of the range of modestly confident econometric projections – it is necessary to cover several topics. First is the nature of technological change and its relation to economic, social and political structures. Secondly, there are the technologies that can already be perceived at, or rising just above, the visible horizon. The third relates to those macroeconomic forces that may discourage or encourage the exploitation of technological potential, and the fourth to public policies that may do the same. Finally, there are the political and social stresses that will be created by evolving technological paradigms.

2. Growth and technological change

Sources of growth

Following Mokyr (1990), economists distinguish three main sources of economic growth:

- *Increases in the size of the market* – Market size can increase for many reasons: new discoveries, as when Europe expanded in the 16th and 17th centuries;

increases in population, such as occurred in the 19th century; reductions in transportation costs, which have been going on for the last two centuries; and reductions in trade barriers, such as have been accomplished by trade liberalisation policies in the last half of this century. All these allow the exploitation of scale economies previously unexploited. Also, a growing economy encourages innovation by reducing risk because it is easier to finance new technologies and sell new things in expanding rather than in static or contracting markets.

– *Capital investment* – In standard economic analysis, pure investment in physical and human capital is distinct from technological change.

– *Technical change* – In the long term, changes in product and process technologies are potent sources of economic growth.

Although this threefold classification can be useful, it is also potentially misleading since these forces typically interact, making the separate contribution of each difficult or impossible to distinguish. Consider two important illustrations. First, market size and technological change are interrelated since the falling transport costs that raise the size of markets are usually driven by technological changes in the transport industry – such as the introduction of containers and the replacement of 10 000 ton tankers and freighters by super-tankers and large container ships in the 1960s. Second, investment and technological change are usually interrelated because most new product and process technologies must be embodied in new capital goods before they can be used. Thus rapid technological change is typically associated with high rates of investment to embody it.

Technological change versus investment

Economists have sometimes debated which is the more important cause of long-term growth, pure investment or technological change. This debate is important here because it concerns the sources of long-term economic dynamism.

The author argues for the importance of technological change with a simple thought experiment. Imagine freezing technological knowledge at the levels existing at some point in the past, say 1900, while continuing to accumulate more 1900-vintage machines and factories and using them to produce more 1900-vintage goods and services, as well as training more people longer and more thoroughly in the technological knowledge that was available in 1900. Today's living standards would then be vastly lower than those we now enjoy (and pollution would be a massive problem). The contrast is even more striking if the same thought experiment is performed comparing today with the knowledge, product and process technologies that existed at even earlier points in time.

This exercise illustrates what economic historians and students of technology are agreed on: technological change is *the* major determinant of long-term, global economic growth. So the problem of explaining growth over time and across countries is mainly one of explaining the generation, adaptation within one country, and international diffusion of new product and process technologies. In the long term, these new technologies transform our standards of living, our economic, social and political ways of life, and even our value systems.

Are we to conclude then that saving, investment and capital accumulation do not matter? The answer is "no", because virtually all new technology is embodied in new capital equipment whose accumulation is measured as gross investment. Technological change and investment are thus complementary, the latter being the vehicle by which the former enters the production process. Anything that slows the rate of embodiment through investment, such as unnecessarily high interest rates, will slow the rate of growth, just as any slowdown in the development of new technology will do so in the long term.

So, just because new investment can statistically "account for" most economic growth, that does not imply it is the main cause of growth. Both technological change and investment are needed. Nonetheless, faced with the choice, most of us would prefer to live in a society in which technology advanced but was only embodied through "replacement investment" since net investment (and hence measured capital accumulation) was zero, rather than in a society in which nothing was known that was not known in 1900 and more and more investment had been made in 1900-style productive facilities to produce 1900-style goods and services.[1]

A *structuralist-evolutionary* (S-E) *model of technological change*[2]

To discuss technological change and economic dynamism, some framework is needed – a theoretical model. The standard neoclassical model, illustrated in Part A of Figure 1, shows inputs passing through a macro-production function to produce the nation's output, as measured by its gross domestic product (GDP). Any structure or institutions are hidden in the "black box" of the aggregate production function where, presumably, they help to determine its form.

The author's model is designed to highlight some of the elements of the neoclassical black box that research in technological change demonstrates to be important for economic dynamism. This model shows the economy's *structure* and is in line with much microeconomic research on the *evolution* of technology (hence the term "structuralist-evolutionary" or "S-E" for short). Its six main elements are shown in Part B of Figure 1.

Technological knowledge is the idea set specifying all things that assist in creating economic value. This includes the specifications of all outputs of goods and services (product technologies), all the processes used to create them (process technologies) and all forms in which production processes can be organised both on the "shop floor" and in management (organisational technologies).

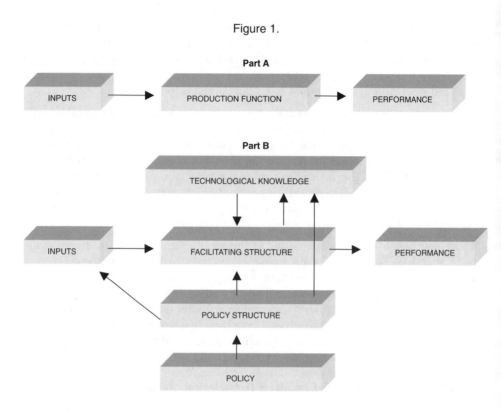

Figure 1.

Part A shows the neoclassical approach. Inputs of labour, materials and the services of physical and human capital flow through the economy's aggregate production function to produce economic performance, as measured by total national income. The form of the production function depends on the economy's structure and its technology, but these things are hidden in a black box, the only manifestation of which is how much output emerges from a given amount of inputs.

Part B shows our structuralist-evolutionary approach. Technological knowledge is the idea set for all products, process, and organisations that create economic value. The facilitating structure is the realisation set and includes the capital goods that embody much of the technology, the internal organisation of firms, the geographical location and concentration of industy, the infrastructure, and the financial system. Inputs pass through the structure to produce economic performance. Policy is the idea set of public objectives and the specification of means. The policy structure is the realisation set that gives effect to policy, including all kinds of public institutions. Policy, working through the policy structure, influences the facilitating structure, technological knowledge and the quantity/quality of inputs.

The facilitating structure is the realisation set for technologies. It comprises 1) all physical capital, 2) all human capital (embodied in people), 3) the organisation of production facilities, including labour practices, 4) the managerial and financial organisation of firms, 5) the geographical location of industries, 6) industrial concentration, 7) all infrastructure, 8) all private-sector financial institutions, and financial instruments. To repeat, the facilitating structure is the embodiment of all technological, product, process and organisational knowledge.

Public policy is the idea set covering the specifications of public policy objectives, which are expressed in such things as legislation and precedent.

The policy structure is the realisation set embodying the means of achieving public policy in the design of public sector institutions, rules and regulations and the human capital of those who administer these public institutions. (Note the parallel with technology and its embodiment in the facilitating structure.)

Inputs of labour and raw materials are fed through the facilitating structure to produce the system's economic performance.

Economic performance covers aggregate GDP, its growth rate, and its breakdown among sectors and among such broadly defined groupings as goods production and service production; GNP and its distribution among size and functional classes; and total employment and unemployment and their distribution among such subgroups as sectors and skill classes.

Economic performance is determined by the interaction between inputs and the existing facilitating structure. That structure is in turn influenced by technology and public policy. It follows that changes in technology typically have no effect on performance until they are embodied in the facilitating structure. Furthermore, the full effects on performance will not be felt until all the elements of the structure have been adjusted to fit the newly embodied technology.

Characteristics of technological change

To study the causes and consequences of technological change, it is necessary to examine a few of the characteristics of the changes that have been going on over the last few centuries and that will go on during the next. This section states in general terms many of the things that are illustrated in later sections.

Endogenous change

Because R&D is an expensive activity which is often undertaken by firms in search of profit, technological change is to a great extent endogenous to the economic system, altering in response to changes in perceived profit opportunities. An abundance of empirical evidence suggests that competition in both product and process technologies drives much endogenous technological change. In manufacturing and many modern service industries, failure to keep up with one's opponents in new technologies is far more serious than the choice of a wrong price or an inappropriate capacity.

Uncertainty

Because innovation means doing something not done before, there is an element of uncertainty (in Frank Knight's sense of the term) in all innovation.[3] As a result, massive sums are sometimes spent with no positive results, while trivial expenditures sometimes produce results of great value. Furthermore, the search for one objective often produces results of great value but for very different objectives.

Uncertainty is involved in more than just making some initial technological breakthrough. There is enormous uncertainty with respect to the range of applications that some new technology may have. The steam engine, electricity, the telephone, radio, the laser, the computer, the VCR, and fibre optics are examples of technologies that were initially thought to have very limited potential, and that did have very limited actual applications during the first decades of their life.

Types of change

The overall technology systems of all growing economies evolve along paths that include both small incremental improvements and occasional jumps. To distinguish these, investigators often define two categories. An innovation is *incremental* if it is an improvement to an existing technology. An innovation is *radical* if it could not have evolved through incremental improvements in the technology that it displaces – *e.g.* artificial fabrics could not have evolved out of the natural fabrics that they displaced in many uses.

An extreme form of radical innovation is called a general purpose technology (GPT). GPTs share some important common characteristics: they begin as fairly crude technologies with a limited number of uses; they evolve into much more complex technologies with dramatic expansions in the range of their use across the economy and in the range of economic outputs that they help to produce. As they diffuse through the economy, their efficiency improves. As mature technologies, they have many complementarities in the sense of co-operating with many other technologies.[4] A mature GPT is defined formally as a technology that is widely used, has many uses, and has many complementarities with other existing technologies. The steam engine, the dynamo and the internal combustion engine are examples of major GPTs in the field of energy generation.

Induced changes in the facilitating structure

The full potential of developing new technologies can only be achieved when they operate within a facilitating structure that fits them. To see what is involved in the link from technology to facilitating structure, a number of points need to be established.

First, when elements of technology change, various elements of the facilitating structure change adaptively. For example, a new method of making steel will have to be embodied in new equipment and possibly new plants. This may affect the optimal plant size and hence the degree of concentration in the steel industry, as well as the location of steel plants. Various elements of the public infrastructure may need to be changed. So, too, will human capital change whenever the new methods require amounts and types of skills that differ from those required by the old methods. These changes are made mostly by self-interested agents who are responding to the price and profit incentives created by the change in technology.

Second, at any moment in time, the facilitating structure may be better or worse adapted to any given state of technology. For example, labour practices with respect to job demarcation, which adapted well to the Fordist production methods, are only slowly adjusting to the new Toyotaist production methods that have already been installed.

Third, there are substantial inertias in most of the elements of the structure. Much capital is highly durable and, as long as its variable costs of operation can be covered, it will not be replaced by new capital embodying some superior technology. The new pattern of industrial location and firm concentration will not be finalised until all the firms and plants are adjusted to the new technology – it took nearly forty years for electric motors to fully replace steam engines in factories after they had demonstrated their clear superiority. The optimal design of plant and management practices may not be obvious after the introduction of a new technology (as was the case with the computer). The understanding of what is needed by way of new infrastructure may take time, as will its design and construction (witness long discussion about the new information highway). New requirements for human capital must be established and the appropriate training devised – both on the job and in school.

Fourth, the period of adjustment is often "conflict ridden" [Freeman and Perez's (1988) term] because old methods and organisations which worked well – often for decades – begin to function poorly in the new situation and often become dysfunctional. Furthermore, the uncertainty accompanying any radical new innovation implies that there will be many different, but defensible, judgements about what adaptations are actually needed.

Fifth, changes in technology and the resulting changes in the facilitating structure can require adaptations in policy and the policy structure. For example, technological changes often turn natural monopolies into highly competitive industries. Thus the post office once had a natural monopoly in the delivery of hard-copy messages, but today's competition comes from fax, e-mail, satellite links, and a host of other technologies that have made this activity highly competitive. A new technology can also do the reverse by introducing scale economies large enough for natural monopolies to emerge in what was previously an industry in which a few firms rigorously competed with each other.

Policy and the policy structure

Reactive changes – How the policy structure reacts to technological change is an important determinant of a society's technological dynamism. However, adjustments typically occur with long lags. Uncertainty can make it unclear what reactions are needed. Inertias in political decision taking, plus the resistance of vested interests who will be hurt, either by the new technologies or by the accommodating changes in policy, can slow the process of adaptation. For example, US legislators spent decades arguing over the revision of the Glass-Steagall Act, long after the information and communications technologies (ICT) revolution made prohibitions on interstate banking obsolete.

Proactive changes – Not only does policy react to changes in technology and in the facilitating structure, it may also be changed proactively in an attempt to alter technology or the structure. For example, a policy that encourages the establishment of R&D labs and richer links between the private sectors and universities is altering the facilitating structure in the expectation that these changes will influence the rate and nature of technological change.

3. Roots of past growth

If we go back through the millennia to the beginning of modern people, some forty thousand years ago, we find a story of continuous technological change at least in the West (defined as the Fertile Crescent through to Western Europe).[5] During that time, there have been a dozen or so major GPTs that have transformed the whole economic, social and political structures of the societies that developed or adopted them. These have been discussed elsewhere (see for example Lipsey and Bekar, 1995 and Lipsey, Bekar and Carlaw, 1998); it will suffice here just to name them to give some perspective: the domestication of crops, the domestication of animals, writing, bronze, iron, the water-wheel and windmill, the three-masted sailing ship, the moveable-type printing press, automated textile machinery, the steam engine, electricity, the internal combustion engine, and the computer. Each of these transformed their societies at least as fundamentally as the current computer-based revolution is doing.

The important conclusion is that massive social, economic and political transformations driven by new technologies are not new phenomena. Qualitatively, we are experiencing nothing new about the transforming potential of major GPTs. Whether the current transformations are quantitatively larger than those of previous centuries is debatable – although there is no clear evidence that they are.

The mechanical age

The period from, say, 1000 to 1870 can be thought of as the mechanical age. In it, Europe mechanised the production of a steadily increasing range of commodities. The process began in the Middle Ages when the water-wheel was used to mechanise a wide range of production activities, from fulling cloth to smelting iron and brewing beer. The scientific revolution in the 15th and 16th centuries solidified a mechanistic view of the universe and contributed to many new mechanical inventions. The steam engine was the culminating power source of the mechanical age.

The electronic age

The period from 1870 to today can be thought of as the electronic age. Of course electricity spread slowly, as does any major GPT, and mechanical means are still important today. But because what happens at the cutting edge of technological development has come more and more to depend on electronics, we now live in a truly electronic age. Our mechanical contraptions would seem understandable marvels to people transported here from 1800, but our electronic technologies would have seemed like magic – something totally beyond their ken.

Electricity is the last major GPT that has worked its way fully through the economy – to the point even of enabling other GPTs such as the computer and the laser. So it is worth studying for the lessons it has to offer about current adjustments.

As is typical of a GPT, electricity's first uses were limited – street lighting and street railways. Slowly, as technical problems were solved, the number of uses expanded, the techniques and locations of production were transformed, and a range of new products and industries arose. For example, an assortment of electrically driven household machines including washing machines, dishwashers, vacuum cleaners, irons, refrigerators, deep freezers, and electric stoves transformed household work; the numerous servants that ran middle class households in 1900 and tended to much of household drudgery were no longer needed.

Electricity has powered an ongoing communications revolution, starting with the telegraph which for the first time in history provided a publicly accessible system that allowed information to travel faster than human messengers. The new communications technologies made possible by electricity evolved through the telephone, the radio, the TV, satellites and the Internet. Electricity also powered the computer and is, therefore, complementary with the new computer-based GPT.

Structural adjustments – As with any major GPT, the full development of electricity's potential required substantial structural adjustments. One of the most important was a drastic alteration in the layout of factories. Water and steam used a central drive shaft whose power was distributed to individual machines via belts. Because of heavy friction loss in belt transmission, machines that used the most power were placed closest to the drive shaft, and factories were built with two stories to get more machines close to the shaft which was situated near the ceiling of the lower floor.

At first, electric motors merely replaced steam or water as the power source for the central drive; they were installed in a design adapted to the old power sources. Later, a separate motor was attached to each machine (the unit drive) and it was slowly realised that the factory could be most efficiently built on one level with machines arranged in the order of the flow of production. Only when this restructuring was completed was the full potential of electric power in factories realised (Schurr, 1990 and David, 1991).

Electricity required a massive new infrastructure for power generation and distribution. In assembly plants, it increased scale economies; in parts manufacture, small-scale production became efficient because an electric motor could be attached to each machine tool. The result was a system of small decentralised parts producers supplying large centralised assembly plants – a method of production that is still used today. The 1890s were also a time of intense merger activity, which was sometimes the cause, and sometimes the effect, of electrification.

Performance effects – Although few new steam-driven factories were built in the United States after 1900, it was not until the end of the 1930s that the electrification of US industry was substantially completed. The long lags were due to many forces, not least of which was the long life of a steam-driven plant. By the early 1940s, the facilitating and policy structures of the US economy had been altered drastically to fit the needs of electricity and the automobile – the result of another concurrent GPT, the internal combustion engine.

There followed a long secular boom from 1945 to the early 1970s in which technological change took place more incrementally, and within a stable structure reasonably well adapted to the underlying technologies. Employment was high, recessions were shallow, productivity and real wages grew rapidly and the human capital requirements for various trades, professions and other occupations were relatively stable and well known.

4. The roots of future growth

When we ask about future dynamism, we must look first and foremost at the GPTs that will create major technological opportunities in the next century.

The first point to make is that we can never identify all of these. Technological development is replete with uncertainties. For almost a century, the steam engine's main use was pumping water out of mines or into reservoirs. Not until the 19th century did the high pressure steam engine allow the many uses that ushered in the Victorian age of steam. When the computer was first commercialised after the Second World War, the world demand was estimated to be fewer than 10. Thus, if the past is any guide, we can be pretty sure that there is some small, ineffective-looking technology that is undergoing its early stages of development but which will surprise us all by becoming one of the 21st century's influential GPTs.

The second point is that we can see some technologies that are well on their way to becoming GPTs. Modern ICTs are well established as full GPTs, although their use is still spreading; the materials revolution is also well under way; biotechnology is in its early stages; new fuel technologies can be foreseen, but their impacts are still uncertain; nanotechnologies are still little more than a glow on the horizon, but their potential is enormous. We consider each of these in the five subsections that follow.

The revolution in information and communications technologies[6]

The electronic computer, combined with various forms of message transmission such as satellites and digital telephones, is in the midst of working one of the most profound economic, social and political transformations in this millennium.

Evolution – As with all revolutionary GPTs, electronic computers came into the world in crude form and were slowly improved as a result of a number of innovations, some incremental and some fundamental, such as von Neumann's substitution of software for hard wiring. Slowly, as their efficiency improved, their range of applications grew. Over the last several decades, computer power has increased and its costs of handling a unit of data have diminished exponentially. The increasing processing power of the computer has led to the shift from analogue to digital methods of recording, analysing, and reproducing all forms of communication, and thereby to immense changes in performance.

Production – It was apparent early on that by managing information flows, computers would have a major impact on the organisation of firms and on financial transactions. What few foresaw was the impact of digitalisation on production and design in both the goods and the service industries. Today, many consumer goods incorporate intelligent reactions initiated by chips. Intelligent buildings will soon be unrecognisable advances over their old "unthinking" predecessors. On the factory floor, computers run robots. In the chemical industry, materials advances are being made that would have been impossible without advanced computing power. In lumber mills, X-rays and computers now decide much more effectively than could an experienced sawyer where to put the first cut in a large tree. Recording, film and TV are all computerised and the virtual band is a reality – one or more musicians who play all the instruments plus technicians who meld the results into a band of as many pieces as desired. Financial industries make extensive use of computers in gathering, storing, analysing, and retrieving information – with mixed results.

Design – In the past, complex products such as a new commercial aircraft were designed in parts which were then joined with the hope that not too many conflicts would emerge at the borders. Whole textbooks were written on which parts of the design should be solidified first and which kept fluid, also on who should talk to whom (as there was so much going on that everyone could not communicate with everyone else). Nathan Rosenberg (1982, Chapter 6) has documented in detail how, until the very latest aircraft, it was necessary to learn by using. One did what one could on the design board, but then there was no substitute for building the aircraft and observing its flight characteristics directly.

In contrast, the evolving design of the Boeing 777 was held in one giant computer, and every night all new design components were fed into the exiting virtual structure. The originators of this procedure thought that individual designers would go to the partially completed virtual plane and figure out how best to fit their own part into it. Instead, designers placed their part into the best spot for it and loaded their specification onto the computer. The computer then discovered any conflicts and told the designers who to talk to. As this example illustrates, no one can fully foretell, even at this micro level, how some new technology will work in practice. Typically, it brings surprises and unexpected gains.

Information generation – Computers generate masses of information as they do their jobs. For example, scanners at checkout counters update inventories and tabulate characteristics of sales, such as time, frequency, and shelf location. This presents management with unprecedented amounts of information and the means of analysing it. As a result, many procedures that used to be handled by intuition are now being rationalised.

Employers know much more about their employees than they used to and can discriminate between the performances of individuals, rather than having to deal with the broad classes that were necessary when information was difficult to obtain. Financial institutions can tell the cost and revenues associated with each customer. For example, banks find that they lose money on the majority of their customers and only a few (not necessarily the wealthiest) yield a profit – a profit which cross-subsidises the majority of customers. How long will banks accept a social obligation to persist in this non-maximising behaviour?

Education – The traditional textbook is under threat. Interactive computerised instruction modes are replacing the older lectures delivered from on high. Distant learning is becoming more and more powerful and is beginning to allow more staff-student and student-student interaction than many traditional face-to-face teaching technologies (to the great surprise of many teachers).

Media – On most days of the week, well-respected and experienced press, TV and radio journalists can be heard lamenting the changes caused by the Internet. In contrast, a few seers laud the Internet's democratisation of information and foresee a new era in which ordinary people have direct access to information unfiltered by the media elite. This debate is characteristic of the conflict-ridden process through which new technologies radically alter facilitating structures.

Military – Computers in tanks, naval vessels, smart bombs, aircraft and satellites have revolutionised warfare. The changes are so fast that strategy, tactics, logistics and countless other military matters are hard pressed to keep up.

The materials revolution

Less well-known but highly important in its impact is the materials revolution. New materials began to become important after the development of the chemical industry at the end of the last century. As with electricity and computers, the first new materials were merely fitted into the structure of the then-dominant technologies. A new material was invented in isolation and usually used to substitute for some existing material in an unchanged structure.

Today, however, the ability to tailor-make new materials constitutes a GPT at the leading edge of a new set of technologies. New products and new processes are designed around new materials expressly created to make the products and processes functional. This is equally true of recent aircraft designs and new undersea methods of extracting mineral and fossil wealth. Indeed, new materials are seen as important to the continued expansion of many important growth sectors including microelectronics, transportation, architecture, construction, energy systems, aerospace engineering, engineering and production practices in the automobile industry – to say nothing of fusion reactors, ersatz human organs and solar conversion cells. Once again we see spillovers creating a cluster of related innovations in often widely differentiated industries.

> Changes in materials innovation and application within the last half century [...] have occurred in a time span which was revolutionary rather than evolutionary. The materials revolution of our times is qualitative as well as quantitative. It breeds the attitude of purposeful creativity rather than modification of natural materials, and also a new approach – an innovative organisation of science and technology (Kranzberg and Smith, 1988, p. 88).

Biotechnology

Biotechnology is an emerging technology developed just enough to be projected as one of the most important GPTs in the first part of the 21st century.

Early history

Although biological engineering through selective breeding is as old as the neolithic agricultural revolution, modern biotechnology begins with the 1953 discovery of the structure of DNA as the carrier of the genetic code. The next breakthrough was the discovery of a family of enzymes called restriction endonucleases, that can recognise a particular sequence in DNA and cut it at the required point, allowing a given set of DNA fragments to be reproduced at will. Another technique allowed the various fragments of DNA to be separated into homogeneous groups. A big step followed with recombinant DNA. Fragments of DNA can be joined by use of a "sealing enzyme", called ligase. Cancer cells, which have the property of unstoppable growth, can then be used to reproduce the recombinant DNA at will. This technique is used to produce masses of monoclonal (single parent) antibodies by fusing white blood cells, which produce germ-fighting antibodies, with cancer cells, which multiply indefinitely.

Like all GPTs, it was not clear just what applications would emerge before each technique was perfected and applied – although it was obvious to most observers in a general way that the possibilities were enormous. As is always the case, the discovery of new knowledge is well ahead of its practical applications, although these are beginning to multiply in the explosive way that is typical of really important GPTs. Below are a few examples.

Applications

Medical

The original use of monoclonal antibodies was to fight disease. But surprising applications have been developed that use their ability to locate and mark any target. This allows them to be employed in a range of techniques for diagnosis, treatment, monitoring, autopsies, drug purification and screening.

New biomaterials are now routinely manufactured from animals' own tissues. The eventual aim is to use the patient's own genetic material to manufacture anything from skin to organ tissue which can then be returned to substitute for defective material with no fear of rejection by the patient's immune system.

Literally thousands of disorders are now known to be caused by defective genes – cystic fibrosis is but one example. Gene therapy offers promise in the cure of many of these.

Vaccines are the second-largest category of over 200 drugs now being produced by American pharmaceutical companies using biotechnology. Other products include hormones, interferons, blood clotting factors, antisense molecules, and enzymes. Most of these drugs are still undergoing clinical testing, and are designed to combat cancer, AIDS, asthma, diabetes, heart disease, Lyme disease, multiple sclerosis, rheumatoid arthritis, and viral infections (Grace, 1997, p. 81).

Only slightly further away is the ability to build up therapeutic molecules from scratch using computer models to discover the best fits for the surface of a protein that is to be treated.

Although successes and failures cannot be predicted, it is clear that a massive range of successful medical applications of biotechnology is on its way, with the early arrivals already in common use. No one can foresee how much will be accomplished in the next thirty years, but it is likely that medical practice will be transformed in myriad ways.

As is usual, predictions about the effects of biotechnology range from disaster to Utopia. What is clear is that those of us alive today are probably the last people on earth whose life expectancy will be determined by the interaction of a given genetic structure with our environment. The latest in a continuing series of dramatic pronouncements is the discovery of how to alter our biology so as to remove the built-in senescence that causes our muscles to atrophy with age. Whatever the final outcome, there is little doubt that people will vote with their pocket-books to read the prophets of doom while embracing technologies that promise a longer life of better quality.

Agricultural

The use of biotechnology in food production is full of uncertainties about harmful side-effects, and so far the results have been less than some of the optimists predicted when genetically engineered plant life was first produced in the 1970s. If nothing else, public resistance to genetically engineered foodstuffs will slow the development, even if a mass of benign applications is ultimately discovered.

The genetically engineered bovine growth hormone mimics the natural product made by cows and stimulates milk production. Genetically engineered resistance to diseases is a superficially attractive way of reducing the use of herbicides, although many fear that the resistance may spread to weeds. Genetic engineering of grains can be used "to modify different stages of crop production, from speeding up early growth of food plants, to increasing yields, to slowing down ripening or wilting. Since much of the form and function of a plant depends on its genes, the ultimate hope is to engineer optimal plants for every growing condition and market niche" (Grace, 1997, p. 110-2). Plants can now be made resistant to fungal diseases by exposing them to a genetically engineered weak version of the disease to activate their immune system – a procedure analogous to inoculation in humans. No doubt other diseases will be treated in this way in the future. Also in

47

the works are more exotic ways of controlling pests, such as genetically engineering plants to secrete substances that harm the bacteria that live within, and are essential to, many plant pests.

Mixed strategies are being developed to combat the development of resistance among the target pests. Immunity of enemies to any treatment usually comes from activating a recessive gene. By planting some non-engineered plants amidst engineered ones, the hope is that the non-engineered ones will harbour more pests and, when these interbreed with pests that have developed immunities by feeding on engineered plants, the immunity will be suppressed. This is an illustration of the continued war between engineers and their enemies. As soon as a new technique is developed, defences evolve and the engineers seek ways of meeting these defences. Critics worry that this never-ending arms race will induce too many unpredictable and potentially harmful side-effects.

Genetic engineering is being used to improve the freezing tolerance of grains and grapes; this could have major effects on extending the area of cultivation of some key crops. In a practice called "genetic farming", genetic engineers are also using plants and animals as factories to manufacture wanted drugs, industrial chemicals, fuels, plastics, medical products and other materials. Here we see a typical GPT development as the procedure branches out to affect more and more industries that initially were unrelated to biology.

Genetic engineering also has promise for environmental control. In an odd reversal, an oil-digesting bacteria was developed only to have its use proscribed by the US Congress. In response to what they had learned, engineers were able to produce a similar bug by selective breeding without genetic engineering, a version now used in selected clean-ups. This technique may also be useful for cleaning up all sorts of accumulated chemical wastes – a possibility that has enormous potential.

One of the biggest roadblocks to development is that so little is known about bacterial communities in nature. Although microbes are the most abundant and widespread organisms on earth, their ecology is largely a mystery. The immediate need is to discover how microbial communities function in the wild, and how they respond naturally to stresses, such as exposure to materials that are toxic to most organisms (Grace, 1997, p. 139).

Here we see another phenomenon typical of a GPT: it can lead to new major research programmes. In virtually all cases, one can be quite sure that masses of useful information will be generated while also being quite uncertain about where they will be applicable.

Mining

Genetically engineered bacteria, fungi, algae and plants have many potential uses in the mining industry. Examples include recovering metals left in tailings, cleaning up contaminated sites after mines are abandoned, and extracting metal from crushed ores when they are first mined, or even *in situ*. Techniques that leach the minerals from the ores without removing the ore-bearing rock itself would be one of the most fundamental revolutions in metal extraction since people first began mining and smelting.

Forests and oceans

Bioprospecting is steadily locating new medicines and other useful materials in forests and seas. Animals that live with others that are poisonous often produce antitoxins of great potency – materials that, once understood, can be manufactured in laboratories. Other possibilities just on the horizon include salt-resistant, protein-digesting enzymes that may be useful in cleaning industrial machinery; compounds made by algae and sponges that help plants to germinate and grow; and marine enzymes that combine readily with other chemicals and are then useful in processing medicines, food production and cosmetics (Grace, 1997, p. 170). Marine farming is becoming widespread and bioengineering can be used to speed up maturation, growth and egg production, and raise survival rates of offspring.

Bioengineering is also being extending into the forest industry. Of the many new techniques, one of the most promising is micropropagation which clones trees. Its advantages include cheap, fast, mechanised production of trees for reforestation; and the ability to genetically engineer and clone stocks of transgenic trees. Currently, industrial plantation of forests is criticised for major environmental impacts. Genetic engineering of farmed trees looks for new species to improve soil fertility and reduce the need for fertilisers and herbicides.

Conclusion

Biotechnology is evolving just as we would expect a major GPT to do. It is a GPT sufficiently developed to clearly offer many potential uses, but not sufficiently developed for us to even guess at some of the revolutionary new uses further down the road.

Commercial risks are great because the industry is operating under conditions of genuine uncertainty. Payoffs are sometimes a decade or more into the future and many dead ends are encountered. Under these circumstances public assistance can be important in influencing the pace and direction of new developments. Indeed, much of the early pre-commercial research is done in universities and government labs. By now, research is heavily financed by companies, but earlier on the technologies would have been much slower to develop had they not been seeded by government money.

The United States is well in the lead in this entire field, which would seem a success of the US innovation system with its mixed private-public base. One important aspect of this is the massive investment in university research – much of which has practical orientation, and much of which is carried on in close contact with the private sector.

One of the unfortunate uncertainties around biotechologies is the large degree of social risk. Risks of unfortunate, even disastrous side-effects are a major concern, especially since uncertainty is everywhere – there is no way we can rule out the possibility of producing a product that does massive harm before we learn how to control it.

New fuels

The end of the age of fossil fuels will be an important landmark, probably to be passed gradually through a good part of the 21st century. Highly efficient batteries may be one of the first steps. Solar energy, already harnessed for some uses, will become increasingly efficient, as may wind and tidal energy. More problematic is the harnessing of the earth's thermal energy. Finally, nuclear fission may sometime in the next century be harnessed to make an inexhaustible, cheap, non-polluting source of energy, first for large power users and later for small sites.

The major uncertainty is in predicting how long the price of petroleum will remain low enough to discourage major research into these alternative sources. Had the price remained at its 1980 level, the massive research that was then under way would already have produced dramatic results. As it is, the continued low price of oil probably well into the 21st century will slow but not stop research into the sources that will eventually supplant all fossil fuels.

No more needs to be said about these developments, not because their effects will be undramatic but because we know from the past experience of steam, petroleum and electricity how dramatic their effects will be. Fundamental changes will be induced in all elements of the facilitating structure, and a host of new derivative inventions will be made possible. Like all GPTs, the new energy sources will establish a research programme that will last for decades, providing new products and new processes, and hence a vast array of new investment possibilities.

Nanotechnology

Compared with the other GPTs considered here, nanotechnology – the technology of producing goods out of individual atoms and molecules – is but a faint glow on the distant horizon. Conceptually, however, this technology promises the greatest revolution in production since the first stone tool was produced by flaking chips off flints.

Basics

Current "bulk technology" takes materials and pares away the unwanted parts to be left from what is wanted. Nano- or molecular technology handles individual atoms and molecules, building them precisely into desired aggregates, which may be no more than two or three molecules, or may be an object observable to the naked eye.

All goods, manufactured or natural, are composed of atoms. When the atoms are rearranged, the resulting goods are changed. For example, the difference between a diamond and a piece of coal is solely in the arrangement of their atoms. The power to rearrange atoms at will, not long ago thought forever out of our reach, will have staggering implications for the production of economic output.

Nanotechnology is already interacting with other GPTs – including biotechnology, the materials revolution and the computer – without which it would have been impossible. The technology does not yet have all the characteristics of a GPT. It has yet to enter the economy in an important way, and many of its applications are either still only on the drawing board or in designers' imaginations. Yet if nanotechnology fulfils even a significant fraction of its potential, it will become one of the most important GPTs of the coming century. If it meets most of its already perceived potential, it could become *the* most important GPT in all of history.

An early example

One early application of the technology was the production of a planetary gear. It was little more than a toy but it demonstrated that such constructs were indeed feasible:

There had been a lot of trial an error involved, and some of the earlier designs hadn't worked so well. When they were put through tests on molecular modelling software, things came unglued. Gears slipped out of their housings. Molecular rings exploded like firecrackers. Atomic wreckage flew hither and yon. But then there was a design that worked perfectly, a gear system that was made out of 3 557 individual atoms – precisely that many, not one more and not one less (Regis, 1995, p. 13).

Key characteristics

Nanotechnology has a number of key characteristics. The first is the ability to produce almost any shape or structure, so long as it obeys the basic laws of physics. The second is the ability to produce goods for a cost only slightly more than the cost of the raw materials. The third, and most important, is the ability to get every atom into its precise place. Manipulating matter at the molecular level allows it to be treated as a computer treats data, transforming it and reproducing it with perfect precision. This one element of nanotechnology will have huge implications. Just as the increase in the quality of materials allowed fundamental changes in the design of aeroplanes, the increase in precision allowed by nanotechnology (affecting hardness and durability, and creating specifically tailored characteristics) will fundamentally change everything from electronics to construction.

Range of applications

Nanotechnology has already started to revolutionise medicine where it underpins many of the advances in biotechnology. It is being used to produce medical machines the size of a few hundred atoms to practice nanomedicine, which includes non-intrusive surgery. The production of new materials will include new polymers with strength and bonding characteristics that have never been seen before. Nanotechnology will be used to reduce the size and cost of computers, and truly molecular computers may not even use electronic effects. One result will be the production of massively parallel computers, which could evolve into intelligent machines. Other nanoproducts will simplify housekeeping. Dirt-digesting machines will make everything from dishes to carpets self-cleaning, while keeping household air permanently fresh. Nanotechnology will also produce fresh food by mimicking cell growth in plants and animals. Nanoreceptors on TV sets will provide high definition only dreamed of today. Tools will be harder, more durable, and separately created for each specific purpose. Batteries will be minute and long-lived. Fuel efficiency of automobiles (should they still be around) will be enhanced when the spark plugs are replaced by nanoplugs. Aeroplanes will fly faster, higher, longer, and safer when made with nanoengineered materials. Medical implants will be more effective and more durable, and so on, and so on.

Not quite in the realm of science fiction are rooms filled with airborne nanomachines no larger that a molecule of air but with substantial computing power. The slightest command would produce any desired action from those machines, from levitating a bottle of beer out of the refrigerator and into your hand, to repelling an intruder.[7]

> [N]anotechnology could have more effect on our material existence than those last two great inventions in that domain – the replacement of sticks and stones by metals and cements and the harnessing of electricity. Similarly, we can compare the possible effects of artificial intelligence on how we think – and on how we might come to think about ourselves – with only two earlier inventions: those of language and of writing (Minsky, 1986).

5.   Structural adjustments

Every new GPT causes structural adjustments. However, the extent and magnitude of these adjustments varies greatly from one GPT to another. Some GPTs, such as the laser, fit reasonably well into the existing structure. Others, such as electricity, require large and extensive structural adjustments before their full potential can be realised. To see what is involved the discussion now focuses on the currently ongoing set of structural adjustments caused by the ICT revolution discussed above, adjustments that will continue into the 21st century. Briefer attention is then given to the other technologies discussed above.

The ICT Revolution

When computers were initially introduced they entered structures designed for the paper world, merely substituting for human hands and minds. Before they could really pay off, administration and production facilities had to be redesigned both physically and in their command structures. Slowly, again as it was with electricity, the whole process of producing, designing, delivering and marketing goods and services was, and is still being, reorganised along lines dominated by computing technologies. As more and more of the needed changes in the facilitating structure are identified and accomplished, we can expect that, as with electricity, the latent power of the new technology to raise productivity will be seen in measured productivity growth – as it is in many sectors already. This section deals with the facilitating structure; policy and the policy structure are considered later, in Section 7.

The organisation of firms

Administratively, the old hierarchical firm, organised on the military command model in which hoards of middle managers passed information and commands up and down, has given way to the new, more flexible management form of semi-independent groups linked laterally rather than vertically. Many middle managers have lost their jobs in the process.

That much has already happened. The uncertainties attached to the structural impact of major innovations are clearly seen, however, in conjectures about what kinds of organisational adjustments will occur in the future as a result of the continuing ICT revolution. Below are two important examples.

Peter Drucker, who has an enviable record as a seer in this area, foresees a new revolution when firms turn outwards from their current ICT-reinforced concentration on internal costs and organisation. He predicts that the next round of ICT-induced organisational changes will be the use of computers to generate and analyse "outside data", which look at external results rather than internal costs. One early advance is that small and middle-sized enterprises are already engaging in "economic chain accounting". This technique, which traces value right through the value added chain, revolutionised the behaviour of such large enterprises as GM in the 1920s, Sears, Roebuck in the 1930s, and Marks and Spencer, Toyota, and Wal-Mart in the postwar world.

> The more inside information top management gets, the more he will need to balance it with outside information – and that does not exist as yet. Within the next 10 to 15 years, developing this data is going to be the next information frontier. This job is already being tackled [...] primarily by top management people in middle-sized and highly specialised businesses in the role as their companies' main marketing executives (Drucker, 1998, p. 54).

Drucker sees this results-centred approach extending to many other fields, such as education and healthcare. He sees the continuing education of professionals during their entire adult lives, with profound induced structural shifts. Education will to a great extent move "off campus and into a lot of new places: the home, the car, or the commuter train; the workplace, the church basement, or the school auditorium where small groups can meet after hours" (p. 54). In healthcare he sees the focus moving from fighting disease to maintaining physical and mental well-being – a results-centred shift aided by computers tracking people's state of health. Again, the structural adjustments will be profound. "Neither of the traditional health care providers, the hospital and the general practice physician, may survive this change, and certainly not in their present form and function" (p. 54).

Malone and Laubacher (1998) foresee an even more fundamental transformation caused by the growth of what they call the "e-lance economy" – an economy dominated by the electronically linked freelancers.

> The coordinating technologies of the industrial era – the train, and the telegraph, the automobile and the telephone, the mainframe computer – made internal transactions not only possible but also advantageous [...] But with the introduction of powerful personal computers and broad electronic networks – the coordinating technologies of the twenty-first century – the economic equation changes. [p. 147] [...] Because information can be shared instantaneously and inexpensively among many people in many locations, the value of centralised decision making and expensive bureaucracies decreases [...] the new coordination techniques allow us to return to the pre-industrial organisational model of tiny autonomous businesses [...] conducting transactions with one another in a market [...] [with] one crucial difference: electronic networks enable these microbusinesses to tap into the global reservoirs of information, expertise, and financing that used to be available only to large companies. [p. 148] [...] The fundamental unit of such an economy is not the corporation but the

individual. These electronically connected freelancers – e-lancers – join together into fluid and temporary networks to produce and sell goods and services. When the job is done [...] the network dissolves, and its members become independent agents again, circulating through the economy, seeking the next assignment [p. 146].

Should anything like this come to pass, the structural adjustment would be enormous. There would be:

fundamental changes in virtually every business function [...] Supply chains would become ad hoc structures, assembled to fit the needs of a particular project and disassembled when the project ended. Manufacturing capacity would be bought and sold in an open market, and independent, specialised manufacturing concerns would undertake small batch order of a variety of brokers, design shops, and even consumers. Marketing would be performed in some cases by brokers, in other cases by small companies that would own brands and certify the quality of the merchandise sold under them. In still other cases, the ability of consumer to share product information on the Internet would render marketing obsolete; consumers would simply "swarm" around the best offerings. Financing would come less from retained earnings and big equity markets and more from venture capitalists and interested individuals [p. 150].

Many e-lance enterprises already exist. The vision of a major e-lance sector, even if it only covers, say, 20% of the whole economy, is unlike anything seen since the first Industrial Revolution destroyed the Putting-Out System.

This discussion illustrates that the major structural changes in the organisation of productive units are not yet over; that they will continue at a rapid rate; and that there are major surprises yet to come.

Economies of scope and scale

As GPTs have done in the past, the ICT revolution is altering scale economies in complex ways. Whereas economies of scale in manufacturing were a driving force in the postwar expansion of many industries, increasingly they are becoming either non-important or redefined. The introduction of computers and other information technologies, plus the use of advanced materials, have drastically lowered the minimum efficient scale of production for many individual product lines. One firm's fixed costs of computers and other facilities are covered by producing many product lines so that economies of scope become more important than economies of scale.

The organisation of service production has also changed rapidly. On the one hand, firms operating on a global scale in law, accounting and other traditional services are replacing many of the older individual operators. On the other hand, computers – plus a host of related electronic devices such as faxes, photocopiers, and modems – allow many independent providers of services to work out of home rather than where their services are consumed. The Internet allows these individuals access to masses of information and the ability to interact with others that was formerly only available to employees of very large corporations. If the first Industrial Revolution took work out of the home, the Computer Revolution is, at least partially, putting it back, with profound social and economic consequences.

Deindustrialisation and servicisation

The new technologies have accentuated a trend observable throughout most of this century. Manufacturing employment typically reached a peak of somewhere between 25-35% of the labour force in most industrialised societies earlier in this century. Since then, the proportion has been steadily declining and shows no signs of stabilising yet. At the same time, the proportion of the labour force employed in services has been growing steadily, to the point where it is now the largest single sector by employment in all industrialised economies. Note, however, that as with agriculture, total output of manufactured goods has continued to rise but productivity has risen even faster, so that manufacturing employment has fallen.

The "servicisation" of the economy has a number of sources. First, some of the apparent shift is definitional. Second, on the demand side the shift to services is partly driven by consumers' tastes. As real incomes rise, people spend a lower proportion of their incomes on durable consumer goods and a rising proportion on such services as medical care, travel, and restaurants. Third, on the supply side the decline in employment in manufacturing is partly a measure of its success in producing more with less inputs, especially labour. A range of service activities that used to be conducted in-house by manufacturing firms, and so recorded as manufacturing activities, is now contracted out to firms specialised in a wide range of activities such as product design, marketing, accounting, cleaning and maintenance, and so recorded as service activities. Fourth, also on the supply side, the ICT revolution has encouraged many service activities by making them more efficient. Travel agents now have real-time access to travel and vacation possibilities; financial advisors monitor the performance of worldwide investment opportunities by the minute; courier services deliver packages worldwide, tracking them at every stage of their journey.

Locational effects: globalisation[8]

Globalisation, the rapid acceleration of which has been going on for over a century, is due in large part to the ICT revolution. The effects on manufacturing follow from three distinct developments. First, the new ICTs have allowed production to be disintegrated into a series of independent operations. Second, ICTs allow independent units to be co-ordinated in ways that were impossible in the past. Seventy-five years ago, even where production was split between many component suppliers, these had to be within relatively short distances of each other so that components could be delivered to assemblers when and where they were required. Third, improvements in transportation technologies, particularly containerisation and the development of very large ships, have greatly reduced the costs of shipping goods around the world. Today, with the ability to co-ordinate worldwide and to ship products at very low cost, component parts can be produced anywhere in the world in the right quantities and shipped to arrive when and where they are needed with little error.

The same is true of many services. Accounting of all sorts is increasingly being decentralised to areas where labour is still cheap. Ireland, the Caribbean and India are all locations in which large transnational corporations, such as credit card and travel companies, do much of their record keeping and accounting. Software firms are also moving much of their coding work to places outside of North America. While India is still a relatively small producer of software in absolute terms, it is now one of the fastest-growing sources of computer coding in the world. When an Indian technician uses the Internet to repair some electronic equipment in Boston, where does the production take place? Where is the value created? Where should it be taxed?

The importance of human capital in many of the new growth sectors has given rise to a need for factor creation, which creates national comparative advantages based on human capital and technological infrastructure. This has had important effects on the old matrix of international comparative advantage.

> By the end of the 1980s, in most advanced industrial economies, not only were natural factor endowments assuming a less important locational role, but also the actions of governments, through their willingness and ability to affect the quantity and quality of these endowments and their organisation, were assuming a new significance (Dunning, 1993, p. 601).

Labour

Flexible, knowledge-intensive production techniques and a global market in low-skilled labour have led to a need to redefine the role of the union. No longer are strict, rigid job descriptions a supportable labour practice. Skill requirements for previously low-skilled jobs have risen as design, production and marketing increasingly involve creating and processing information.

Effecting the required changes quickly has been a conflict-ridden process. To many labour leaders, the need to change procedures that were worked out painfully over decades early in this century and that worked well for further decades seems like some plot by employers to exploit employees instead of an inevitable adjustment to new technologies.

European and Canadian labour markets have shown high unemployment since the mid-1970s. Although there is controversy about causes, market rigidities are thought by many to bear some part of the blame. Technological displacement has also accounted for some of the unemployment, as the restructuring of finance and industry has caused a shedding of jobs and left people at least temporarily unemployed, sometimes for quite long periods.

Both firms and workers are going through an evolution where structural relationships are adapting to changes in the technology. This sorting out process should bring productivity gains in the long term, but there are likely to be casualties in terms of job demarcations and other structural dislocations and relocations as the process evolves. Currently it is the well-paid and well-educated who are benefiting most from the introduction of the computer in the workplace; thus, computerisation is reinforcing the polarisation of incomes and jobs.

Dealing with long-term unemployment and finding ways to diminish the proportion of the labour force that is unskilled and therefore in competition with unskilled labour worldwide are urgent matters for public policy in the developed nations.

Social organisations

Ways of life are changing with the changing patterns of work. With electronic communication, groups of like-minded individuals are finding it easier to get together. Technologies have effectively redefined our notions of time and distance (and in some ways have created the much-heralded global village).

> By linking people and groups, e-mail encourages work across space, time and group boundaries. Indeed, the absence of constraining non-verbal cues and social controls in e-mail may make it easier to communicate with unknown or peripheral people than through face-to-face means. Such wide-ranging ties are especially useful for linking socially diverse people, obtaining innovative information and integrating organisations (Wellman and Buxton, 1994, p. 12).

Conclusion

The scale of R&D in the new applications of ICT, the extraordinary growth of the software industry and related business services, the scale of investment in computerised equipment and in the telecommunications infrastructure, the rapid growth of industries supplying the ICT products and services, and the use of computers within every function in every industry have led some observers to characterise the ICT

Revolution as a structural change in the economy comparable to the first Industrial Revolution. Peter Drucker argues, with not much exaggeration, that:

> We are clearly in the middle of this transformation [...] already it has changed the political, economic, social, and moral landscape of the world. No one born in 1990 could possibly imagine the world in which one's grandparents [...] had grown up, or the world in which one's own parents had been born (Drucker, 1993, p. 3).

The future is hard to predict but the ICT Revolution is still in full swing. Many applications of new products, new processes and new ways of organising activities have yet to be invented. Their effects will continue to reverberate through most economies during the first half of the 21st century.

Other technologies

The other GPTs discussed above will also have major effects on structure and economic performance. The full discussion of ICTs above is intended to provide a foretaste of the changes that the other technologies may have in store over the next decades; thus there will be only brief mention of the adjustments that will be induced by the other technologies.

New materials

In certain industries the materials revolution will have significant effects on the organisation, geographic location and degree of concentration of firms. Most of these changes can, however, be accommodated within the existing structure and so will not themselves cause the kinds of deep-seated structural adjustments caused by the ICT revolution.

Biotechnology

In contrast, biotechnology will cause deep and widespread changes in the facilitating structure. Many of biotechnological processes have large-scale economies and so the size of firms will increase in many lines. Also, intellectual property rights are currently being redefined in quite fundamental ways. There is ongoing conflict between innovating countries that want tough new property rights and the adopting countries that want weaker control for inventors and innovators. Some researchers feel that it has already become much too easy to patent a bio-engineered product or process (see for example Eisenberg, 1996).

Biotechnology will transform many basic industries such as agriculture, forestry and mining, changing them almost beyond recognition. Although the details are still hard to predict, we can be sure that massive adjustments will occur throughout the facilitating structure as biotechniques begin to transform these and other industries.

More importantly, the impact of the medical applications of biotechnology will be profound. Increasing average life spans from 70 to, say, 110 years over the course of half a century will require enormous adjustments in all aspects of the facilitating and policy structures. Imagination rapidly proves inadequate when predicting the pervasive adjustments that will have to be made in response to just this one medical advance – to say nothing of the many other advances, including big alterations in the prevalence of many human ailments (and the possible introduction of new ones).

Non-fossil fuels

The end of fossil fuels will also bring about major adjustments in the facilitating and policy structures that are hard to imagine in detail. At one extreme, major shifts in global power balances will occur when oil and coal cease to be important commodities. At the other extreme, local pollution and city layouts will alter greatly. The decommissioning of the vast infrastructure of production and distribution of petroleum products will cause profound upsets that will coexist with the rise of a new infrastructure adapted to the new fuels, and take forms that cannot be predicted today.

Nanotechnology

Guessing at the adjustments in the facilitating structure that would be brought about by a major shift to nanotechnology is still in the realm of science fiction. Just as our electronic world would look like magic to people transported from 1800 to 2000, the world of nano, bio and materials technology will look like nothing on earth to us if we could be transported to 2100 or even 2050.

Opportunities for great technological dynamism are surely offered by this radical new technology. Adjustment problems that may tax the ability of societies to manage them will probably also arise.

6.   The anatomy of long booms

What does all that has been said so far suggest about the future? Will there be boom or stagnation, or some of both? The possibility of a continuing boom depends a great deal on what one means by the term. The concept that seems to underlie the topic of this book is a very long boom of a century or more. The concept that emerges from our S-E theory is a boom lasting several decades followed by a period of rapid structural adjustment and pervasive uncertainty.

Century-long booms

In a very long-term perspective, there is one long boom covering the period stretching to the present time and starting with the second Industrial Revolution in the latter part of the 19th century. This revolution was characterised by the rise of science-based industries often depending on organised R&D, and the spread of electricity through the entire economy. If that is to be our perspective we must be willing to see the 1930s and the 1980s and 90s as lesser cycles within that long boom. Given this perspective, it seems pretty clear that a boom of this sort will continue well into the 21st century. Everything that we know about the GPTs that are either in full bloom or in obvious bud suggests that investment and employment related to the new technologies will persist at high levels, at least into the first half of the 21st century.

Decade-long booms

In another perspective, the period 1945-75 was a secular boom which was preceded by a period of major upheaval which culminated in the Great Depression (whose depth was very probably magnified by poor macroeconomic policies) and was followed by the structural upheavals of the 1980s and 1990s. This is the kind of boom that we have associated with the mature stage of an entire technological system (or paradigm) after the facilitating and policy structures have become fairly well adjusted to it.

To deal with this type of boom Freeman and Perez (1988) develop the concept of a "techno-economic paradigm" It describes a socio-economic technology system which includes all of the items covered here under technology, facilitating and policy structures. They see these as coming together into a systemic whole. Occasionally the whole paradigm changes, as when electricity replaced steam, or electronic ICTs replaced the paper world.

Here, the S-E model with its explicit disaggregation is preferred; nonetheless, it is acknowledged that these ideas grew out of theirs. Both treatments expect a major new system of interrelated technologies grouped around some really important evolving GPT, to be accompanied by massive readjustments to every element of the facilitating structure and many elements of policy and the policy structure, some of them in a conflict-ridden process.[9] Then, after the whole new set of technologies is developed and the facilitating and policy structures have adapted, a period of secular boom can ensue as the full potential of the new technologies is worked out. This can be a period of rapid technological advance, but mainly in incremental and lesser radical inventions. These develop the potential of existing GPTs, which take place within stable and well-adjusted facilitating and policy structures.

Booms of this sort tend to have several characteristics. The facilitating structure is fairly well-adapted and further inventions and innovation fit fairly well into it. For this reason, the areas of uncertainty are substantially diminished compared with the preceding period of rapid structural adjustment. The requirements of the labour force become fairly well known so that young people understand the kinds of education that are needed to fit into the new economy. Business is profitable as new incremental improvements, applications and derivative inventions are made and marketed. These are likely to be associated with a higher rate of productivity growth than were earlier innovations which had to be fitted into facilitating and policy structures that were not well adapted to them.

Such was the period between 1945 and 1975 in the United States. The new electric age had been well established, factories had been remodelled to suit machines driven by unit drive electric motors, the system of mass assemblers and decentralised parts manufacturers was in place, the infrastructures for electricity generation and petroleum refining and their respective distribution systems had been installed, and the adjustments to the internal combustion engine and automobiles were well under way. Within this stable structure, the full potential of the new technologies was developed in what is seen with hindsight to have been a period of strong and rapid growth. (Because of the disruption of the Second World War and because mass production was later in being accepted in Europe, the timing was a little later in Europe than in North America – the time frame to which this discussion applies.)

There was a similar period of about fifty years that started around 1840, when the full potential of the steam engine, driving railway engines, ships, automated machines in factories, etc. was being worked out in a structure that had been painfully adapted during the transition from the early stages of the first industrial age, in which the water-wheel was the main motive force for stationary engines and the horse for movement.

It seems reasonable to see the ICT revolution as being at about the same stage as was the electric and motor car revolutions in the late 1930s. Much has been worked out, and the full potential of the computer is foreseen but not yet realised. Many of the structural adjustments in the organisation of offices and plants, design, and information control, as well as the infrastructure of the information highway, are already in place, at least in embryo form. The near future should see vast improvements in the efficiency of the new technologies increasingly taking place, as well as a widening of their range of applications, within a structure designed for electronic rather than paper ICTs.

If the past is any guide, and to the extent that other forces such as wars or poor public policies do not upset expectations, we might expect a secular boom starting about 2000 and extending into the 2020s or 2030s. This will not necessarily preclude large sections of the population from remaining unemployed or cyclical fluctuations from occurring but, like the 1950s and 1960s, the fluctuations should be mild and grafted onto a rising trend of output and productivity.

Of course, during such a boom the economy is only stable relative to the period of transition that preceded it. Change and uncertainty are always present. Also, each technology carries its own characteristic costs and benefits. If the ICT technology has speeded up the pace of innovations, which seems pretty clear, more rapid product cycles may lead to lower profits, lower rates of return on capital that rapidly becomes obsolete, and higher uncertainty than accompanied previous booms. Change will always destroy some jobs and if labour markets are rigid, substantial structural unemployment may persist.

Alternative possibilities

Of course, these theories, combined with the evidence of the past, can only suggest possibilities, or at most broad probabilities. Thus, many things could upset the prediction of a coming secular boom, aside from the always-present possibility that the whole theory could be wrong. The current Asian crisis, or some new one that is mismanaged by monetary authorities, might develop into a deep, worldwide depression. A shift to inward-looking, protectionist and anti-growth policies might drastically slow (although it would be unlikely to fully stop) the pace of technological advance. The pace at which one fundamental GPT follows another might accelerate so much that facilitating and policy structures never become well enough adjusted to create the stable conditions needed for the full development of any one GPT, and the secular boom that often accompanies its later stages.

On the first item, there is nothing to add about the possibility that some crisis unrelated to the technological dynamism of Europe and North America might create a severe worldwide recession. On the second, government policies are considered in the last part of this chapter. This leaves the possibility of problems caused by too much technological change, rather than too little, to be discussed now.

Past periods of sustained development of the new GPTs' full potential have taken place after the facilitating and policy structures became fairly well adjusted to a new set of prevailing GPTs. For this to happen, those major new GPTs that require extensive adjustments to the facilitating structure must be introduced far enough apart for the structure to have sufficient time to become well-adapted to the prevailing set of GPTs. Although not easy to measure, it seems that the pace of technological change is speeding up. Among other things, the late 19th century institutionalisation of invention and innovation, which in all previous times was mainly in the hands of non-scientists, has led to a cascading advancement of knowledge and a shortening of the time between the discovery of fundamental scientific knowledge and its commercial application.

Currently, no fundamental new GPT is sufficiently well-developed to destabilise the facilitating and policy structures that are becoming increasingly well-adapted to the current ICT and materials revolutions. Of the new GPTs discussed earlier, biotechnology, nanotechnology and a pervasive new energy source probably have the characteristics capable of causing upheavals in the facilitating and policy structures comparable to those caused by the factory, steam and electricity. It must also be remembered that it is often impossible to identify a technology in the early stages of its development as one that will develop into a fully fledged GPT. Given the three fundamental GPTs already coming into place and the possibility of further ones not yet identified, we cannot rule out the possibility of the reverse of secular stagnation. In this case there would be a succession of upheavals due to a series of new GPTs, each one of which would outdate many of the facilitating and policy structures that are relevant to the established GPTs.

7. Policies to exploit potential

It is one thing for there to be a potential for dynamism; it is another for that potential to be realised. The latter depends on many things, including public policy.

New policy views

Events over the last couple of decades have forced many governments to revise their views on appropriate economic policies. Among other things, it is now understood that there are massive and often unpredictable technical changes that are difficult to predict and to manage; the facilitating structure is constantly changing; and global competition is restricting any government's ability to act unilaterally. According to the new policy paradigm, sustaining dynamism into the 21st century requires that governments cease to do many of the things they routinely did in the mid-20th century, and that they newly take on, or increase their existing emphasis on, other activities.

Some accepted key government functions are:

– Macro policies must provide a stable background in terms of low inflation, reasonable investment incentives, a stable fiscal regime with either balanced budgets or sustainable deficits and micro policies without excessive disincentives, such as high marginal rates of taxation, high indirect labour costs, and excessive regulatory burdens. Among other things, this requires the scaling back of entitlements that seemed supportable in the postwar era.

– Appropriate market supporting institutions must be provided, such as the justice system, property rights, freedom of contracts, ensuring a sound money and a well-functioning financial system, and providing quality control product standardisation and consumer protection.

- An efficient infrastructure is also required. The realisation that technological dynamism is needed in these areas, as well as the growing belief that production should be left to the private sector except where there are compelling reasons for public control, has led to the privatisation of many government-owned infrastructure activities, particularly in the United States and the United Kingdom.

- Human capital must be created for the new knowledge society, a need which extends from providing the substantial minimum level below which people become unemployable, to higher education, to providing adequate staffing for private- and public-sector R&D.

- Strong support for R&D, including assistance in the creation of emerging technologies in the pre-commercial stage. For example, much of the early basic US research on biotechnology and nanotechnology was done, and some still is being done, in publicly funded universities and research labs.

Policies for technological dynamism

Economists debate what kinds of S&T policies are needed to support technological dynamism. Neoclassical economics is structureless. Its equations apply to all markets everywhere, and it produces a single set of policy prescriptions applicable to everyone: remove market imperfections. In the case of invention and innovation, a positive externality is recognised and, therefore, a generalised non-distorting subsidy to R&D is recommended. As Ken Carlaw and the author have pointed out in detail in a series of publications, (See, e.g., Lipsey and Carlaw 1996, 1998a and 1998b), this advice does not take into account what is known through both empirical studies and S-E theory concerning endogenous technological change. S-E theory, like Romer's macro endogenous growth theory, recognises that unique optimal policies cannot be derived in the case of knowledge creation. Romer emphasises the non-rivalrous nature of knowledge, which invalidates the standard conditions for an optimal allocation of resources – perfect property rights and competitive markets. S-E theories emphasise the uncertainty of technological advance which creates a context-specific, path-dependent world in which there are better and worse polices but no unique optimal set for all times and all places. Both of these approaches prescribe policy approaches that practical policy makers and advisors have come to accept as a result of observing the changing knowledge-intensive world and the failures of some past policies. Here are a few examples.

Assisting pre-competitive research

Many economists, particularly in the United States, argue that governments have little potential to influence the process of technological change in a useful way. The reality is that many important technologies have been encouraged in their early, largely pre-competitive stages by public sector assistance in the United States, as well as in other countries. Here are a few US examples of this important point.

Publicly funded US land grant colleges have done important agricultural research from their inception in the 19th century. The 20th century "green revolution" was to a great extent researched by public funds. In its early stages, the US commercial aircraft industry received substantial assistance from the National Advisory Committee on Aeronautics (NACA) which, among other things, pioneered the development of large wind tunnels and demonstrated the superiority of the retractable landing gear. The airframe for the Boeing 707 and the engines for the 747 were both developed in publicly funded military versions before being transferred to successful civilian aircraft. Electronic computers and atomic energy were largely created in response to military needs and with military funding. For many years, support for the US semiconductor industry came mainly from military procurement, whose rigid standards and quality controls helped to standardise practices and to diffuse technical knowledge. The US Government's activities in the software industry produced two major spin-offs to the commercial sector: an infrastructure of academic experts built largely with government funding, and high industry standards.

Knowing when and how to use public funds to encourage really important new technologies in their early stages is one of the most important conditions for remaining technologically dynamic.

Created assets

Many of the new technologies are knowledge-based in the sense that human capital is the most important resource required. Governments have always played an important part in creating human capital, for example by establishing elementary schools, trade schools and institutions of higher education. Uncertainty surrounds the design of education most suitable for today's rapidly changing world. Today's monolithic state education systems encourage less diverse experimentation than would occur if education were provided by the private sector (and universal access provided by vouchers or some other similar system). As with commercial innovation, the best response to uncertainty is to maximise experimentation, as a free market in education would do.

Policies concerning FDI

To be technologically dynamic, a country needs to be a part of the global economy, which normally requires two things. First, a substantial presence of TNCs within its borders is required. Second, where firms need to be international in scope, outward-bound FDI is an important step in turning successful domestic industries into truly global competitors, rather than an undesirable export of jobs.

A key part of government policy is the treatment of foreign-owned relative to home-owned firms. The technology-support initiatives of many countries are often open only to home-owned firms, as was the US SEMATECH. As a result, foreign firms that are major creators of domestic jobs are denied support, while domestic firms that do most of their production in foreign countries are included. There is a strong case that countries that wish to remain technologically dynamic should treat all firms based in their jurisdictions equally (as, for example, the three NAFTA countries must do to firms owned in any NAFTA country).

Fixed costs of acquiring knowledge

Acquiring codifiable knowledge about new technologies, as well as tacit knowledge of how to operate given technologies, often requires heavy fixed costs. Thus small firms often operate in "rational ignorance" of existing relevant technologies. Government bodies can disseminate technological knowledge by operating on a scale that makes the sunk costs bearable, even trivial, where they would be prohibitively high for small firms. The institutional design of such programmes is critical if they are to succeed in this difficult area. The very successful Canadian Industrial Research Assistance Program (IRAP) is a case in point. (This programme is described and evaluated in Lipsey and Carlaw, 1998*b*, Chapter 4.)

Catch-up and leading-edge economies

The recognition that technical change is endogenous makes S&T policies become context-specific in many ways. For one example, the problems of catch-up are very different from the problems of trying to stay on the cutting edge of technological advance. Catch-up economies, especially in their earlier stages, have the advantage of dealing with already established technologies. Although there are still uncertainties associated with tacit knowledge and local adaptations of generic technologies, many of the main uncertainties of cutting-edge advances are removed. Many market-oriented Asian countries in the catch-up stage have championed consultative processes whereby the government agency and the main private sector agents pool their knowledge and come to a consensus on where the next technology push should be and then jointly finance it. This policy worked well in the catch-up phase and it still works well when all private agents are pushing for a fairly well defined small-to-intermediate advance in technology. Consensus and co-operation can then eliminate wasteful duplication of pre-competitive research. But when more major breakthroughs at the cutting edge are being sought, the inevitable uncertainties call for a multiplicity of investigations, each pursued with the minimum required funds. Here concentrating effort, even after a national consensus has been reached, is likely to be worse than the apparent "wastefulness" of unco-ordinated experimentation that occurs in the free market. Possible illustrations are Japan's costly failures in high definition TV, which was overtaken by the digital revolution, and in the 5th generation chip, which proved too big a technological jump to succeed against the more conservative US approach.

Changes in structure

Policies may also indirectly target technological change by altering elements of the facilitating structure. Examples of such policies include attempts to integrate some university, government and private sector research activities, attempts to create technology information networks, and attempts to change private sector attitudes toward adopting new or different technologies. Furthermore, a government can give funds to firms to develop technologies that they would have developed anyway but then attach structural conditions. This has been done by more than one government to encourage the development of long-range research facilities. All of these initiatives would fail narrow tests that measure only direct changes in specified technologies, but would pass wider tests that consider alterations in the structure which would not have happened without the government pressure. Two prime examples are the aforementioned US military procurement policy that virtually created the US software industry, and Canada's Defence Industry Productivity Program (DIPP) which helped firms to create R&D facilities in the early stages of what is now Canada's very successful aerospace industry.

Institutional competence

Policies are given effect by the policy structure, and their success depends to a great extent on the institutional competencies of those administering them. The ability of government to carry out some types of policies aimed at technological dynamism will vary across governments partly because of constitutional differences (e.g. first-past-the-post or proportional representation and cabinet or decentralised powers); partly on the power relations between various special interest groups (e.g. are government required to broker regional differences? and how strong are the Greens?); partly on the nature of their civil services (e.g. professional or amateur, well or poorly paid); and partly on the accumulated learning-by-doing in operating their country's typical set of policy instruments over the past. Policies need to be tailored to suit a nation's institutional competence.

Conclusion

This discussion only scratches the surface of specific policies to promote technological dynamism. The author and his colleagues have studied the reasons for success or failure in 30 such individual policies (Lipsey and Carlaw, 1996). A second publication drew lessons about the conditions that lead to success and those that lead to the all-too-many failures (Lipsey and Carlaw, 1998*b*). In the former publication, our general position was summarised as follows.

An innovation policy will work well or poorly depending on how well adapted it is to such elements of the facilitating structure as the pattern of industrial concentration, the structure and behaviour of financial institutions, the mobility of labour, the way in which the political system brokers regional interests, and the ability of special interest groups to capture particular policies and public bodies. It is useful to ask how well adapted a country's policies are to its structure. It is useful to ask if other countries have elements of their innovation policy that work well and could be easily transferred to one's own structure. It is not useful to think of copying completely another country's set of innovation policies, especially when their structures are as radically different as are, say, those of Japan and Canada or the US (Lipsey and Carlaw, 1996, page 299).

8.   The need for social consensus

The shift of policies from those of the middle-20th century to those appropriate to the new conditions is unlikely to be accomplished or sustained in the absence of a social consensus that change is needed. French Colbertist policies had that social consensus uniting the elite who were technologically oriented and the populace who approved of reducing foreign domination. There seems to be no such French consensus for adopting new policies consistent with the new technologies, and a diminished place for government in production of goods and services. The German Government is having trouble persuading the populace that levels of entitlements that seemed feasible in the postwar boom are no longer affordable. The Canadians achieved such a consensus and then jeopardised it when the opposition party got elected on a platform of undoing all of the reforms and then reneged on all of their important promises. This left the Conservative government that imposed the changes one of the most hated governments in Canadian history, while the current Liberal government is under pressure from the electorate and many of its own rank and file to reactivate some of its Luddite promises.

There is space to mention only in passing a few of the forces that may make reaching and/or sustaining the new policy consensus difficult. First, continued high unemployment makes it difficult to impose reforms that impose further short-term pain, although structural rigidities in the labour market need to be alleviated as part of the new policy package.

Second, increasing disparities in the distribution of income create a "have" and "have-not" dichotomy that is inimical to social consensus. In the United States, this has been exacerbated by the tendency to cut entitlements for the poorer groups while leaving some key middle class entitlements in place, contributing to social stress. It is worth noting here that there are forces in current technological change that contribute to rising inequality. New technological paradigms always create inequalities between those lucky enough to have human capital suited to the new techniques and those who do not. The current ICT technologies add some new forces. They make it easier to gain information about the contributions of individuals and so to reward each separately rather than in the broad groups needed with cruder information systems. Also, globalisation, by uniting formerly separate markets, leads to greater stratification and hence greater income inequalities.[10] Offsetting to some extent these demand-side tendencies, there should be some supply-side adjustment as the education system begins to train a larger fraction of the labour force in the skills needed for the new economy.

Third, there is a strong desire to maintain old entitlements, particularly on the part of older people who counted on them. This is an argument for grandfathering some vested interests that are threatened by reforms. But this gives rise to intergenerational jealousies.

Finally, the rapid pace of technological change and structural adjustment has led to a fear of big business, globalisation, and technological change. This could lead to a reversion to more inward-looking policies, particularly in the United States and possibly in Canada as well. A turning away from the postwar outward-looking stance, as seen for example in the reluctance of the United States to embrace the extension of NAFTA, could have serious repercussions for world dynamism.

9. The policy structure

The current structure of government is still the old hierarchical departmental structure that was found in most firms in the middle of the 20th century. Many matters that civil servants now have to deal with cut across these traditional structures and hierarchical information channels. But unlike firms, many of whom have changed in response, there has been little alteration of the structure of government departments. Lacking bottom-line constraints, governments find it difficult to alter the structure of their operating institutions. Societies that manage to reform governments along lines made efficient by the ITC revolution, may be those that make the most of the dynamic opportunities in the area of private-public sector co-operation in the 21st century.

Government power

Aside from creating the need to change the operating institutions, the ICT revolution is altering some of the very basics of government power. All governments are being impacted by globalisation and the other structural adjustments associated with the ICT revolution.

Diminished power

Sophisticated communications and vast amounts of short-term capital in the hands of TNCs make it impossible for governments to control international capital movements in the ways that they routinely did in previous times.

Many of today's most important assets are both created and internationally mobile. A country whose government policies reduce the value of these assets significantly more than do the policies of other governments loses many of these assets. The resulting limitations on policy independence are profound.

The increasing difficulty that governments face in dictating what their citizens will see and hear has greatly curtailed the efficacy of information-restriction policies exercised in the interest of many purposes, from supporting a repressive dictatorship at one extreme to encouraging local cultural industries at the other.

Increased power

In other areas, governments have gained power. Computers allow the collection and cross-referencing of masses of data about individual citizens and firms. The technology exists today to locate any inconsistent statements given to two different government authorities and, unless it is controlled by political means, this possibility may soon be realised. Developments in genetics have provided breakthroughs in crime prevention and detection. As a final example, traffic control will see major changes in the next decade as it becomes possible to track cars through urban streets and to monitor speed with advanced technologies.

The more distant future

No one can be sure how the full development of ICT technology, by say 2030, will affect the powers of the state. Some, such as Davidson and Rees Mogg (1997), see a great deterioration of state power as assets disappear into the untraceable cyberspace in which business is increasingly transacted. We can be sure that the government's power to track and tax wealth and income transactions will diminish, but we do not know by how much. One disturbing observation is in order. In the final analysis, taxes are voluntary and if enough transactions do escape, the sense of injustice among those who still pay may reach a point where widespread tax evasion disrupts the whole system. If the social consensus that taxes should (more or less) be paid breaks down in the face of cyberspace evasion, a real crisis of the state could ensue. How this affects growth and technological dynamism will depend on all sorts of imponderables, including how the nation state responds to its loss of power and how the private sector copes with the resulting dramatic restriction of state activity.

Reallocations of power

Reallocations are tending to transfer some of the powers of national governments upward to supranational bodies and others downward to more local levels of government.

Pulling in one direction, globalisation is requiring supervision at the international level of many issues involving trade and investment. The importance to most countries of a relatively free flow of international trade has led them to transfer power over trade restrictions to supranational bodies such as the World Trade Organisation (WTO), the EU, the NAFTA, and MERCOSUR. The interrelation of trade and investment brought about by the ICT revolution has caused modern trade liberalising agreements to be expanded to include measures to ensure the free flow and "national treatment" of foreign investment.

Due to globalisation of trade and investment, policies with respect to such matters as labour practices, industrial competition, R&D support, subsidies and intellectual property protection, which were formerly of purely domestic interest, now affect international flows of trade, FDI and factors of production. Trade liberalising arrangements are now working towards "deep integration" in which the sources of these "systems frictions" are brought under international control, which implies major transfers of power from national to supranational levels of government (Ostry, 1990).

In contrast, consciousness of regional identities and the decline of broad identification with the nation-state, which are also related to the globalisation caused by the ICT revolution, are causing pressures for the devolution of some powers to lower levels of authority. Provided that acceptable allocations are achieved, there is no need to find these two pressures contradictory. If common markets (or at least modern free trade areas) are maintained among the local authorities, there is little reason to oppose the devolution of considerable power with respect to cultural and community matters to local authorities, although making the transition is often a conflict-ridden process.

Determining an appropriate allocation of functions between local, national and international levels of government, and willingness to pass some power upwards to supranational authorities and some downwards to state and local authorities, are two of the most important tasks facing modern national governments. How well this is managed will be one important determinant of a nation's technological dynamism in the 21st century.

Notes

1. The author argues that the split between pure investment, as measured by increases in physical and human capital, and technological change, as measured by total factor productivity, is only possible under a strong set of assumptions never found in reality. In practice, new investment embodies some existing and some new technologies and it is impossible to separate how much of any increase in GDP is due to "pure" investment and how much to technological change. (See Lipsey, Bekar and Carlaw, forthcoming.)

2. The author has developed this model in a series of publications starting in the early 1990s. The fully elaborated version is in Lipsey, Bekar and Carlaw (forthcoming) and one published brief account is in Lipsey and Carlaw (1998*a*).

3. Risk occurs when outcomes have both well-defined expected values and probability distributions. In uncertain situations, it is often impossible even to enumerate all the possible outcomes, let alone assign an expected value to each.

4. For a detailed consideration of these characteristics and a development of the definition that follows in the text, see Lipsey, Bekar and Carlaw, Ch. 2 in Helpman, 1998.

5. Technological dynamism was found in China from the beginning of civilisation until a time that is debated but was probably between the 16th and the 17th centuries. It was also found in the Islamic countries for a shorter period running from about the 11th to the 14th centuries.

6. These issues are discussed in more detail in Lipsey and Bekar, 1995.

7. For a description of such airborne machines see Crandall, 1996.

8. The author has discussed the implications of the new ICTs on globalisation at length in Lipsey, 1997.

9. Whether a new GPT fits into the existing facilitating structure or requires a whole new structure depends on the technological characteristics of each individual GPT.

10. To illustrate this important point, consider a set of markets. Each market has 100 clients with incomes spread out evenly between $1 000 and $100 000 and each is served by two professionals with different abilities whose fees are proportional to their client's abilities. The professional with the greatest ability gets the clients with the highest incomes. When the markets are isolated, each will be served by the two local professionals, the better of which will have clients with an average income of $75 000 while the other's clients will average $25 000. Now let the two markets be united. Now the four professionals will each serve a quarter of the combined market and the average

incomes of their clients will be $87 500, $62 500, $37 500 and $12 500, respectively. The more markets unite, the more the stratification according to ability and the more the inequalities in the professionals' incomes.

Bibliography

CRANDALL, B.C., ed. (1996),
Nanotechnology Molecular Speculations on Global Abundance. Cambridge, Mass: MIT Press.

DAVID, P. (1991),
"Computer and Dynamo: The Modern Productivity Paradox in a Not Too Distant Mirror" in *Technology and Productivity: The Challenge for Economic Policy*. Paris: OECD.

DAVIDSON, J.D. and William REES-MOGG (1997),
The Sovereign Individual. London: Macmillan.

DRUCKER, Peter F. (1993),
Post Capitalist Society. New York: HarperCollins.

DRUCKER, Peter F. (1998),
"The Next Information Revolution", *Forbes* ASAP, 24 August, pp. 47-58.

DUNNING, J.H. (1993),
Multinational Enterprises and the Global Economy. Reading: Addison-Wesley.

DUNNING, J.H., ed. (1997),
Governments, Globalisation, and International Business. Oxford: Oxford University Press.

EISENBERG, Rebecca (1996),
"Patents: Help or Hindrance to Technology Transfer?" in Rudolph and McIntire (1996), pp. 161-174.

FREEMAN, C. and C. PEREZ (1988),
"Structural Crisis of Adjustment" in Dosi *et al.* (eds), *Technological Change and Economic Theory*. London: Pinter.

GRACE, C.S. (1997),
Biotechnology Unzipped: Promises and Realities. Toronto: Trifolium Books Inc.

HELPMAN, Elhanan, ed. (1998),
General Purpose Technologies and Economic Growth. Cambridge: MIT Press.

KRANZBERG, M. and C. S. SMITH (1988),
"Materials in History and Society" in T. Forester (ed.), *The Materials Revolution*. Cambridge, Mass.: MIT Press.

LIPSEY, R.G. (1997),
"Globalisation and National Government Policies: An Economic View", Chapter 2 in Dunning (1997).

LIPSEY, R.G. and C. BEKAR (1995),
"A Structuralist View of Technical Change and Economic Growth", Bell Canada Papers on Economic and Public Policy, Vol. 3, Proceedings of the Bell Canada Conference at Queen's University. Kingston: John Deutsch Institute.

LIPSEY, R.G., C. BEKAR and K. CARLAW (1998),
"What Requires Explanation" and "The Consequences of Changes in GPT's", Chapters 2 and 8 in Helpman (1998).

LIPSEY, R.G., C. BEKAR and K. CARLAW (forthcoming),
Time, Technology and Markets: Explorations in Economic Growth and Restructuring.

LIPSEY, R.G. and K. CARLAW (1996),
"A Structuralist View of Innovation Policy" in Peter Howitt. (ed.), The Implications of Knowledge Based Growth. Calgary: University of Calgary Press, pp. 255-333.

LIPSEY, R.G. and K. CARLAW (1998a),
"Technology Policies in Neo-classical and Structuralist-Evolutionary Models", STI Review, No. 22. Paris: OECD.

LIPSEY, R.G. and K. CARLAW (1998b),
Assessing Innovation Policies: Taking Schumpeter Seriously on Technology Policy, Industry Canada Working Paper No. 25. Ottawa: Industry Canada.

MALONE, Thomas W. and Robert J. LAUBACHER (1998),
"The Dawn of the E-Lance Economy", Harvard Business Review, September-October, pp. 145-152.

MINSKY, Marvin (1986),
Foreword to Eric K. Drexler's Engines of Creation. Garden City, New York: Anchor Press/ Doubleday. Also available on the Internet: http://www.foresight.org.EOC/ EOC_Foreword.html

MOKYR, J. (1990),
The Lever of Riches: Technology Creativity and Economic Progress. Oxford: Oxford University Press.

OSTRY, Sylvia (1990),
Governments and Corporations in a Shrinking World: Trade and Innovation Policies in the United States and Japan. New York: Council on Foreign Relations Press.

REGIS, E. (1995),
Nano. New York: Little, Brown.

ROSENBERG, N. (1982),
Inside the Black Box: Technology and Economics. Cambridge: Cambridge University Press.

RUDOLPH, F.B. and L.V. McINTIRE, eds. (1996),
Biotechnology: Science, Engineering, and Ethical Challenges for the Twenty-First Century. Washington DC: Joseph Henry Press.

SCHURR, S. et al. (1990),
Electricity in the American Economy. New York: Greenwood Press.

WELLMAN, B. and B. BUXTON (1994),
"Work and Community Along the Information Highway", Policy Options 7, pp. 11-15.

3

The Emerging Global Knowledge Economy

by

Peter Schwartz, Eamonn Kelly and *Nicole Boyer*
Global Business Network

1. Introduction: A tale of two countries

There is an old South American legend that when God created the continent he tripped over the Patagonian Andes and accidentally emptied the bulk of His riches in the land of Argentina. One can see how this myth got started. Argentina is indeed blessed with a surfeit of natural resources: vast, fertile "Pampas" flatlands which yield a bounty of grains and support countless livestock; a solid range of forests for lumber; a long triangular coastline with a rich fishery; an ample supply of water for hydroelectric power; and lastly, a beautiful high mountainous terrain that both attracts travellers and provides minerals to fuel industry.

Throughout its history, these natural endowments have served Argentina well. As far back as 1535, they lured the Spanish to colonise it as a territory. By the early 1880s-1900s, the former colony had become a formidable economic and political power, boasting the seventh largest economy in the world. With an educated and sophisticated population, high culture and the arts flourished. Buenos Aires' natural beauty and architecture earned it the distinction of being the "Paris of Latin America". Argentina was clearly a country on the rise, set to be an important presence on the world stage for the coming century.

Now imagine the island of Singapore around the same time. As one of Britain's "Straits Settlements", the city was a sleepy trading outpost in 1900 compared to the bustling streets of Buenos Aires. An island just 647.5 square kilometres in size, it had little in terms of natural resources. While it did have a protected harbour and was strategically located in the South China Sea, the lucrative tea and spice trade had made its sister cities – Penang and Malacca – long-standing rivals and equal competitors in capturing the business of traders. So at the turn of century, Singapore must have looked like a poor bet for future success.

Enlisting the entrepreneurial energies of characters like Sir Stanford Raffles, Singapore eventually did earn its place in the Empire's sun. It quickly became a key naval base and commercial centre in British Malaya, acting as a hub for exporting agricultural commodities to the rest of the world. Then in 1965, Singapore's future was again in doubt. Shortly after it won independence, it joined the Malaysian Federation but was quickly forced to leave. (In essence, the Malays were suspicious of their Chinese partners in Singapore.) So with strained relations among its neighbours, and few natural resources to stand upon, Singapore faced grim prospects. How could this small city-state survive in the modern world? Many observers were highly sceptical.

In 1999, the stories of these two countries have taken very different turns. Argentina, its improved performance in the past decade notwithstanding, has experienced drastic decline, dashing the buoyant expectations and future promise. With a population of 35.4 million, Argentina's GDP per capita is $8 030 in 1995 figures. In contrast, with a population one-tenth the size of Argentina's (3.1 million), Singapore had a GDP per capita of $26 730 in 1995, exceeding many parts of Europe, including the United Kingdom. Ranked consistently by the World Economic Forum as the most competitive nation in the world, Singapore is now the envy of both developed and developing countries. From a policy point of view, the island country has managed the unimaginable, transforming itself in just thirty years from a have-not state to a leading global economic entrepôt.

The recent histories of these countries have been informed by a range of deep and complex factors – political, social, economic – that are beyond the scope of this chapter. But they are perfect illustrations of the emerging global knowledge economy because they highlight the evolution from an economic order in which the clever and organised use of natural resources was sufficient for success – illustrated by Argentina at the end of the last century – to an economic order based on knowledge, in which the exploitation of natural resources is not only insufficient but, as Singapore demonstrates, not *even necessary*. Those individuals, organisations and countries that recognised this early are well-placed for the next century; those still struggling to understand the seismic shift we are undergoing may suffer friction burns and relative decline for some time to come.

Section 2 of this chapter puts the knowledge economy in context, explaining what makes it different from an industrial-based economy, and highlighting the key driving forces that enable this transformation.

Section 3 then surveys the numerous dilemmas facing society. When we take stock of today's challenges – whether finding a new set of metrics for knowledge-based activities, reinventing how we educate our citizens or employees, reconciling antitrust laws in an economy based on increasing returns, or enabling developing countries to participate in an increasingly high-tech world – we get a profound sense that our institutional, legal, organisational and social arrangements are lagging behind events, and that we lack the analytical and conceptual tools to deal with these dilemmas. Our thesis is that these dilemmas are symptomatic of a clash between two economic paradigms and values – the uneven collision between the industrial age and burgeoning knowledge age. But as Albert Einstein noted, we cannot solve our current problems with the same level of thinking that created them. In the same way, to resolve these dilemmas we need to step back and clearly understand the different assumptions driving the two different economic models and reperceive the various problems through the lens of knowledge. This perceptual shift is critical for the realisation of what we call "The Long Boom", a sustained period of global economic growth, prosperity, openness, and integration.

Section 4 takes some of the key dilemmas or critical uncertainties and weaves them into two broad-brush scenarios for the future of the knowledge economy. For example, in a world where innovation is highly rewarded, where the slow must compete against the fast, who will be the winners and losers? How widespread will the economic impact of the knowledge economy be? How rapidly will it occur? One can envision two very different scenarios. If the effects of growth are substantial and rapid, and access to education and technology is very wide and deep, then a high-growth, socially convergent future is plausible. If, on the other hand, the effects of growth are slow to materialise and access is more limited and narrow, then a slower growth and socially divergent future is more likely. In terms of the implications for the OECD countries, the central policy question for governments is how to achieve the first outcome and avoid the second. The answer lies in providing cheap and easy access to a high-quality knowledge infrastructure, especially in education.

2. Understanding the global knowledge economy

At times of momentous change in culture and society, our use of old words to describe new things can hide the emerging future from our eyes.

Charles Handy (Drucker *et al.*, 1997)

The naming of an economic system is usually long in the making. Indeed, over the past couple of decades there has been a profusion of terms emerging in popular discourse. We have heard about the post-industrial economy, service economy, post-capitalist society, digital economy, network economy, the new economy – and more recently, the knowledge economy. So amid this diversity of terms, it is worth asking, why now the "knowledge" economy? This section will answer that question, and in the process will detail the three fundamental forces driving the transformation. Inextricably related, each representing one aspect of a complex feedback loop, they include:

- The qualitatively different assumptions governing knowledge inputs.

- The proliferation of IT networks.

- The globalisation of the economy.

Toward the tipping point

In the same way that an algae blight goes unnoticed until just before the tipping point – the day before it takes over the entire pond – we often fail to see the nature of deep trends and structural changes until they are upon us (Kelly, 1997). Today we are at one of these thresholds, where the proliferation of knowledge-intensive activities is irrevocably transforming the shape of our economic systems.

We have been approaching this tipping point for some time. As historian Fernand Braudel details (1992), the changing nature of capitalism has favoured different inputs over the past three centuries. "Favoured" here means, that which was scarce became the source of wealth creation. For instance, the focus shifted from land in an agrarian society to capital in an industrial society. Now we are see-ing the balance move from capital to knowledge. In the language of economists, knowledge is now the source of wealth creation and the most important factor of production. This means that while traditional factors – land and natural resources, labour, and capital – are still important for economic activity, they are becoming secondary (Drucker, 1993). Capital, once the pre-eminent factor, is no longer scarce. This can be seen in high-technology centres like the Silicon Valley. If one has knowl-edge, as is the case with promising new start-ups, capital and labour quickly follow. Furthermore, in the last few decades, we have seen how the input of knowledge has been remaking the economic landscape, lending knowledge-intensity to other inputs. The revolution in manufacturing is one example, where entire supply chains are now wired from beginning to end with just-in-time delivery systems.

Knowledge, however, is more than just the next critical factor of production. From an economic perspective, it has two roles: it is a source of renewal and is also the glue that binds and co-ordinates other factors of production. In fact, the evolution of our collective knowledge may also be the key to *our* evolution and progress over time. Taking the long view, each major economic and social transfor-mation throughout the ages has been triggered by new breakthroughs in knowl-edge. During the Agricultural Revolution tens of thousands of years ago, a new society emerged (in different parts of the world at different times) as a result of the new knowledge about how to grow, cultivate, and harvest food from seeds (Chichilnisky, 1998). In the 18th century, the invention of the steam engine, together with the knowledge of how to harness the power of this new machine, initiated the Industrial Revolution.

As we move into the 21st century, we are learning to exploit information technology (IT) to create wealth from knowledge (Chichilnisky, 1998). In a post-modern way, we are now learning to use the tools of IT to mine our "knowledge about knowledge". IT has shown us that information is not knowledge, and that while digitisation, IT networks and technological innovation are all key aspects of the new economy, the common DNA driving these changes is knowledge.

Lastly, from a human perspective, the quest for knowledge is an integral part of what it means to be Homo sapiens. So in this context, the word "knowledge" commands a certain emotional appeal that "capital" and other inputs fail to invoke. Thus, while the prefix "knowledge" may be place-holder for the next epithet to emerge in popular discourse, the notion of the knowledge economy may have more enduring conceptual power because it tells us how to do things and how we may do them better (Davenport and Prusak, 1998).

The birth of knowledge economics

In the end, the location of the new economy is not in the technology, be it the microchip or the global telecommunications network. It is in the human mind.

Alan M. Weber (1993)

Manifestations of the knowledge economy are now appearing in many aspects of our economic lives. As we approach the tipping point, we see evidence of this transition everywhere. In the stock markets, corporations are increasingly being evaluated for their knowledge and ideas, e.g. new technology, patents, copyright, brand names and human talent. For instance, Microsoft, a company that has only 3% of the physical assets of General Motors, now has the highest capitalisation in the market. In terms of job creation, the fastest-growing sectors are all knowledge-intensive industries, including software, biotechnology, consulting, healthcare and education (Wilson, in Conceição et al., 1998); meanwhile, we will continue to see a jump in the number of displaced workers from manufacturing and resource extraction sectors. Overall, however, the number of new jobs being created is greater than the jobs lost (Kelly, 1998.) For instance, 1998 saw the United States experiencing its lowest unemployment rate (4.3%) in twenty-eight years (The New York Times, 5 February 1999).

A special issue of Technological Forecasting and Social Change on "The Emerging Importance of Knowledge for Development: Implications for Technology Policy and Innovation", found ample evidence to sustain the idea of a knowledge-based economy (Conceição *et al.*, 1998). While the subject of the knowledge economy remains controversial in their view, the "safe" evidence includes:

- Workforce movements from manufacturing to service jobs. Service jobs were interpreted by the journal as more knowledge-intensive because they have intangible inputs and outputs. This shift has been strongest in developed world.

- Growth in investment in intangible assets.

- The growth of new employment in knowledge-intensive fields such as consulting, education, high technology and healthcare.

- Evidence that "knowledge work" requires higher education levels and that knowledge workers are increasingly better paid.

Another important indicator is a change in popular discourse. As we approach the tipping point, the discussion of "knowledge about knowledge" has increased exponentially. Already there is a growing body of empirical and theoretical literature explaining the development of the knowledge economy. Entire new disciplines and areas of study have been born, and with them a flurry of new journals, websites and magazines devoted to understanding various aspects of knowledge creation, application and dissemination. The University of California at Berkeley recently appointed its first professor of "knowledge". In the private sector, we have seen the birth of the "knowledge movement" and the rise of "chief knowledge officers". Recognising where their future work will be, all of the "Big Six" consulting firms are now reinventing their core business around the platform of knowledge management.

Not everyone, however, is comfortable with this shift. In particular, the process of re-perception has yet to penetrate the halls of many economic departments. In fact, when it comes to talking about the "new economy", the sheer religiosity of views on the subject is astounding. Varian and Shapiro (1999) write in the beginning of their book *Information Rules*, "Technology changes. Economic laws do not." Indeed, when it comes to key economic laws such as supply and demand, this is surely the case. But there are some noticeable and widening cracks in conventional economic theory that cannot be addressed within current economic thinking. Take the concept of scarcity, for instance. According to traditional economic thinking, the main factor of production was also scarce. Does this mean, now, that knowledge is scarce? With the exponential growth of the world's knowledge stock, how can knowledge be scarce? Whether economists like it or not, knowledge is different. The rest of this section addresses that difference, one that conventional thinking struggles to reconcile.

Knowledge is messy

There is good reason why economic thinkers have avoided the use of knowledge as a primary unit for analysis: quite simply, knowledge is hard to measure and quantify. Clearly, as Verna Allee (1997) notes, "There is no convenient way to isolate knowledge as a discrete phenomenon." In systems thinking terms, knowledge exists in, as she puts it, "a system of interacting problems". Because of this, the study of economic growth has been focused on more tangible manifestations, such as technological innovation. But even then, economists have had a hard time incorporating technology into their economic models. Knowledge and technology growth, therefore, have typically remained outside or "exogenous" to economic models and measures.

The Nobel Prize winning work of Robert Solow (1957), however, started to highlight the shortcomings of this approach. Solow found that after accounting for the impact of increases in labour and capital, the "residual" – *i.e.* technology – was the key driver of growth. With so much of technology accounting for economic growth, a full 85% according to Solow's calculations, it did not seem to make sense to treat it as if it occurred in a black box. This work led to a measure called Total Factor Productivity (TFP), which gives an indication of the overall improvements in all factors of production. But even this yardstick has been inadequate in furthering our understanding of how knowledge drives economic activity.

In recent years, a band of pioneering economists called "new growth" or "endogenous" theorists have tried to incorporate knowledge and technology into the production function. Paul Romer (1993, 1995), one of the leading proponents of new growth theory, has gone as far as to reframe how we see the production function. The traditional factors of production fall into fairly distinct categories: land, raw materials, capital equipment, and labour. Romer argues that the term "factors of production" is very industrial age, invoking the metaphor of "factory". As we move away from factories and industrialisation, a more appropriate way to see economic activity is through a computer metaphor: hardware, software, and "wetware" (see Figure 1). Hardware includes all physical inputs, such as land, buildings, and capital investments in technology. Software is codified knowledge that is stored outside the human brain: in a book, CD-ROM, computer hard drive, blueprint, or schematic. Wetware includes the tacit knowledge stored in the human brain, including skills, talents, and beliefs (Conceição *et al.*, 1998).

There are further distinctions within each broad category. Software – knowledge that is codified – includes information or knowledge about facts (know-what) as well as knowledge about how things work in the world (know-why). Wetware, embodied in the minds of knowledge workers, includes a person's abilities and skills to carry out their function (know-how). Another

Figure 1. **Taxonomy of knowledge**

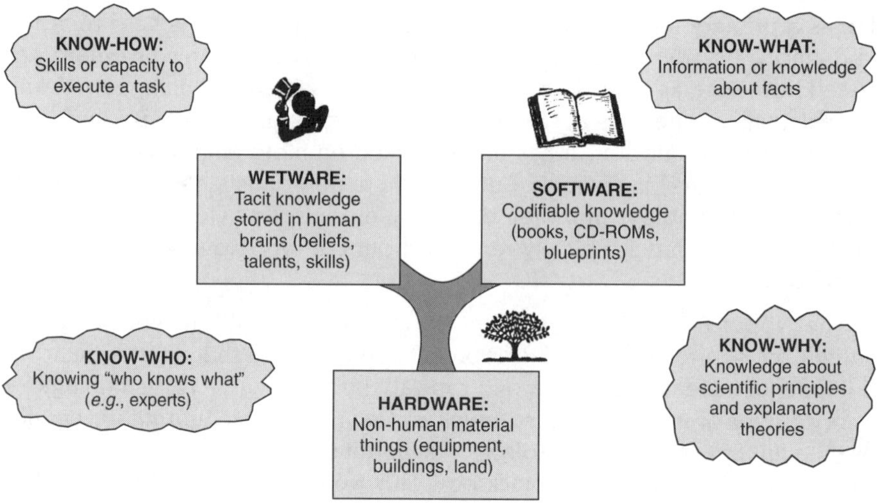

KNOW-HOW:
Skills or capacity to
execute a task

KNOW-WHAT:
Information or knowledge
about facts

WETWARE:
Tacit knowledge
stored in human
brains (beliefs,
talents, skills)

SOFTWARE:
Codifiable knowledge
(books, CD-ROMs,
blueprints)

KNOW-WHO:
Knowing "who knows what"
(*e.g.*, experts)

KNOW-WHY:
Knowledge about
scientific principles
and explanatory
theories

HARDWARE:
Non-human material
things (equipment,
buildings, land)

Sources: Foray and Lundvall, in Conceição, *et al.* (1998).

aspect includes knowledge about knowledge relationships, *e.g.* knowledge about other people's wetware (know-who) and who the experts are in the organisation – the "who knows what and who knows how to do what" (Conceição *et al.*, 1998).

This new taxonomy deals with the individual as the primary unit for analysis, but one can also see how the concepts of hardware, software and wetware can be extrapolated to a firm, a country, or a region. For instance, although Singapore is lacking in hardware, its economic strength comes from key investments in its software and the wetware of its citizens. Even as the city-state experiences the full brunt of the Asian financial crisis, it is cognisant of this reality more than ever. Its strategy for the future is firmly grounded in the virtuous circle of investment in the knowledge stock of its people. Argentina, by contrast, has an economy focused on hardware, including its natural resources and more industrial-age activities. While the population is highly educated, with 25 national universities and a 95% literacy rate, the typology of Figure I raises some interesting strategic questions about how well they are marshalling their national wetware and software. As this example shows, seeing things through the lens of knowledge, with human resources in its centre, can fundamentally recast people's thinking and priorities.

Knowledge is abundant, not scarce

Contrary to traditional economic thinking, knowledge follows the law of abundance rather than scarcity. As Romer discusses (1993), the economics of "ideas" follow very different assumptions from the economics of "objects". Objects, or physical inputs to production, are finite resources subject to the laws of physics. Their meaning is derived from their physical performance (*e.g.* the strength of steel). Ideas, on the other hand, are intangible and abstract. Their meaning is not derived from the physical realities of ink on the page; rather, meaning is created in the interaction of a reader with the words on the page.

The shift away from a resource-intensive economy to a knowledge-intensive economy means that economic growth is constrained only by our ability to create new knowledge. As Romer explains, economic growth occurs whenever people develop new "recipes" or ideas that rearrange physical things and resources in ways that add more value. New discoveries in material science, for instance, are ideas that will create cheaper, stronger, and possibly more sustainable products for automobiles. In this way, knowledge amplifies the value and capacity of other factors while creating new processes and products (Stevens, 1996).

Although knowledge is not scarce, what may be scarce is human attention. To quote the Nobel Prize winning economist Herbert Simon, "what information consumes is rather obvious: it consumes the attention of the recipient. Hence a wealth of information creates a poverty of attention."

Knowledge creates increasing returns

Another key difference in a knowledge-based economy is the existence of an "increasing returns" dynamic that contrasts with the traditional concept of "diminishing returns". The latter is based on the notion of scarcity of resources. A mining company, for instance, will inevitably face certain limitations as it depletes the natural resource it mines. In theory, this prevents one company from dominating the market and ensures an equilibrium of prices. As we have already established, knowledge and the economics of ideas is not based on scarcity – thus the dynamic of "increasing returns". Industries based on increasing returns lend themselves to "natural monopolies", where markets are unstable and perfect price competition does not occur. This is because increasing returns are based on "mechanisms of positive feedback that operate – within markets, businesses, and industries – to reinforce that which gains success or aggravate that which suffers loss" (Arthur, 1996). Kevin Kelly (1998) calls these "network superwinners" because they essentially dominate the industry ecosystem. Microsoft, Cisco and Oracle are classic examples of this in the high technology sector. In brief, three things drive this winner-take-most logic:

- Large up-front R&D investments but with falling costs per unit as sales increase. It may cost $50 million to create a piece of software, but only $3 per unit to produce. Companies that seize early market share stand to gain further advantages.

- The need for products and services to be compatible with a network of users. The company that gains market advantage also influences the rules and standards of the network.

- The customer lock-in that occurs when a product requires a certain level of knowledge to use it, *e.g.* Microsoft Windows (Arthur, 1996).

As Brian Arthur notes, we are seeing the coexistence of both increasing returns and diminishing returns in different industries, and often within the same company. The dynamic of diminishing returns is found mostly in traditional, industrial age industries, whereas increasing returns is a hallmark of high-technology, knowledge-intensive industries and companies. Importantly, each dynamic elicits and requires different economic and organisational behaviours. As Arthur puts it:

[...] diminishing returns is characterized by planning, control, and hierarchy. It is a world of materials, of processing, of optimization. Observation, positioning, flattened organizations, missions, teams, and cunning characterize the increasing return world. It is the world of psychology, of cognition, of adaptation.

As Arthur and Kelly both argue, the bifurcation of the economy into these two worlds is becoming less distinct. Increasing returns is migrating to other parts of the economy as industrial age sectors adopt more knowledge-intensive products and processes with "smart" technologies. This deeper shift toward the knowledge economy is pulling with it the old economy as well.

Increasing returns can also happen within a region. As AnnaLee Saxenian (1994), author of *Regional Advantage*, makes clear, Silicon Valley's sustained success has been driven by the powerful forces of increasing returns. Many regions have subsequently tried to emulate the same initial conditions of Silicon Valley by nurturing positive feedback loops to drive growth: the recruiting of a talent pool, the presence of world-class institutions and R&D facilities, a risk-taking venture capital sector, and fast broadband networks and technology. Singapore, for instance, has been moving down this checklist very consciously. In an attempt to stimulate increasing returns, Singapore has been systematically luring top talent and corporations to participate in its state-of-the-art multimedia network called "Singapore One". Its goal is to be the "giga-hub" for Southeast Asia. Other examples are proliferating around the world: South Africa's "Cyber-townships"; Malaysia's

"Multimedia Corridor"; "Smart Toronto" in Canada; the "Redline" project in the Netherlands; and the "Stockholm Project" in Sweden (Boyer, 1996).

Knowledge feeds on itself

The second form of increasing returns in the new economy is embedded in the very cycle of knowledge creation and innovation. Scientific discoveries and technological breakthroughs do not happen in a vacuum, with a solitary researcher finding the silver bullet to a key problem. One scientific discovery in a given discipline builds on the cumulative knowledge stock of that particular field. According to Romer (1997),"the more we discover things, the better we get at the process of discovery itself. Knowledge builds on itself." The more we learn about how innovation happens, the more we realise it is driven by a series of feedback loops between a network of scientists, universities, labs, think tanks, investors, corporations, and even consumers; it is a dynamic, organic, and iterative process.

Growth in the knowledge stock of science, therefore, has nonlinear, biological characteristics. This creates certain problems when it comes to public perception and even analysis. The human mind is notoriously bad at intuitively comprehending exponential growth. For instance, when someone is told that they will get paid 1 cent at the beginning of the month, with it doubling in value every day, it is hard for them to grasp that by the thirtieth day they will have earned in excess of $5 million dollars. In a similar way, with each scientific discovery building on others, we systematically underestimate the potential for scientific discovery in the future. For instance, who knows what kind of jump human knowledge will make after the completion of the Human Genome Project? The answer is most likely far beyond our predictions or imagination.

Knowledge resets the limits for economic growth

In the bigger picture, we can see how the biological growth of new ideas and knowledge has stimulated technological innovations throughout human development. In categorising technological breakthroughs over time, Perez has argued that different waves of technology profoundly reinvent the "techno-economic paradigm" of the day (1985). Such a shift occurs when a certain technological development becomes pervasive and fundamentally affects other technologies, industries and services. An increasing returns dynamic takes hold as knowledge about how to use and apply these technologies spreads widely throughout society. Electricity was one such technology at the turn of the last century. Information technology is at the centre of another paradigm shift today.

Returning to Romer's metaphor, these waves of technology are not only "new recipes" that unleash economic wealth; they are also entirely new ways of cooking that creatively push the outer boundaries of what was once thought possible in terms of economy growth. In Wheels of Commerce, Braudel (1992, Volume 2) makes a compelling

Figure 2. **Changes in economic leadership**

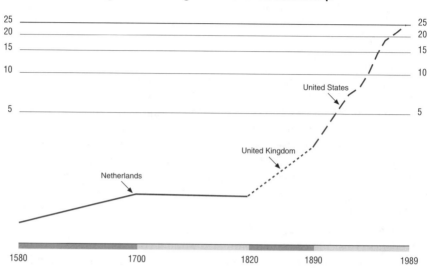

Locus of Productivity Leadership, 1580-1989 (GDP per man-hour in 1985 US$).
Source: Maddison, 1991.

case for how this has happened with each techno-economic shift. In the 15th century, Holland, a small trading country, dominated the world economy because of its mastery of sailing technology and knowledge of navigation and the seas. At that time, the global rate of growth was about 0.5%. During the Industrial Revolution, capitalism began to spread throughout the world and brought with it steam power and new modes of manufacturing. The United Kingdom rose as the key economic player, partially because of its early adoption of and pioneering efforts using machines driven by steam. The worldwide rate of growth jumped to 1.5%. Then, based on early exploitation of new technologies and resources – *e.g.* electric power, the telephone, the internal combustion engine and petroleum – the United States assumed economic leadership in the latter part of the 19th century. Another factor fuelling this hegemony was that US industrialists, mainly in the East and the upper Midwest, had mastered mass manufacturing, surpassing the techniques first developed by the British. By then, the global economy was growing at approximately 3% annually.

New waves of technology – computers, communication, bioengineering, fuel cells, and the like – are just beginning to impact the world economy. Once again, the drivers of growth may be relocating (this time toward the Western United States and the Pacific Basin) and accelerating growth to levels perhaps as high as 4-5% annually. Conventional economic wisdom holds that as economies mature they will converge toward lower growth (*e.g.* 1-2% annually). But clearly, this view is being challenged as we learn more about the impact of these techno-economic paradigms. In particular, we are seeing that new technologies can de-mature an economy if it successfully adopts the new capabilities. Singapore, for example, has de-matured itself several times.

The impact of these new technologies, especially the powerful web channel, will increase the amount of turbulence in the world economy, a turbulence driven largely by uncertainty. Developing an e-commerce strategy for most companies is still one grand experiment because there are no clear "recipes". At present, we see a wide variety of business models sprouting up around e-commerce going in different directions, each hoping that their model will stick or set the standard for others. But once these recipes evolve and take hold, a much larger number of people and companies will start to imitate them – and that in turn will drive another spurt of economic growth.

Knowledge is both a public and private good

When one asks the question "What is knowledge in an economic sense?", there are usually two answers. Knowledge can be either a private or public good, depending on what aspect is considered. Using Romer's typology, "wetware" is a private good until that knowledge is codified into "software". The problem with software is that once produced it is hard to make it "excludable", given the marginal cost and ease of reproduction. This is a problem because most knowledge-intensive products, such as pharmaceuticals or a new CD-ROM, are costly to produce. In many cases, the innovators do not capture the full economic benefit of their work. Put another way, "traditional market mechanisms do not provide the rules for efficient resource allocation in the production of software" (Conceição *et al.*, 1998). Public goods, which have private goods qualities, are very hard for the market to price. This is a dilemma that will be discussed further in the next section.

Knowledge involves human beings

If the new economy is rooted in the human mind, this is likely to produce new values and behaviours in our institutions, corporations, and society. One example is that the traditional power relationships are likely to change significantly, making the economy more decentralised in nature. In a knowledge economy, for instance, "knowledge workers" own the mode of production. In this sense, knowledge, unlike capital, equipment, or land, can walk out the door on any given day. This will considerably shift the dynamic between employer and employee. Similarly, while a country or state may invest money in educating its citizens, the global competition for highly skilled workers is making it easier to move to another country where there are more lucrative and rewarding jobs. The current "brain drain" of highly skilled scientists from Russia is a good example.

Also, if corporations are seeking to increase the productivity of knowledge workers, they can use very different types of incentives. The quality of the work environment, for instance, is becoming a priority. What motivate a knowledge worker are things such as learning, equity sharing, interesting and important work, and fun. Knowledge generation also follows nonlinear, organic cycles that contrast strongly with industrial age production cycles. As Allee (1997) writes, "knowledge wants to happen, just as life wants to happen, and both want to happen as community". Prime examples are the on-line knowledge communities currently blossoming on the Internet. Physics researchers were among the first to exploit the community of knowledge made possible by the Net. Within these communities, no one is in charge of the knowledge-creation process. Knowledge also seeks community when issues are complex and uncertainty abounds. We see this happening at the policy-making level and among scientific groups, but also within industry. The whole idea of "co-opetition" is based on the idea of co-operating and sharing knowledge to solve a particular issue (*e.g.* standard-setting) while still competing in the wider market-place.

Values of trust might also become a business imperative in the knowledge economy. With the free flow of information across a multitude of networks, concerns about privacy are going to increase. IT enables corporations to know more about their consumers. While this can help customers, it also gives corporations the ability to make market-based choices (or to discriminate) based on a consumer's socio-economic profile. This is raising a number of social and political concerns. As Kevin Kelly (1998) writes: "The network economy is founded on technology, but can only be built on relationships. It starts with chips and ends with trust."

IT *networks and connectivity*

Knowledge is the content, information is the medium. The content is driving change, facilitated by the medium.

Graciela Chichilnisky (1998)

As we have argued, the very nature of knowledge is driving change. The most important catalyst, however, has been the tremendous growth of IT and digital networks. Without question, this aspect of the emerging knowledge economy is something new. Transcending both spatial and temporal boundaries, IT networks are creating an entirely different competitive space and social experience. As a result, the "network economy" has been an important focus in recent literature.

In brief, the widespread application of networks and information technology has enabled and accelerated the knowledge-based economy by:

– Increasing the codification, dissemination, and creation of knowledge.

– Enabling the commoditisation of knowledge.

- Creating a global information infrastructure for communication, discovery and commerce.

- Facilitating a functional convergence between the spheres of commercial activity.

- Accelerating the pace of change towards a state of disequilibrium.

The power of connectivity

Although scientists and experts have been communicating via IT networks for decades, the rapid rise of the World Wide Web was a largely unanticipated development. The desire to communicate, interact, and engage in commercial transactions seems to be an insatiable human need. Already 100 million people can access the web. By the year 2002, this figure will have jumped to 320 million. Another indicator of increasing connectivity is the growth of data traffic on telecommunications networks. According to Bell South Chairman Duane Ackerman, voice traffic will drop to 10% by 2008. But as he explains, "It's not that voice is declining, on the contrary, it continues to grow, doubling every twelve years, but data traffic over the internet – e-mail, orders from retail businesses and the like – continues to double every 100 to 120 days." That is indeed astounding, exponential growth.

In response to this emerging economic and social platform, governments around the world, together with the private sector, have been creating information infrastructures so that more people can participate in the economic and social benefits. The opportunities for developing countries to leap-frog into knowledge-intensive activities are therefore greater than ever. The new generation of low-earth-orbit communication satellites (LEOs) will extend the range of communication options to nearly everyone on the planet in just six years. This is a historic discontinuity: today, 70% of the world has never made a telephone call but soon, most will have full broadband access to the Net. As increasingly large sections of global society become connected to networks, the result is bound to be profound. Even so, the globalisation of the knowledge economy does create numerous dilemmas for society's policy makers, a point taken up in the next section.

The acceleration of knowledge creation

Developments in IT and networks have been driving tectonic changes in almost every scientific and technology field by magnifying the acceleration and sharing of knowledge. Revolutionary innovations are occurring across the board. Alternative, "clean" energy technologies and fuel cells are on the horizon. Industrial ecology and intelligent materials will change the way we build. Genetic engineering will enable us to cure major diseases and improve agricultural productivity. New computational and simulation methods are improving the productivity of scientific, engineering and design talent. Meanwhile, the creation of information networks and enhanced connectivity among scientists is enabling the free flow of ideas and knowledge from diverse cultures and fields at a global level. The economic rewards for technological innovation have never been higher. The metabolism of discovery and innovation is continuing to accelerate. To put this into perspective, of all the scientists who ever lived, more than 90% are alive today. It's estimated that the stock of scientific knowledge is currently doubling every five to six years; by the year 2020, it will double every 73 days.

The speed and development of new knowledge is exemplified by the US Government's human genome project. Initially, the government estimated that mapping the human genome would take twenty-five years to complete. The private sector, however, could not wait that long. In 1997, a biotechnology company named Human Genomic Sciences jumped into the race and concluded that it could perform the work not in half the time, but in three years. This in turn forced the government to rethink – and speed up – its research to match the private efforts. Now, the entire human genome will be mapped by the year 2002 instead of 2015.

Technological convergence

IT, itself the convergence of communications and computing, is accelerating the creation of new knowledge and new technologies. Most technologies today are products of many other supporting technologies. The development of the modern VCR, for instance, required, over time, the convergence of approximately 16–18 technologies and innovations.

Another important functional convergence is also happening between the modes of commerce. On an abstract level, commerce can be reduced to three circles of activity or goals (Alliance for Converging Technologies, 1997):

- *Value creation* – which occurs mainly through physical labour and tangible goods.

- *Communication* – either externally (with customers) or internally (with employees), using various forms of media such as the human voice, print, telephones, TV, and radio.

- *Distribution* of goods and services – which has utilised a variety of technologies of transport (*e.g.* by hand, ship, railway).

For the first time in the history of commerce, all three activities are converging around a common digital platform (Alliance for Converging Technologies, 1997). This is why some observers dub our current world a "digital economy" (Tapscott, 1995.) However, the real story is centred around enhanced access to the knowledge housed in the other modes of commercial activity. For instance, what we mean by value creation is starting to change. The way we communicate with our employees and customers is being transformed, with consumers becoming "prosumers": customers who co-create the value being produced with their suppliers. For example, the success of Scott Adams' "Dilbert" cartoon strip, which lampoons the social and economic perversions of modern corporate life, did not take off until he distributed his e-mail address on the web. The result: people from around the world sent him a flood of e-mails detailing their real-life experiences as corporate employees. The quality and power of his strip were strengthened because he reflected the very issues and concerns of his audience. In this sense, the content was being created by both Adams and his readership.

This functional convergence via IT has sped up nearly every process in the world of business. This has led to much wider and deeper integration among economic actors and has blurred the boundaries between them. The fusion and cross-fertilisation of three pillars of commerce – value creation, communication, and distribution – is creating, in the words of Stan Davis and Christopher Meyer (1998), a "blur of desires, blur of fulfillment, blur of resources".

Toward creative disequilibrium

Contrary to what many people thought, ecosystems and other complex adaptive systems in the natural world exist in constant flux at the cusp of disequilibrium and breakdown. In recent years, the rise of "chaos theory" and "systems thinking" has taught us that our organisational and economic institutions operate very much like a complex, adaptive living system. This has certain implications for creating the right conditions in which new ideas and insights flourish. For instance, Kevin Kelly (1998) advises: "To achieve sustainable innovation you need to seek persistent disequilibrium. To seek persistent disequilibrium means that one must chase after disruption without succumbing to it, or retreating from it." Dee Hock, founder of Visa International, calls this the "chaordic" organisation. Building these companies, however, is very hard to do in practice. Clearly, the realisation that creative disequilibrium reigns supreme in organisations and economic systems is a discomforting thought for managers and policy makers, creating numerous dilemmas that defy an intuitive response.

Forces of globalisation and integration

The third driver making this economic transition truly novel is the manifold thrust towards globalisation and economic integration. The rise of transnational networks, the market power of connectivity, and the global demand for real-time information and knowledge have been pushing the trend. Critics are quick to point out that this is not a historical precedent, which is true enough. In empirical terms the world is probably no more integrated economically than it was in 1913 (Dicken, 1998), but the type of global economic integration we are seeing is faster, deeper, and more profound than ever before. The following indicators offer good examples:

- World exports were 14 times greater in 1994 than they were in 1950 (Dicken, 1998).

- Since 1985, foreign direct investment (FDI) has been growing at an average annual rate of 28%. Although the 1993 recession dampened investment, FDI outflows quickly rebounded in 1995 by 40% (Dicken, 1998).

- Daily foreign exchange turnover has increased from $15 billion in 1973 to $1.2 trillion in 1995 (The Economist, 1997).

Perhaps the best examples of globalisation are the growth and transformation of the South East and East Asian economies. While a large part of manufacturing remains in developed countries, the Asian tigers and other newly industrialised economies (NIEs) have become the new centres of production for global trade and manufacturing (Dicken, 1998). This has, in turn, increased the level of interconnectedness between national economies and transnational corporations. Value-added processes are now diffused around the world. A new cellular phone, for instance, may be designed by a team in London, manufactured in northeast China with parts from Canada, the United States and Sweden, and then brought to various national markets by the global marketing and sales headquarters in Helsinki.

The depressed state of the Asian economies, post-financial crisis, will not change this pattern, unless developed countries put in place more protectionist barriers to prevent the dumping of cheap commodities on their markets. Singapore, our bellwether for the knowledge economy, has been at the forefront, developing into a value-added production centre for the rest of the world. The city-state has clearly positioned itself well in the cross-hairs of two important trends: the rise of the knowledge-intensive economy and the thrust toward globalisation.

3. Reperceiving the knowledge economy

As we move further into the knowledge economy, profound dilemmas seem to proliferate in almost every aspect of our lives. This section tries to articulate a few, focusing on issues likely to be of interest to policy makers. At the highest level, what do these dilemmas tell us? They are indicative of a clash between two economic paradigms and values, the collision between the industrial age and the burgeoning knowledge age. These dilemmas also suggest that we need to reperceive the future through the lens of knowledge. As Drucker notes, changing our assumptions – within economic policy, educational models, or management – is critically important because, unlike scientific theories or paradigms, these assumptions affect behaviour and human institutions.

Governance dilemmas

Over the past 200 years, the modern organisation – in both private and public sectors – has evolved into a model based on "command and control" hierarchies and the view that the world was relatively certain and predictable. Most organisations today are still structured around and functioning on this familiar logic, mainly because it has worked so well in the past. We metaphorically call these "citadel" organisations. This model was ideal for industrial-based activities where cost efficiencies, increased productivity, and economies of scale were of paramount importance. As knowledge becomes a critical resource, however, we will see more organisations based on the "web" metaphor. This model springs from the contrary belief that the world is increasingly complex, full of rapid discontinuous change, and unpredictable. As Figure 3 highlights, the difference in assumptions and behaviours governing the two models are pronounced.

The dilemma here, however, is that the web model will not necessarily replace the citadel organisation. Both models will continue to coexist in different parts of government (*e.g.* the Department of Defense), in different industries, and – interestingly – often within the same organisation. So, while over the long term the balance may be shifting towards a more web-based structure, the challenge today is in managing the *interface* between these two very different worlds. Already numerous tensions are emerging.

Dilemmas for governments

Finding the right institutional arrangements to govern an emerging global knowledge economy is creating many problems for governments. Governmental departments are notorious for operating in a citadel-like way. As the knowledge economy penetrates our society more deeply, dilemmas about the very nature of governing will persist. For instance, in an industrial economy, the government was concerned about the allocation of scarce resources, whereas in a knowledge economy the goal will be to foster knowledge-creation and the discovery of new things. In this model, governments are more focused on creating "framework" policies that set the context or "road-map" from which knowledge activities happen (Stevens, 1996). This model is more about nurturing and stimulating such drivers of growth as technological innovation, and being open to new ideas and outside influences. Like corporations, bureaucracies will have to become nimble learning organisations. The character and style of policy making may come to resemble "action-oriented" research, which tests several directions or pilot projects at the same time and then makes modifications and directional decisions through a series of learning loops. This is a more grass-roots, responsive, and experimental way to govern. As Kevin Kelly describes it (1997, 1998), a knowledge economy is about "letting go at the top" and trusting in the power of decentralised and autonomous networks to

Figure 3.

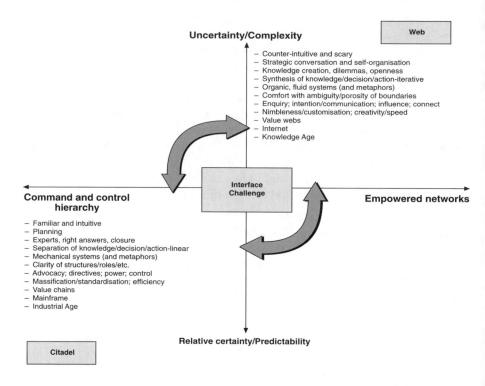

Uncertainty/Complexity

Web

- Counter-intuitive and scary
- Strategic conversation and self-organisation
- Knowledge creation, dilemmas, openness
- Synthesis of knowledge/decision/action-iterative
- Organic, fluid systems (and metaphors)
- Comfort with ambiguity/porosity of boundaries
- Enquiry; intention/communication; influence; connect
- Nimbleness/customisation; creativity/speed
- Value webs
- Internet
- Knowledge Age

Interface
Challenge

Command and control
hierarchy

Empowered networks

- Familiar and intuitive
- Planning
- Experts, right answers, closure
- Separation of knowledge/decision/action-linear
- Mechanical systems (and metaphors)
- Clarity of structures/roles/etc.
- Advocacy; directives; power; control
- Massification/standardisation; efficiency
- Value chains
- Mainframe
- Industrial Age

Relative certainty/Predictability

Citadel

Source: Eamonn Kelly, 1994.

generate wealth. The problem with this, however, is that it runs counter to modern notions of the nation-state and sovereignty.

This web-based model is problematic for countries that want to maintain a more closed system with a particular ideology and way of life. Singapore today is a classic example. Until recently, a key part of the country's success came from its top-down approach to governance. Ensuring stability in a politically charged region has been the first goal of the government. Over the past thirty years, any semblance of serious dissent or opposition has been squashed. Political stability in exchange for political liberty was a tolerable trade-off for most of the local population, many of whom were immigrants who had fled "revolutionary regimes". The government also worked hard to create an environment of economic freedom. By behaving like a corporation actively seeking new markets, Singapore quickly earned the reputation of being "Singapore Inc." By placing its best and brightest at the wheels of the government (and earning private sector wage equivalents), Singapore has successfully sustained its competitive advantage over the years.

The problem Singapore is facing today concerns fostering an environment where local innovation and knowledge-creation happen. Singapore's strategy thus far has relied on the spin-off effects of technology and knowledge from foreign multinationals based on the island (there are about 2 000.) This has not happened to the extent that economic policy makers had initially hoped. Singapore has few global high-technology companies to speak of. The direction, therefore, is clear to the Singaporean leadership: it needs to move up the knowledge value-chain. There are big questions, however, about how to do this in practice without com-promising the current political system. If innovation is key to continued success, how can an orderly society be sustained while allowing for the creative disequilib-rium within which innovation thrives? As Prime Minister Goh describes, "[...] this is the kind of dilemma we are in: How paternalist should we be, and how much room can we give to the people?" (Dolven, 1998). In the past couple of years, Singapore has been experimenting with new approaches to break its culture of conservatism and stimulate freer thinking. A first step has been to revamp its entire educational system, with a great emphasis on "teaching" creativity. But teaching creativity, in characteristic top-down style, may be exactly the problem. Deeply ingrained cultural traits are bound to collide with the imperatives of the knowledge economy, causing both social and economic tensions within that society.

There are other country examples. Recently in China, an Internet entrepre-neur was thrown in jail for sending 30 000 e-mail addresses to another company apparently affiliated with a pro-Chinese democracy organisation. The man claimed he was simply selling addresses for profit, a common practice on the web, but the PRC, ever fearful of outside influences, dismissed this explanation. In the final analysis, however, the networked global knowledge economy is forcing these more closed countries open. Compared to ten years ago, very few economies remain "closed" today, and the trend towards openness is likely to continue.

There are many other dilemmas for governance. For example, immigration and taxation policies will be challenged by this new economy. Global knowledge workers, although not a new phenomenon, will become even more prevalent. The archetype of the future is to be found in high-technology centres such as Silicon Valley that are host to a diverse mix of highly skilled workers from all over the world. A country's competitive advantage is therefore partially driven by its ability to recruit and attract the best knowledge workers. This thinking is already part of Singapore's strategy. Also, in Malaysia's Multimedia Super Corridor project, a key feature is the creation of "Cyber Jaya", designed with the ideal aesthetics and modern conveniences for the high-tech knowledge worker. This trend has many implications for the future of nation-states as we know them. A worldwide value-added tax could very well be in the offing.

Dilemmas for organisations

As they are closer to the market, organisations in the private sector have been on the forefront of trying to manage this "web" *vs.* "citadel" interface. Already we have seen many organisations restructure themselves through a system of empowered networks and decentralised decision-making (Kelly, 1996). This has been a difficult transition for some. Barings Bank, for instance, thrived for the past hundred years using the citadel model. But Barings Securities, a newer, more web-based organisation, quickly found itself out of business because of the mis-guided actions of one of its workers. This example raises a host of dilemmas about knowledge workers. As the story of Barings Securities illustrates, a company's knowledge workers are often far more powerful than their managers. As owners of their knowledge, they can create great wealth as well as create tremendous sys-tem-wide disruptions, either by leaving or by precipitating a series of disastrous mistakes. How do we make knowledge workers accountable? How do managers "manage" knowledge workers when the latter's' motivations are no longer purely based on monetary factors? To recruit and retain top talent, leading companies in Silicon Valley, for instance, go to great pains and cost to build campuses that more resemble hotel resorts than traditional offices. In the quest to create the right envi-ronment for knowledge workers, these offices are complete with health clubs, com-fortable furniture, works of art, and even concierges to help with errands and life's time-consuming minutiae. For industries steeped in industrial age *modus operandi*, however, this jump to more holistic thinking about the work environment is a far one indeed. In this context, Drucker argues for a reconceptualisation of what we mean by "management." Instead of being responsible for the performance of people, the focus should be on "the application and performance of knowledge" (Neef, 1998).

Dilemmas for economic policy

Economic policy makers are faced with a complex of dilemmas. As noted ear-lier, we are in the midst of a transition governed partially by industrial era rules of the game and partially by knowledge era rules. Policy tools that were useful for an industrial era, such as the impact of interest rates on the cost of physical goods, have little relevance to the value of knowledge. Most of the dilemmas arise because we do not have an adequate empirical or theoretical understanding of a knowledge-based economy. In 1998, for example, the US Federal Reserve Board struggled with monetary policy, not knowing if the old rules of thumb linking capacity, employment and prices still applied when dealing with the new eco-nomic realities. Neither research nor extensive debate among the Fed governors could satisfactorily resolve these questions. Our tools for crafting economic policy are glaringly blunt. As Kevin Kelly describes, "The dials on our economic dashboard have started spinning wildly, blinking and twittering as we head into new territory. It's possible that the gauges are all broken, but it's much more likely the world is turning upside down" (Kelly, 1998).

In the field of economics, what is now required is the analogue of Thomas Kuhn's notion of scientific paradigm shift, where there is a wholesale change of world view (1962). Based on the new insights from Romer and his fellow growth theorists, it is possible that we are in "phase two" where the weaknesses in conventional thinking become increasingly apparent, anomalies become the rule, and where new theories and methods start surfacing as their replacements.

Measuring economic growth

The quest for economic measures has always been fraught with difficulty. The debate over developing the measure for GDP, for instance, was a long and hard process, earning economists Nobel Prizes. But compared to some of the issues faced today, measuring the value of an economic investment in the industrial economy was fairly straightforward and easy to understand. If an improved, steel-making blast furnace allowed workers to make more steel in less time and use less energy, then the productivity gain was obvious. If the word processing software we are using to produce this article enables the authors to spend more time on creative thought and less time on the mechanics of production, then the improvement is clear but harder to measure. In developing software, creativity may be the most important success factor. How to measure and value that creativity in any meaningful economic sense is conceptually and practically difficult. Ironically, since software is considered an intermediate good, all the productivity improvements at Microsoft that produced enormous shareholder value in the past decade do not show up in the GDP. The dilemma here is that we cannot throw the baby out with the bath-water; we need to work within the existing system of measures while devising more appropriate measures for the knowledge economy. This is already an urgent research priority, and some progress has been made. Work commissioned by the United Nations Commission on Science and Technology for Development (UNCSTD) has produced an indicators approach called INEXSK – **In**frastructure, **Ex**perience, **S**kills, and **K**nowledge – to map the strengths and weaknesses for technology and knowledge accumulation in developing nations (Mansell and Wehn, 1998).

The productivity paradox

For most of the OECD nations, the seventies, eighties, and nineties have seen low productivity growth – around 1% – compared to the fifties and sixties when productivity grew at more than twice that rate. Prosperity is a direct result of increases in productivity. Thus, any expectations about future prosperity are linked to expectations of productivity growth. Many economists argue that the expanding investments in IT have not yielded increases in productivity, and growth is therefore likely to remain low. Even if there appear to be some signals of increasing productivity growth, the debate in the economics profession remains lively.

The challenge we face today is understanding how to harness knowledge as a productive resource. Only recently have we started to shift our attention to knowledge, and especially how it interacts and amplifies the other inputs of capital, labour and land. As we have discussed, knowledge is messy and confusing because it is a process, a thing, and now a commodity. Increasing the productivity of knowledge and service-based workers is nonetheless critical to the future of the new economy. Given the nature of knowledge, the precise meaning of "productive" might have to change dramatically for this to happen. For Bill Joy of Sun Microsystems, productivity is not related to efficiency but creativity. The creative process rarely follows notions of efficiency; its goes in fits and starts, and happens through iterations. A software engineer might spend a whole year working on a project, with small marginal improvements in the value they are creating for the company. Then all of a sudden, in just a night's work, they pay for their annual salary (and then some) by creating a new product idea that has the potential to generate tremendous value. Importantly, this idea was an indirect result of working on the year-long project. Innovations build on other innovations.

Provocatively, Kelly (1998) asserts that productivity "is exactly the wrong thing to care about in the new economy." As he explains: "The task for each worker in the industrial age was to discover how to do his job better: that's productivity [...] But in the network economy, where machines do most of the inhumane work of manufacturing, the question for each worker is not 'How do I do this job right?' But 'What is the right job to do?'" This latter question, now decided by managers, is about exploration, curiosity, and discovery. Companies and institutions will continue to struggle with these two very different ways of perceiving productivity for some time.

Natural monopolies

As we saw earlier, in a knowledge-based economy, "natural monopolies" arise due to the logic of increasing returns. Today we see Microsoft dominating the operating systems market, and Cisco Systems dominating the network equipment market. This is perceived as a problem because innovation is the engine of growth in a knowledge economy and monopolies tend to inhibit innovation. Kelly (1998) calls this problem "monovation". Microsoft, the first great monopoly of the knowledge economy, is now under extensive legal attack for the success it achieved in capturing the dominant position in the software market. While they may have engaged in some predatory practices, abusing their market power, they got that power by winning in the market-place. The knowledge economy may continue to generate such natural monopolies. The key role for regulators will be to find a way to encourage "polyvation" in a world of monopolists (Kelly, 1998).

Digging deeper, another dilemma is trusting in Joseph Schumpeter's idea of "creative destruction" when public perception and our legal system still rest on industrial-age notions of competition. In a knowledge economy, competition within industries will come from new and substituting technologies rather than price. The introduction of these new technologies often destroys the natural monopolies created by increasing returns and opens up the competitive field for new players. For instance, the makers of transistors did not win in the integrated circuit market. Microsoft is quite conscious of these precedents of creative destruction. Its key competitors are not necessarily companies within its own industry, but the inventors of the next "killer app," whether they be the R&D scientists of Xerox PARC, a professor at MIT, or some talented hackers in a suburban garage.

Balancing innovation and diffusion

The debates over the evolving notion of "intellectual property" are another indicator of how our mental maps are no longer adequate in understanding the emerging terrain. Innovation is central to the production of knowledge. Rewarding innovation by providing economic incentives is essential for inventors to continue to create new ideas, products and services. One of the reasons Silicon Valley has done so well, despite the increasing costs of labour and other inputs, is that lucrative rewards are offered for innovation. The dilemma is how to reward innovators without restricting the dissemination and distribution of knowledge. This boils down to the theoretical economic problem of pricing knowledge. Once created, knowledge can be shared at a marginal cost. We see this in software development: the up-front costs are huge, but once the software is created, additional costs per unit are marginal and decrease over time. In this respect, knowledge has aspects of a public good: it can be shared by all with positive social and economic benefits. Society has tried to solve the reward problem through intellectual property laws. With the easy replicability of knowledge goods such as software, and the use of the web as a distribution channel, the merits of the existing system are being questioned. Academics and policy makers are coming up with hybrid regimes. Chichilnisky (1998), for instance, argues for "compulsory negotiable licences" that enable the unrestricted use of knowledge with the creator getting paid per use of that knowledge. In this model, compensation would directly reflect market demand.

The dilemma of "jobs" versus "work"

Of all the challenges faced by people in developed economies over the past twenty years, perhaps one of the most urgent, divisive, and agonising has related to the erosion of the traditional job. Reflect, for example, upon media coverage of the collapse of any large company, or popular demands for government interventions to save failing giants. People do not ask, "What will we do without Acme's products and services?" They ask, "What will we do without these jobs?"

The job – a relatively static, secure, and lifelong form of work, clearly definable and boundaried, requiring a specific and known set of skills – became, very quickly, one of the defining features (and benefits) of the industrial economy. Within only two or three generations, it came to inform and drive our expectations. Governments worldwide still implement policies based on this model, despite the fact that the mass, highly structured, and protected "job" was a brief curiosity in the history of work (see Figure 4).

One hundred and fifty years ago, the vast majority of people (even in the more developed economies) were engaged in agricultural work or domestic service – both of which were flexible, ever-changing and often "portfolio" in nature, certainly not like jobs as we came to know them. Even those involved in physical

Figure 4. **Work, wealth, jobs... coming full circle**

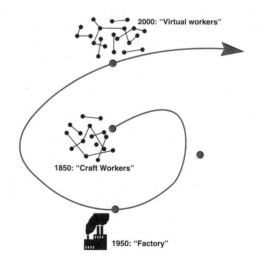

2000: "Virtual workers"

1850: "Craft Workers"

1950: "Factory"

Source: Eamonn Kelly.

production, especially craft workers, were working individually or in small groups in flexible and fluid ways, usually from home. Indeed, the webs of craft workers and their various market-places, generally co-ordinated by a "factor", bore some resemblance to the virtual organisations of today. The industrial age encouraged the factor to centralise production in a factory and routinise work into jobs. Today the centrifugal forces of the knowledge economy and information networks are driving many organisations back in the opposite direction.

Today, therefore, people tend to change their employers more frequently, or work for several employers simultaneously, or work as independent contractors, or work flexibly from home. We often have to learn new skills, change career tracks several times, and pursue new opportunities in growth areas of the economy that we had never even imagined. In short, people are having to adapt to the "post-job" economy, and concentrate instead on ever-evolving and rather fluid work opportunities and challenges, not unlike their forebears four or five generations ago.

For policy makers everywhere, this transition point generates a significant dilemma as to whether and when to revise long-standing policies based on the public's expectations of work in the form of "the job". For example:

- Today many governments – national, regional, and local – are under some pressure to support or initiate job creation or programmes, often predicated on historic notions of work.

- Often, attempts to attract foreign direct (or even out-of-state) investment are driven by policies related to the volume of jobs attracted, rather than broader measures of work, value, and economic activity.

- In many countries, pension planning and other benefit arrangements assume long-term, steady jobs as the normal form of economic engagement for individuals.

- Just as the physiocrats once argued that all true wealth creation was sourced only in agriculture, economic policies appear to value manufacturing activity ahead of services – as if wealth could only be created by the making of things. This may in part be driven by, as well as reinforce, a rather nostalgic focus on the traditional job as the desired form of work.

Over time, even our approaches to spatial planning will be seriously impacted by the new geography of the knowledge-intensive, work-rather-than-job society unfolding today.

The jobs-versus-work dilemma is deep, and it will take time for public policy making and public opinion to come into alignment with new economic and social realities. However, in the knowledge society there is real potential for new, rewarding, and ever-changing types of work. Those who linger too long with an outmoded set of expectations – related to the relatively short-lived era of the static and permanent job – will suffer more than those who move fast to embrace new work opportunities. Public policy makers may find it their duty not only to revise their own policies as quickly as possible, but also to help shift public attitudes and expectations.

Dilemmas for education

If our economy is in fact shifting towards knowledge-intensive activities, education will have to move to society's centre stage. Already, our educational institutions are feeling pressures to reform and adapt. The dilemma, however, is how to actually achieve this without penalising the students and people who do not have the education or socio-economic means to participate. The central issue in the competitive race ahead is how to create the right education for the new economy while improving access for more (all) people. Singapore amply demonstrates the value of investing in the quality of the labour force. In addition to the basic issues of cost and access, questions regarding the purpose of education will also arise. How do we balance the goals of economic gain and human development? Is human development also a goal? If creativity and innovation are essential success factors, can you educate for these abilities?

These dilemmas are highlighted in debates on educational reform. For example, in the United States there is a push toward making educational standards more rigorous. On the one hand, we need some benchmarks to improve the quality of education, while on the other we know that what gets measured and rewarded in schools is the only thing that receives attention from students. However, these measures often fail to capture what is truly important for the knowledge economy – intangible skills, the ability to think independently, and creative instincts which in themselves often defy measurement. Meanwhile, in North America (and elsewhere) the private sector continues to be disenchanted with the types of skills and abilities the secondary and post-secondary education systems seem to foster. This is why corporations are increasingly entering the training and education business so as to ensure they get a skilled workforce trained to meet to their needs. Of course, this in turn raises a host of other dilemmas about the ability of corporations to deliver a well-balanced and unbiased education.

Dilemmas for world development

Many of the key problems confronting world development are rooted in a lack of knowledge. Diarrhoea, for instance, is a simple ailment, yet it kills millions of children in developing countries because their parents do not know how to treat them. Many of the diseases in these countries are brought about by people drinking contaminated water supplies, yet they continue to drink and wash from them because they do not know any better. Population growth also continues to be a problem even though we learned in the past twenty years that it can be significantly curbed if women are educated. So in this sense, the world has always been divided between the "knowledge-rich" developed world and the "knowledge-poor" developing world. However, with the dynamic of increasing returns driving much of the knowledge economy, this gap is likely to get wider. Thus the dilemmas for global institutions relate back to creating the right incentives for continued innovation while distributing knowledge to the "knowledge-poor" areas of the globe.

Environmental dilemmas

A sign of the clash between economic paradigms is that we have yet to find a satisfactory solution to the "tragedy of commons" dilemma. Meanwhile, the extraordinary success of worldwide industrialisation is now turning on itself and hurting the earth. With the continued erosion of our planet's biodiversity and signs of rapid climate change, we are quickly approaching a critical threshold where long-standing and irreversible damage is being done. And despite the progress of new regimes and agreements such as those made at Rio and Kyoto, our attempts to create the right incentives for sustainable development have been only partially successful. Pricing public goods, as we have seen with the pricing of knowledge, is quite problematic within current intellectual property regimes.

These shortcomings have been driven by the structural underpinning of the industrial-age paradigm. Economic growth in the industrial economy was driven by the exploitation of resources and the consumption of fossil fuels. To use Romer's (1997) analogy, growth was achieved by cranking up the volume of cooking, and doing more with more. In our debates aimed at finding solutions to environmental problems, the underlying dilemma concerns balancing long-term sustainability with the continued need to exploit resources for industrial activity. But as we move away from industrial-based activities toward a knowledge economy, there is an opportunity to reperceive this dilemma. For instance, in theory, the economics of ideas is inherently less resource-intensive. If the right incentives and measures were created – such as a new regime of intellectual property rights and pricing schemes – that would initiate a fundamental shift in the way people view "environmental assets". Under such a scheme, an Amazon rain forest would have far more economic value in terms of future discoveries, biotechnology product ideas, patents, and even insight into how complex adaptive systems operate than it would as lumber. Until such a recalculation can occur, many of our pressing environmental problems will remain burdened with that principal dilemma. What Romer calls for is another creation of a "meta-idea" that could radically transform the way an economic system operates and yet increase the flow of ideas and knowledge. The British invention of the patent system is one example. It is time to find others.

Ethical dilemmas

Ethical dilemmas are not new; they have provoked philosophers and governments throughout history. But we are in an historical moment during which they are becoming particularly acute. As social, technological and commercial boundaries blur, new ethical challenges present themselves that have direct or indirect implications for economic policy. In Europe, for instance, with the historical memory of Nazi eugenics experiments during the Second World War, the idea of patenting human recombinant DNA met with considerable resistance. This in turn had serious consequences for the future success of European biotechnology companies. Another example concerns the regulation of unsavoury content on the Internet, such as pornography and the predatory practices of paedophiles. How should we regulate this? Or should we? Many people argue that the free and unfettered nature of the web drives its vitality and is the source for creative expression.

These ethical dilemmas will proliferate in the near future. Already, developments in bioscience are reaching a point where we will be able to "design" our children and create the first "immortals" by extending life by a factor of 2 or 3. As we create tools that have the potential to fundamentally enrich and transform our existence, we simultaneously open a Pandora's Box of ethical issues which could serve to seriously damage social cohesion and drive deep divisions within society. In a negative scenario, for instance, one can easily imagine the Religious Right in the United States or the Green lobby in Europe taking up some of these emerging ethical issues, and driving public opinion away from acceptance and application of these important technologies and discoveries in bioscience.

Indeed, one of the most important roles for public policy makers in the first years of the next millennium will be to prevent such a scenario. This might involve two things: first, anticipating where technology and commerce may generate ethical challenges; and second, creating the conditions for open and inclusive civic dialogue from which a more complex value system might evolve.

4. Scenarios for the future of the global knowledge economy

The way we use and distribute knowledge casts very long shadows on human societies.

Graciela Chichlnisky (1997)

Assuming that we are perceiving the new economic realities accurately and that a knowledge economy is emerging, that economy's future could unfold in two distinct ways. The fundamental uncertainty at the heart of the discussion is the degree to which the transformation will be socially inclusive. Will an ever-growing number of people in the near future share in this economic development and increasing prosperity? Or will the benefits flow mainly to a fairly small elite, while the great majority of people lose ground by almost every measure?

Most of the darker visions of the knowledge economy share common fears...

High friction world

This is a winner-takes-all economy where a small knowledge elite captures most of the economic value. The economic structure rewards a few and leaves the great majority behind. The resulting social friction of a two-tier society consisting of "knows" and "know-nots" consumes much of the economy's potential in a vicious circle.

The fruits of innovation drive economic growth in some parts of the world, creating local islands of prosperity. Highly educated knowledge workers do very well, but a modest education produces little economic benefit. Low wages characterise most service and manufacturing work. Overall, organisations evolve very slowly and remain mainly traditional in form. The "fast" gradually pull away from the "slow". Highly divergent outcomes result as a few countries do well behind high-security shields and others fall further behind. Intellectual protectionism is rife and the free flow of ideas is highly constrained by both those who want to protect the value of their intellectual property and those who want to prevent the informational "pollution" of their populations.

But there is another possibility...

The knowledge take-off

After a fairly brief transition, the emerging economic structure allows value to be added and captured by people with a wide range of skill levels and intellectual capabilities. Eventually most people benefit economically from the evolving knowledge economy. The computer-enhanced deliveryman of today is an early example.

Two major forces drive the successful knowledge take-off: the continued development of human capability and massive expansion of the technological infrastructure. More and more public and private resources are devoted to the two priorities of education and information infrastructure. Public education and business training become universally available. Public policies encourage investments in R&D. In addition, government and private sector expenditures create new capacity which leads to abundant, cheap bandwidth, inexpensive and easy-to-use devices, and an information-rich web.

This is a world characterised by open flows of information and rapid, nearly universal innovation. It is a high-speed economy of change. A side benefit is reduced environmental impacts of growth as value is added by knowledge-intensive rather than resource-intensive activities. Innovators are disproportionately rewarded. Network organisations become common and facilitate diverse new forms of economic participation.

5.   Conclusion and implications for the OECD

The movement toward an economy and society where knowledge is highly valued is more or less inevitable. There are, however, important uncertainties about the pace, distribution and consequences of this transformation. No benefits come without a cost. An assessment of the policy implications will require an understanding of both the benefits (and how to increase their likelihood and pervasiveness) and the downsides (and how to minimise their likelihood and impact).

The experience of Singapore over the last thirty years is a very clear demonstration of the ability to harness effectively the power of knowledge and create enormous economic potential. Knowledge economies have the potential to grow ever richer, and they are largely unconstrained by the limits of physical resources and environmental carrying capacity. Indeed, as the knowledge component of economic output grows, the environmental impact per unit of economic activity is likely to fall. The result is, at least in theory, greater wealth on the road to a more ecologically sustainable economy.

But often such transitions are accompanied by the loss of huge numbers of jobs. With retraining, many of these displaced workers may find new employment opportunities and in some cases even better jobs. However, many will struggle with unemployment, falling job levels and reduced incomes. Others may find the insecurity of the new dynamic job market very stressful: while opportunities may be abundant, the competition may be equally plentiful. It is also possible that it will be a very long time before the technology of the knowledge economy will advance sufficiently to give a relatively unskilled worker the ability to earn a middle class income in the way that industrial technology did. Some people may be left permanently behind, with very limited prospects.

The spread of useful knowledge is the key to the widening circle of growing economic potential. This implies that nations need to be fairly transparent to information flows. However, a consequence of transparency is the near impossibility of control. Thus, with the useful knowledge comes unwanted information, ranging from foreign entertainment to pornography. Open flows of information in the form of telecommunication networks, freedom of the press and the free flow of people are essential to encourage the continuing innovation that is key to competition in the knowledge economy. The increasing integration of the world, both physical and through information, also leads to another widespread concern: the potential for cultural homogenisation. For example, the ubiquity of English as the language of the knowledge economy is a powerful force. The impact of American television and movies is felt all over the planet.

Many nations will find such openness a threat to the current order. But the frictions created by this transition to a knowledge economy might be even more fundamental. China, for example, has millions of people out on the leading edge of the knowledge economy and hundreds of millions living in subsistence agriculture. The economic and social tensions of such vast difference in ways of life will be very difficult to manage. China will also confront frictions created by its different approaches from the west to some aspects of the knowledge economy, such as intellectual property laws.

Thus a core policy dilemma is the tension between the need for openness and the need for control. Singapore finds this a difficult dilemma. Also, many think that the USSR failed to handle this in part because they tried to control too much and so cut themselves off from external inputs. Maintaining a balance between the two extremes can produce a very dynamic society like the United States, but one whose high mobility creates great social tensions as winners accelerate away from the losers. Getting this balance right will be one of the keys to policies that sustain growth.

Policy makers in both the public and private sectors are also struggling with another aspect of the transition. What are the appropriate metrics of a knowledge economy? How, for example, do we measure the productivity of a knowledge worker? Automobiles made per hour made sense in the industrial age, while the notion of ideas per hour in the knowledge economy is obviously silly. A major and fairly urgent intellectual challenge is to develop new models and measures.

These issues translate into critical policy questions. For example: How will governments deal with taxation in an economy driven by electronic commerce? What is the right level of regulation, especially with regard to such key systems as banking and finance? Does government need to subsidise access to new information networks as every citizen's basic right? How do you help those who are getting left behind? Some of the traditional activities of government, such as the development of infrastructure and the provision of education, will become increasingly important in a knowledge economy.

The private sector obviously has critical roles to play in innovation, investment in new capabilities, provision of employment and education for its workforce. As the great engine of growth, the private sector can contribute to reweaving the fabric of social equity by making technology easier to use for a wider range of skill sets.

The policy issues and dilemmas created by this transition are mainly about increasing the likelihood and distribution of the economic benefits and mitigating the potentially damaging social consequences. The transition to a knowledge society and an economy driven by knowledge creates great challenges and tensions. In the end, a key question remains: how to increase and liberate the potential of the winners and how best to assist the losers.

Bibliography

ALLEE, Verna. (1997),
   The Knowledge Evolution: Expanding Organizational Intelligence. Boston: Butterworth-Heinemann.

ALLIANCE FOR CONVERGING TECHNOLOGIES (1997),
   Strength in Numbers: How Cyber-commerce Communities Create Value in the Digital Economy. Toronto: Alliance for Converging Technologies.

ARTHUR, W. Brian (1996),
   "Increasing Returns and the New World of Business", *Harvard Business Review*, July-August, pp. 100-109.

BRAUDEL, Fernand (1992),
   Civilization and Capitalism, 15th-18th Century, translated by Siân Reynolds. Berkeley: University of California Press.

BOYER, Nicole-Anne (1996),
   "Working Paper on the Growth of Smart Cities." Singapore: International Development and Research Council.

CHICHILNISKY, Graciela (1998),
   "The Knowledge Revolution", *The Journal of International Trade & Economic Development*. 7, No. 1:39-54.

CHICHILNISKY, Graciela (1997),
   "The Knowledge Revolution: Its Impact on Consumption Patterns and Resource Use". Human Development Report 1998: UNDP Development Program. Draft for discussion only.

CONCEIÇÃO, P. *et al.* (1998),
   "The Emerging Importance of Knowledge for Development: Implications for Technology and Policy and Innovation", *Technological Forecasting and Social Change*, 58:181-202.

DAVENPORT, Thomas and Laurence PRUSAK (1998),
   Working Knowledge: How Organizations Manage What They Know. Boston, Mass.: Harvard Business School Press.

DAVIS, Stan and Christopher MEYER (1998),
   Blur: The Speed of Change in a Connected Economy, Ernst and Young Center for Business Innovation.

De GEUS, Arie (1997),
   The Living Company. Boston: Harvard Business School Press.

DICKEN, Peter (1998),
   Global Shift: Transforming the World Economy. 3d ed. New York and London: The Guildford Press.

DOLVEN, Ben (1998),
"Let's All Be Creative", *Far Eastern Economic Review*, 24 December.

DRUCKER, Peter (1998), "Management's New Paradigms", *Forbes*, 5 October, pp. 152-176.

DRUCKER, Peter, P. and E. DYSON, C. HANDY, P. SAFFO and P. SENGE (1997)
"Looking Ahead: Implications of the Present", *Harvard Business Review*. September-October, 18-32.

DRUCKER, Peter (1993),
The Post-Capitalist Society. New York: HarperBusiness.

The Economist (1997),
"One World?" 18 October, pp. 79-80.

The Economist (1997),
"The Survey of the World Economy", 20 September.

HALAL, William *et al.* (1998),
"The George Washington University Forecast of Emerging Technologies: A Continuous Assessment of the Technology Revolution", *Technological Forecasting and Social Change*, 59:89-110.

HEILBRONER, Robert (1994),
21st Century Capitalism. Toronto: CBC Massy Lectures Series.

JARBOE, K.P. and Robert D. ATKINSON (1998),
The Case for Technology in the Knowledge Economy: R&D, Economic Growth, and the Role of Government. Washington DC: Progressive Policy Institute.

KELLY, Eamonn (1996),
Presentation on "The Knowledge Economy". Emeryville, California: Global Business Network.

KELLY, Kevin (1998),
New Rules for the New Economy: 10 Radical Strategies for A Connected World. New York: Viking.

KELLY, Kevin (1997),
"New Rules for the New Economy", *Wired* 5, No. 9.

KUHN, Thomas [1962 and 1996 (3rd Edition)],
The Structure of Scientific Revolutions. Chicago: University of Chicago Press.

KURTZMAN, Joel (1997),
"An Interview with Paul Romer", *Strategy & Business*, First quarter. Booz-Allen & Hamilton. Reprinted from Paul Romer's home page (www.stanford.edu/~promer).

MADDISON, Angus (1991),
Dynamic Forces in Capitalist Development: A Long-Run Comparative View. Oxford: Oxford University Press.

MANSELL, Robin and Uta WEHN (1998),
Knowledge Societies: Information Technology for Sustainable Development. Oxford and New York: Oxford University Press.

NEEF, Dale, ed. (1998),
The Knowledge Economy. Boston: Butterworth-Heinemann.

NONAKA, Ikujiro and Hirotaka TAKEUCHI (1995),
The Knowledge-Creating Company: How Japanese Companies Create the Dynamics of Innovation. Oxford and New York: Oxford University Press.

PEREZ, C. (1985)
"Microelectronics, Long Waves and World Structural Change", *World Development.* 13:441-463.

ROMER, Paul M. (1997),
personal communication.

ROMER, Paul M. (1995)
"Beyond the Knowledge Worker", *Worldlink*, 56-60.

ROMER, Paul M. (1994),
"Beyond Classical and Keynesian Macroeconomic Policy", *Policy Options*, July-August.

ROMER, Paul M. (1993),
"Economic Growth" in David R. Henderson (ed.), *The Fortune Encyclopedia of Economics*. New York: Time Warner Books.

ROMER, Paul M. (1990),
"Endogenous Technological Change", *Journal of Political Economy*, 98, No. 5:S71-S107.

ROSELL, Steven *et al.* (1995),
Changing Maps: Governing in a World of Rapid Change. Ottawa: Carleton University Press.

SAXENIAN, AnnaLee (1994)
Regional Advantage: Culture and Competition in Silicon Valley and Route 128. Cambridge, Mass.: Harvard University Press.

SHUMPETER, J.A. (1952),
Capitalism, Socialism, and Democracy. 4th ed. London: George Allen & Unwin.

SOLOW, Robert (1957),
"Technical Change and the Aggregate Production Function", *Review of Economics and Statistics*, 39:312-320.

STEVENS, Candice (1996),
"The Knowledge-Driven Economy", *The OECD Observer*, No. 200:6-10.

TAPSCOTT, Don (1995),
The Digital Economy: Promise and Peril in the Age of Networked Intelligence. New York and Toronto: McGraw-Hill.

VARIAN, Hal and Carl SHAPIRO (1999),
Information Rules: A Strategic Guide to the Network Economy. Boston, Mass.: Harvard Business School Press.

WEBBER, Steve (1999),
Informal Conversation. Global Business Network.

WEBER, Alan M. (1993),
"What's So New About the New Economy?", *Harvard Business Review*, January/February, 27.

4

Towards Global Competition: Catalysts and Constraints

by

Horst Siebert and *Henning Klodt*
Kiel Institute of World Economics, Germany

1. Introduction

When the turn of a century approaches, perceptions of the future tend to become gloomy. As we enter the 21st, one of the gloomy catchwords is "globalisation", which is associated with concerns and sorrows about the economic prospects of highly developed countries. It is feared that they will not be able to withstand the storms of a global competition that will eventually destroy the wage gap against poor countries and will raze social standards to the ground all around the globe. *One World, Ready or Not* is the title of a bestselling book (Greider, 1997), and many observers are concerned that people are indeed not yet ready.

The basic message of this chapter is that the public debate strongly overrates the risks of globalisation and almost completely ignores its opportunities. Most of the concerns raised today against globalisation could similarly have been raised against the expansion of international trade in the 1960s. Import competition in those days was also threatening domestic jobs, and put labour-intensive and standardised industries in advanced economies under strain. In retrospect, however, the sixties seem like a "Golden Age", when an increased international division of labour opened up rich export opportunities, created numerous new jobs, and fostered economic growth and welfare in all open, internationally oriented economies. There is good reason to believe that the current wave of globalisation will also be regarded as a tide of rich opportunities which will eventually lift all boats.

The structure of the chapter is as follows. Section 2 analyses the concept of globalisation within the context of international economics theory; Section 3 examines the driving forces for a more integrated world economy; Section 4 discusses the constraints involved; and Section 5 concludes with a look at the future of globalisation and the potential gains.

2. Visions of an integrated world economy

No doubt, globalisation is an increasingly fashionable term. A person researching the number of publications that contain the word in the title at the library of the Kiel Institute of World Economics will find not more than 36 entries for the year 1990. For the year 1997, the number of entries increases to 212, equivalent to a growth rate of 30% per year.

There is still no unequivocal definition of what globalisation means and what it does not mean. For some observers, it describes the tremendous increase of trade and capital flows in the recent past; for others it is a catchword for the ubiquitous availability of all kinds of information, for the emergence of worldwide production networks, or for the assimilation of lifestyles in the global village. All these perceptions share the notion that globalisation raises the level of integration in the world economy.

As the suffix "isation" indicates, globalisation describes a process, not a state of affairs. From an economist's point of view, the word can be defined as the process of converting separate national economies into an integrated world economy. This conversion is basically achieved through three channels:

– International trade, which is still the basic and most important link between national economies.

– International factor movements, which are mainly confined to capital flows; the international mobility of workers is still rather low.

– The international diffusion of technology, which is only partly a by-product of international flows of goods and capital; increasingly, it is based on intangible cross-border flows of information.

Figure 1 illustrates the main features of a world economy where national borders have lost their significance and global competition is prevalent. It is a simple model with two countries, two production factors (capital and labour), and an independent government in each country. Production factors are employed by firms which compete with each other in the domestic market and with foreign firms in world markets.

The immediate result of globalisation is an increase in competitive pressures in virtually all areas of the economy. *Product competition* can be expected to eliminate substantial differences in product prices between countries. Standard models of trade theory tell us that this equalisation of product prices will also equalise real wages and interest rates. However, this factor price equalisation theorem rests upon a number of restrictive assumptions that are not very realistic. For instance, it assumes the complete absence of any transport costs or other types of trade barriers. And, more importantly, it postulates identical technologies all over the world.[1] In the real world, where shipping goods across long distances is costly,

Figure 1. **Basic elements of global competition**

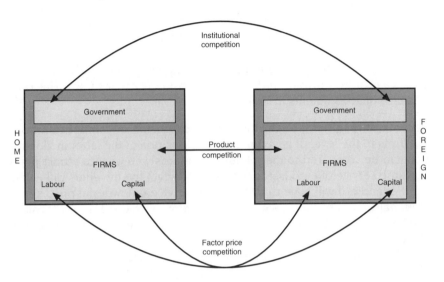

where some countries are technologically ahead of others, and where labour represents different levels of human capital, it can be expected that international trade – while it might tend to level factor prices – will not succeed in completely eliminating any international factor price differentials.

Those that remain are the stimulus for international factor flows which give rise to *factor price competition*. If capital is free to move across national borders, interest rates will differ between locations only with respect to different risk premiums, not with respect to the capital endowment of countries. Real wages in rich countries will no longer benefit from a higher amounts of physical capital, because capital will flow to those places where the rate of return is highest. If capital mobility is supplemented by unrestrained international flows of technology, factor price equalisation will also apply to real wage levels – even if international mobility of labour is low. In these conditions, international wage differentials will only be sustainable if they reflect corresponding differences in the qualification of the labour force or in the general economic conditions of the respective countries.

In centuries past, when governments were small and nature was a dominant production factor, general economic conditions depended mainly on geographical features, *i.e.* on climate, the quality of soil, or the availability of ports and navigable rivers. Nowadays, the economic capacity of locations depends much more on institutional settings, which are largely under the influence of governments.

Among these settings are the quality of communication infrastructure, the level and structure of taxes, the soundness of legal protection, the intensity of social conflicts, and the stability and convertibility of the national currency. If countries want to attract internationally mobile production factors, their governments have to engage in institutional competition with foreign governments. In a perfectly integrated world economy, where distance costs have completely vanished, the relative wage level of regions depends to a large extent upon the relative performance of governments in *institutional competition*.

The major result of globalisation is the extension of competition from the level of firms to the level of governments. The position of the latter in global competition can be compared to that of hotel landlords who want to attract potential guests. If the service offered is poor or too expensive, the travellers will just move on and the landlord will have to improve the service or lower the price. Similarly, internationally mobile investors will chose locations with either low costs and poor infrastructure or with high costs and excellent infrastructure – but they will surely avoid locations with high costs and poor infrastructure. This type of competition, labelled as "institutional competition" in Figure 1, can also be referred to as "locational competition" (a translation, far from perfect but the best available, of the German term *Standortwettbewerb*), because it is concerned with the relative attractiveness of business locations for internationally mobile factors.

Generally speaking, it can be expected that all types of global competition will increase aggregate welfare: product competition will enrich consumption opportunities and erase production inefficiencies; factor price competition will improve capacity utilisation and help avoid allocative distortions; and institutional competition will eliminate excessive and inefficient government activities. A truly integrated world economy holds the promise of substantial "gains from globalisation", which basically result from the deepening of the international division of labour. Hence, the pessimistic perceptions of globalisation held by the public are not shared by the internationally oriented economists.

3. Catalysts of globalisation

Globalisation is an ongoing process which continues to gain momentum. A whole string of tendencies can be observed in the world economy, which together have the effect of reducing market segmentations and increasing interdependence of world markets. Some of these factors have been in play for decades, others are fairly new, but almost all of them will continue to exert an influence in the future. This section examines those factors which appear to be the most important.

Reduced transport and communication costs

Transport and communication costs are falling significantly – a phenomenon as true for the traditional costs of covering distances by sea and air (reduced to approximately one-fifth since the twenties and thirties, respectively) as for the costs of telecommunication. For instance, a three-minute telephone call from New York to London in 1930 cost $250 (in constant prices from 1990), in 1950 $50, and in 1990 $3.32; the price for processing information fell from $1 per instruction per second in 1975 to one cent in 1994 (World Bank, 1995, p. 45). The costs of using satellites have also fallen dramatically. In the future, transport costs may continue to fall when technological progress is sufficiently strong to overcome environmental costs incurred by transport activities.

This decline in costs is illustrated in Figure 2. The "death of distance" (Cairncross, 1997) facilitates the establishment and monitoring of international production networks, enlarges trading areas, and enables firms to exploit international cost differentials through the fragmentation and relocation of production and global sourcing.

Information technology is a veritable revolution. In 1998, 180 million Internet stations made up a worldwide information network; the number will be half a

Figure 2. **Costs of transport and communication**

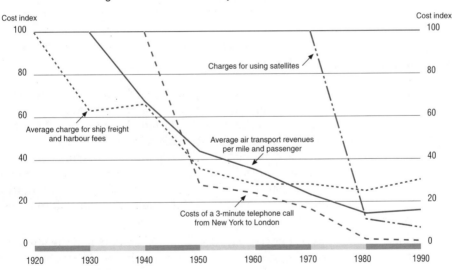

Source: World Bank, 1995, p. 51.

billion in 2002. Information costs are likely to fall even further in the future, because the microelectronics revolution is far from over. Physical transport costs can also be expected to decline, although limited fuel supply and/or "green taxes" to protect the environment may counteract the technology-driven trend.

At present, integration into the global network of information is much easier for rich countries than for poor ones. The availability of information and communication equipment is significantly greater in countries such as the United States or Singapore than in countries such as China or India (Table 1). As the relative prices of these appliances are declining, however, it can be expected that the connection of poor countries to the world pool of information will improve considerably in the near future. Hence, an important aspect of globalisation in the near future will be the eventual inclusion of virtually every region of the world into the global village.

Table 1. **Information and communication equipment per 100 inhabitants
in countries grouped by income, 1995**

GNP per capita	PCs	Telephones	Television sets
Low: <$726	0.3	2.0	12.9
Middle: $726-$2895	1.1	9.1	20.5
Upper: $2896-$8955	3.3	14.5	26.3
High: >$8955	20.5	53.2	61.2

Source: Cairncross (1997, p. 22).

Dismantled trade barriers

National economic policies have changed, and adopted an approach of greater openness. The radical change in the former centrally planned economies of Central and Eastern Europe and the opening of China have brought important regions of the world within the scope of the international division of labour. If India is also taken into account, it is clear that an historical process is taking place, one in which more than 40% of the world's population is becoming integrated into the world economy. This implies that the limitation of the size of markets, formerly a potential barrier to extending the international division of labour, will be a less important factor in the future.

Regional efforts towards integration, for example in Europe, and the strengthening of multilateral trade agreements have also eliminated impediments to trade. Most developing and newly industrialising countries have changed their strategies for development and foreign trade, and are now much more open.

Forty-four countries have joined GATT/WTO between 1986 and 1998. As of 1998, 31 countries want to become members of the WTO, a clear sign of a forceful process of liberalisation in the world economy. Finally, the reduction of political tensions (*e.g.* cold war, apartheid in South Africa) has provided a better political environment for openness.

National and regional liberalisation policies are supported and complemented by international negotiations on trade and investment barriers in the GATT/WTO framework. The significance of declining trade barriers is illustrated in Figure 3, which describes the development of average tariff rates for the United States since the 1940s. By and large, the tariff rates of other industrial countries are at a similar level, whereas those of developing countries are in general higher. Over time, however, the latter have also substantially declined.

Of course, the international trading system is still far from free trade in several areas, notably agriculture, textiles and clothing. And severe problems will have to be solved before international trade in services will really become free. Nevertheless, there should be no doubt that trade liberalisation has significantly contributed to the integration of the world economy over the past decades. At present, several far-reaching agreements from the Uruguay Round, for instance on trade-related intellectual property rights (TRIPS), trade-related investment measures (TRIMS), trade in

Figure 3. **Weighted average US tariff rate after GATT Rounds**
Pre-Geneva = 100

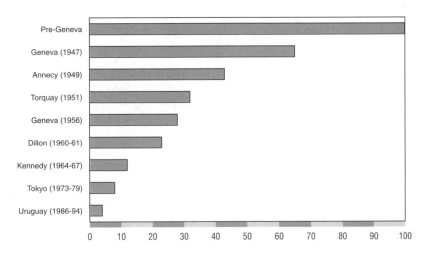

Source: Bhagwati (1989); own calculations.

services (GATS) and improved dispute settlement procedures, are being implemented and brought into effect. Furthermore, initial negotiations are commenced for establishing a new GATT/WTO round (the Clinton Round?). Hence, global economic integration will continue to benefit from multilateral liberalisation approaches in the future. Apart from measures which explicitly restrict trade, national regulations are increasingly being reviewed. They are continuously adjusted in the process of institutional competition, which also results in less impediments.

Expansion of trade and foreign direct investment

Globalisation is not a new phenomenon, but there are signs that indicate the process is accelerating. A rather simple although highly instructive indicator of globalisation is provided by the growth rates of world output and world trade. Generally, the volume of international trade is growing twice as fast as the volume of world output. This development suggests that the international division of labour is deepening and the world economy is becoming increasingly integrated (Figure 4). The gap between export growth and GDP growth has further widened in the recent past – yet another indication of this acceleration.

Contrary to popular belief, world economic integration is not accompanied by a replacement of manufactures by services in international trade. The share of

Figure 4. **World output, exports, and foreign direct investment**
1973 = 100

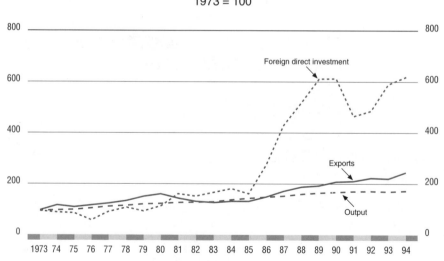

Source: Siebert (1997b, p. 15).

services in world trade stagnates around a level of 20% (Table 2), although the share of services in domestic output and employment is significantly rising in virtually every country. Moreover, modern information and communication technologies have facilitated the international tradability of services – at least those that are provided in a "disembodied" manner (Klodt, 1988). The seeming contradiction between rising trade potentials and constant shares of services in world trade can be explained by the fact that the transition to the service society is mainly achieved by a rising share of services in intermediate inputs, whereas the ratio of services to industrial goods in final demand is fairly stable (Klodt, 1997). Hence, the true importance of international trade in services is not reflected by statistics, because a significant portion is incorporated into trade in goods. Nevertheless, further steps towards liberalising trade in services (for instance in the context of GATS) appears to be an essential ingredient of further world economic integration, because a significant fraction of the international division of labour is achieved by foreign direct investment in service industries.

Table 2. **Share of services in total trade**
Percentage

	1975	1980	1985	1990	1996
World	19.6	18.2	18.2	20.1	20.1
Industrial countries	20.5	20.6	19.6	21.3	21.1
United States	17.9	16.9	22.3	27.5	27.7
Japan	/	/	11.4	12.8	14.5
Germany	17.1	16.9	15.7	13.9	14.0
France	22.4	29.2	27.3	26.8	24.5
United Kingdom	28.4	25.1	23.4	23.6	23.4

Source: IMF (current issues); own calculations.

Foreign direct investment (FDI) can be regarded both as an international relocation of capital and as a basic means of establishing international production networks. Up to the early 1980s, the development of world FDI more or less kept pace with the development of world exports, but in the recent past there have been two distinct waves of globalisation via FDI, which peaked around 1990 and 1995. Hence, international capital flows can indeed be regarded as an increasingly important channel of globalisation.[2]

Among the larger OECD countries, FDI dominated in Germany, France, Japan and the United States, whereas in Italy and the United Kingdom globalisation was mainly driven by exports (Figure 5). On the other hand, it should be kept in mind that the international integration of production networks can be achieved not only by outward FDI (presented in the figure), but also by inward FDI, which is especially important for the United Kingdom. With respect to the elimination of international factor price differentials, outflows and inflows of foreign investment are working in the same direction.

The role of capital flows

Figures 4 and 5 look at investment capital and ignore international flows of financial capital, which have reached impressive levels in recent years. According to the Bank for International Settlements, international currency transactions (which are only a fraction of international financial transactions) account for $1.49 trillion per day in 1998, an increase of 26% against 1995 and an increase of 150% against 1989 (Neue Zuercher Zeitung, 19 October 1998, p. 10). Nevertheless, there are still reasonable doubts whether the world capital markets can really be regarded as perfectly integrated.

These doubts were originally raised by Feldstein and Horioka (1980), who argued that a perfectly integrated world capital market could be regarded as a financial pool where savers put their money in and investors take their money out – irrespective of the national origin of savings and investment. Under such conditions, there should be no systematic relationship between the savings ratio and the investment ratio of a country, because only by accident would a high propensity to save go hand in hand with rich and promising investment opportunities.

However, Feldstein and Horioka found a rather stable relationship between the savings and investment ratio across countries. This observation, which became known as the Feldstein-Horioka Puzzle, was confirmed in several other studies. Moreover, Taylor (1996) found that international capital mobility among the G7 countries was even higher in the late 19th century than in the 1970s and 1980s, and only slightly lower than in the 1990s.

There are several objections to these findings that cannot be discussed at length in this chapter. For instance, Taylor's argument ignores the fact that international capital mobility today covers many more countries than it has in the past century. And more importantly, it covers countries with much larger differences in wage rates and technological levels, which allows more room for exploiting international cost and productivity differentials by relocations of capital. With respect to the Feldstein-Horioka argument, the basic objection is that countries may be affected by external shocks that influence savings and investment behaviour in the same way. Therefore, a parallel development of national savings and investment ratios does not necessarily reflect a segmentation of national capital markets. Nevertheless, most observers agree that the Feldstein-Horioka coefficients

Figure 5. **Increase in gross domestic product, exports, and foreign direct investment of selected countries, 1981-1996**

At constant prices; 1981 = 100

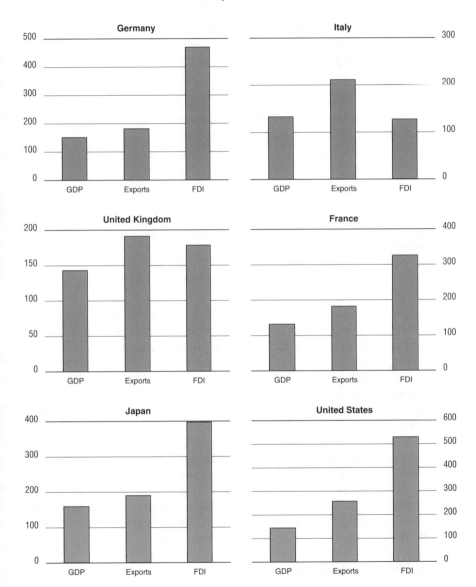

Source: OECD, *International Direct Investment Statistics Yearbook*, 1998; OECD statistics; OECD, *National Accounts, Main Aggregates, Vol. I*, 1999.

at least contain some relevant information about the integration of world capital markets.

More recent studies have revealed that the correlation between savings and investment ratios is still significant, but declining over time (Table 3).[3] Hence, it can be argued that world capital markets are still far from being perfectly integrated. But integration obviously continues, which implies that globalisation via trans-border flows of capital is an ongoing process which will probably carry on into the future.

Table 3. **Feldstein-Horioka coefficients for OECD countries**

	Regression: $(I/Y)_i = \alpha + \beta \, (S/Y)_i$	
Period	β	t-value
1960-69	0.86	14.3
1970-79	0.77	7.0
1980-89	0.63	6.3
1990-93	0.61	6.8

Source: Bayoumi (1999).

In essence, the decline of the Feldstein-Horioka coefficients reflects the enhanced opportunities for internationally mobile investors to enter foreign markets. An important prerequisite for this development is a well-functioning international banking system that relies on transparency of financial markets, liberal regulations of cross-border capital flows, and political stability. In the European Union, complete capital market liberalisation was achieved in 1990 (as one of the four freedoms in the single market). East and South East Asia opened up to foreign capital as early as the 1960s and 1970s, whereas several Latin American countries lacked the necessary political stability until the 1980s. If there exist reasonable risks of sovereignty, foreign countries become mousetraps: they are easily entered but difficult to leave. The reduction of sovereignty risks helps to reduce capital flights and allows access to the international supply of capital. Further steps towards an integrated world capital market will remain an important topic on the agenda of the International Monetary Fund, the World Bank and – with respect to international trade in banking services – the World Trade Organisation.

4.   Constraints of globalisation

The driving forces of globalisation – technological reduction of distance costs and removal of artificial economic barriers between countries – have surely not reached an end. It can be expected that the trend towards the integrated world economy will forge ahead in the years to come. It should be kept in mind, however, that history has never been, and will never be, a one-way street. The success of globalisation will breed its own constraints, which may slow down if not reverse world economic integration. These endogenous constraints and a few others are discussed in this section.

Demand for more redistribution and an expansion of the Welfare State

Resistance to further globalisation can be expected especially from those groups that fear they will be among the losers. In highly developed countries the main losers are low-qualified workers, because they are increasingly exposed to direct and indirect factor price competition from low-wage countries. There is still an ongoing debate among economists about the relative importance of globalisation for the income and employment opportunities of skilled and less-skilled workers (Siebert, 1999b), but there is no doubt that the integration of China, Eastern Europe and other labour-rich regions into the world economy will put the wage levels in Western industrial countries under strain. In a globalised world, high wages can only be earned if they correspond to high labour productivity which stems from a high qualification level of workers.

In the United States, the United Kingdom and, to some extent, Japan, the national labour markets have reacted to the increased adjustment pressure from global competition in the form of increased wage differentials (Table 4). In continental Europe, by contrast, wage dispersion remained constant or even declined. Consequently, low-qualified workers had to face a severe deterioration of their employment opportunities in those countries. Inadequate and inflexible adjustment

Table 4. **Wage dispersion between different income deciles[a] across countries**

	D5/D1		D9/D5	
	1979	1995	1979	1995
United States	1.84	2.13	1.73	2.04
Japan	1.71	1.63	1.76	1.85
Western Germany[b]	1.65	1.44	1.63	1.61
France[c]	1.67	1.65	1.94	1.99
United Kingdom	1.69	1.81	1.65	1.87
Italy[d]	1.96	1.75	1.50	1.60

a) D1: lowest income decil; D9: second-highest income decil.
b) 1983 to 1993.
c) 1994 instead of 1995.
d) 1993 instead of 1995.
Source: OECD (1996).

to global competition can be regarded as a major determinant of rising structural unemployment in continental Europe (Siebert, 1997a).[4] Presumably, globalisation's potential losers will try to minimise their adjustment costs by calling for redistribution from gainers in order to participate in the aggregate welfare gains from globalisation. In principle, this strategy meets with open arms in the European approach to economic policy – for instance in the concept of the "Social Market Economy", where social insurance helps accommodate structural change. It is therefore not surprising that, as Rodrik observed (1997, p. 53), open economies tend to spend more on social security and redistributive policies than less open economies. In his view, "the social welfare state is the flip side of the open economy".

The potential for compensating globalisation's losers through an extended social policy are limited, however, because institutional competition restricts the power of governments to raise taxes for financing such policies. Rodrik may be right in concluding that the demand for redistributive policies will rise, but he ignores that the supply of redistributed income will decline. Politicians will increasingly face the dilemma that rising claims for redistribution will be accompanied by shrinking tax revenues. The social security systems in Europe are under pressure in any case because they create severe distortions in the labour market (tax wedge), and because with an ageing population these systems are running the risk of not being sustainable. The scope for redistribution is limited; an increase in the Welfare State is unlikely; instead, the industrial countries in Europe are faced with choosing which income risks (in case of unemployment) are so relatively small that each individual can carry them on the basis of their own economic capacity, and which risks are so large for the individual that society needs to carry them (Siebert, 1998a).

Like national security systems, the transfer system of the European Union (structural funds, the common agricultural policy) can be interpreted as an attempt to make structural adjustment more acceptable. With monetary union, the political demand for transfers can be expected to rise. As the EU budget is limited to 1.27% of the EU GDP, however, there is a severe hurdle for an extension of transfers that would eat away the efficiency gains expected from the single market.

Trade unions and political systems under strain

It seems unlikely that the increased pressure on the labour market could result in stronger trade unions. In the United States and the United Kingdom, trade unions have seen an erosion of their power, and in most continental European countries membership is down. New production processes involving teams in which the individual worker has more responsibility, the rising level of human capital requirements, the decline of industrial-type jobs and the rise of new jobs in information technology and the service sector in general – all these tendencies make it more difficult for trade unions to organise members. The most important aspect, however, is that the rising international mobility of investors and capital increases the elasticity of labour demand, and thus reduces the monopoly power of unions (Lorz, 1997). The attempt to Europeanise wage policy will not be a way out for them, because the European Union itself is increasingly integrating into a globalising world economy.

In a sense, the limited ability of unions to adjust to globalisation's require-ments is part of the more general question of whether the political decision-making system is able to cope with larger shocks or the reversal of eco-nomic trends that prevailed in the past. Japan, accustomed to high growth rates until the early nineties, seems to be a case in point: its political system may appear to have lost its capacity to solve economic problems. Is that also true for the three major continental countries in Europe – Italy, France and Germany? Like Japan, these countries are based on consensus, and not unlike Japan, they seem to be less and less able to solve major issues such as high unemployment and the necessary reforms of the social insurance system.[5]

Pressure for protectionism

When advanced countries lack the flexibility that is required for coping with the challenges of globalisation, it must be expected that politicians will increas-ingly be tempted to rely upon another strategy: the establishment of protectionist barriers against global competition. Such barriers can take various forms: tariffs, non-tariff trade barriers, capital controls, Tobin taxes, social and green standards, etc. It would appear necessary, therefore, to keep a watchful eye on the development of protectionist policies in the future.

In the area of trade-related instruments, the imposition of anti-dumping actions is one of the most prevalent protectionist measures. In the 1990s, the incidence of these measures has strongly increased (Table 5). It would perhaps be misguided to interpret the data of the table as the beginning of protection-istic struggles against global competition, but the large increase in the number of actions per year should at least be taken as a first warning signal.

A second warning signal results from the calculations of Table 6, where the share of intra-bloc trade is provided for different blocs. Except for the EU, intra-bloc trade has gained importance both in exports and imports.[6] The numbers are not dramatic, but they may well indicate that governments are beginning to look for ways of escaping from global competition and the associated adjustment pains of the integrated world economy.

Table 5.   **Anti-dumping actions by region**

Countries initiating actions	Average actions per year[a]	
	1985-90	1990-96
North America	56.8	62.7
Western Europe	28.2	30.7
Australia/New Zeeland	33.6	47.5
Latin America	5.6	38.5
Asia	1.4	7.8
Other	0.0	12.6
Total	**125.6**	**199.8**

a)   Years run from 1/7 to 30/6.
Source: Calculated from Spinanger (1997, Table 2).

Table 6.   **Share of intra-regional trade in total flows**[a]
Percentage

Trading bloc	No. of participating countries	Exports		Imports	
		1990	1996	1990	1996
APEC	18	69.1	73.0	67.0	70.9
EU*	15	62.5[b]	62.2	62.1[b]	64.0
NAFTA	3	42.7	47.5	34.4	39.2
ASEAN	7	19.5	24.7	15.9	19.3
MERCOSUR	4	8.9	22.6	14.5	20.0

a)   Without associated members.
b)   1993.
Source: WTO (1998, Vol. II, p. 7).

Social standards and international policy co-ordination

In public debate, harmonising social norms is proposed as another strategy in the era of globalisation. The starting point of this position is that social protection should not stop at national borders, but should also apply to countries that are the source of imports to advanced countries. The logic behind this approach is that employers in developing countries would be forced to improve their working conditions; otherwise they could not obtain access to the markets of developed countries. As a variant, minimum social norms are required. This leaves open what minimum means, i.e. whether it is related to bare necessities or whether it is simply a step towards a more comprehensive form of harmonisation. Harmonising social norms could prove to be as formidable a constraint to the international division of labour as protectionism.

In many cases, the demand for social standards in international trade is not motivated by solidarity with exploited workers in poor countries, but basically aims at sheltering high-wage jobs in advanced countries from low-wage competition. The price of such "social protection" would have to be paid by developing countries, which would face reduced opportunities of integrating into the world economy, and by consumers in developed countries, who would have to face higher import prices.

In any case, the logic behind harmonising social norms is fallacious for different reasons. Firstly, from an employer's point of view, social standards are just another form of non-wage labour costs. They can only be increased at the expense of the wage level. As the demand for social protection is income-elastic, rich countries should refrain from imposing their conceptions about social security upon poorer countries, which probably prefer higher wages instead of higher social standards. Secondly, social standards in international trade may cause substitution effects between the international sector and the domestic sector in developing countries. For instance, if advanced countries banned the import of goods that are produced from child labour, children would probably be driven into local industries where working conditions may be even worse. Hence, it may be difficult to achieve well-intended social goals by imposing respective barriers to trade.

The social standards approach can be viewed as the tip of an iceberg: the more general approach of "co-ordinating" international arrangements – including taxation. Although this is unlikely to proceed on a worldwide level, attempts can clearly be seen such as harmonising taxes, including taxes for business in the European Union. This can be interpreted as the response of national governments that see their manoeuvring space reduced in locational competition and that are trying to redefine some common institutional setup that would limit the exit opportunities of internationally oriented investors.

At present, the debate about international policy co-ordination is concentrating on exchange rates and international financial markets. The financial crisis in South East Asia, the fragility of the banking sector in Japan, the crisis in Russia, the potential instability of Latin American countries such as Brazil, and the increased risk aversion in the US financial sector have made clear that volatility in the financial sector has an impact on the real sphere of the economy. Globalisation also means more globalised financial markets.

Many solutions to these issues have been discussed, but the bottom line of all approaches is that each country must anticipate the negative impact that a financial crisis will have for its own development. Thus, countries cannot rely on international efforts to help them. They have to take stability at home more seriously by applying stricter banking regulations, by including investment banks and hedge funds in a regulatory framework, by preventing a bubble from developing, and by implementing more stability-oriented policy. "Stability begins at home" will be an important slogan for the new world economy. This implies, however, that stability constraints have to be taken into consideration early on. That will restrain excessive growth; it will also be helpful in steering economies to a long-run growth path.

Environmental sustainability

In a long-term perspective, considerable constraints on globalisation and world economic growth could result from the limited capacity of the environment as a sink, *i.e.* as a receptacle of wastes. The major issue is no longer national environmental quality as a restraint on national development; the issue of the next century is global environmental goods.

If the appraisal of the overwhelming majority of natural scientists is taken seriously, global warming is a severe risk for the world; the risk has to be taken into account by a precautionary environmental policy. There are competing uses for the global environment: its role as a public good for consumption *versus* its role as a sink for greenhouse gases (Siebert, 1998*b*). Reconciling these facets requires determining the optimal level of the global environment (the atmosphere), *i.e.* the quantity of greenhouse gases to be tolerated. That means comparing the costs of reducing emissions and the benefits of improved environmental quality, including a diminished risk of global warming. It also entails signalling the global scarcity to individual countries. The problem is that in determining the tolerable global quantity of emissions, countries can behave as free riders. Thus it is necessary to allocate the total quantity of emissions to individual countries. This allocation of property rights poses severe incentive problems: accepting a global treaty, ensuring that an international contract among sovereign states is not revoked in the future. This presupposes that the allocation of emission rights is "incentive-compatible" and that the increased demand for emission rights of countries in the process of economic development is taken into account (Sachverständigenrat zur Begutachtung der gesamtwirtschaftlichen Entwicklung, 1998). According to the Kyoto Protocol, emission reduction obligations will be defined for the 1990 level, and will be tradable.

The extent to which the atmosphere's limited capacity to absorb greenhouse gases will be a restraint for economic growth is an open question. The institutional arrangement envisioned by the Kyoto Protocol and the results of the 1998 Buenos Aires Conference so far do not represent a specified restraint. National environmental policy has had structural effects in the last twenty years, in that it has reduced the competitiveness of emission-intensive sectors in industrialised countries. Until now, environmental policy has not been a severe restraint for national economic growth. The situation could change, however, if environmental scarcities become more noticeable.

5. The future of globalisation

As the preceding section has demonstrated, a simple linear extrapolation of current globalisation trends would be premature; several drawbacks have been identified that could considerably slow down the speed of future world economic integration. Most of these drawbacks originate from advanced countries, where low-qualified labour has to bear significant adjustment costs. These potential globalisation losers may try to revert to a disintegrated world economy and reshape the international economic order in favour of protectionism and "fair" instead of free trade relations. All in all, however, it can be expected that the positive engines of globalisation and integration will eventually predominate, for two major reasons.

First, the industrialised countries as a whole will gain, which enables them to at least partly compensate the losers. A case in point is the development of the terms of trade, *i.e.* the relative change of export prices as compared to import prices. If this ratio rises, the respective countries are better off because they have to give in less export goods for the same amount of import goods, or in other words, can afford higher imports at a given level of exports.

As a matter of fact, the terms of trade of industrial countries have substantially improved during the past two decades (Table 7). The basic reason is the integration of large, labour-rich countries into the international division of labour. China alone accounts for about one-fifth of the worldwide labour force, and India is not much smaller. The contribution of these and other newly integrating countries to world output is much less, because they are provided with little physical and human capital and a rather low technological level of production. Hence, it can be expected that labour-intensive goods (which are mainly importedby advanced countries) will become relatively cheap on world markets, whereas technologically sophisticated and capital-intensive goods (which constitute the major portion of

Table 7. **Terms of trade in international trade**

	Export prices		Terms of trade of industrial countries[a]
	Industrial countries	Developing countries	
1980	100	100	1.00
1985	99	92	1.08
1990	148	115	1.29
1995	181	130	1.39
1996	178	129	1.38

a) Ratios of export prices of industrial countries to export prices of developing countries.
Source: Gundlach, Nunnenkamp (1997).

export goods of advanced countries) will face increasing demand and rising prices on world markets. These gains from globalisation would be at stake if the world economy fell back into protectionist practices.

The second reason is the historical experience of several countries, which strongly supports the case for further liberalisation. According to a pioneering study from the World Bank (Michaely *et al.*, 1991), economic growth after trade liberalisation was higher than it was before in 23 out of 31 cases. The most prominent examples are presented in Table 8, which concentrates on the success stories of trade liberalisation, but also presents the average growth performance for all countries. That average clearly supports the view that an intensified international division of labour is a major source of economic growth and wealth.

The country-specific results of Table 8 are in line with the region-specific calculations of Stoeckel *et al.* (1990) which are based upon a general equilibrium model of the Centre for International Economics at the University of Canberra. The status-quo situation on world markets was compared to a scenario with completely liberalised trade on the one hand and a scenario with strong protectionism in the United States and the EU on the other. In the case of completely free trade, world output would increase by about 5%, whereas a relapse into protectionism would reduce world output by 3%. Moreover, unilateral steps towards free trade either by the United States or the EU would be beneficial to each region, although the welfare gains would be smaller than the gains from complete liberalisation. Of course, the results of these simulations depend upon the specific features of the underlying. model, but the calculations of Stoeckel *et al.* at least demonstrate that trade liberalisation is not a zero-sum game.

Table 8. **Annual real GDP growth before and after trade liberalisation**
Percentage

	Start of trade liberalisation	Before[a]	After[b]
Brazil	1965	2.90	3.43
Chile	1974	2.30	3.74
Greece	1962	4.90	6.20
Indonesia	1996	6.13	8.95
Israel	1962	0.80	6.38
Korea	1965	5.77	10.40
Portugal	1970	5.32	6.48
Singapore	1968	1.60	4.20
Turkey	1970	2.80	6.81
Uruguay	1974	2.90	4.00
Average of 31 countries		4.45	5.57

a) Average of three years up to liberalisation.
b) Average of three years after liberalisation.
Source: Maurer (1998).

The advanced economies would be well advised, therefore, to resist protectionist pressures from special interest groups and to proceed on the road towards the integrated world economy. Flexible adjustment to changing world economic conditions will probably require some painful offerings in the short run, but will eventually turn out to be beneficial to all participants. History has repeatedly demonstrated that those who try to escape from structural adjustment will not only not be able to preserve their Elysium, but will have to face an even harder landing when their protectionist shelter is washed away by the relentlessly rising tide of global competition.

Notes

1. Gottfried Haberler (1955) even argued that the factor price equalisation theorem actually proves the opposite of what it claims to prove, because its assumptions are much too restrictive to ever be fulfilled.

2. For a detailed analysis of the structure and determinants of foreign direct investment, see Klodt (1998).

3. In a perfectly integrated world capital market, the coefficient β in Table 3 should be zero, whereas it should be unity in case of completely segmented national capital markets.

4. For the European Union as a whole, unemployment reached a level of 12.6% for low-qualified workers, 8.6% for the medium-qualified, and 5.9% for highly qualified workers in 1996 (EUROSTAT, 1997).

5. According to Olson (1982), the diminishing ability of consensus-oriented countries to cope with structural adjustment basically reflects the rising power of special interest groups that obstruct aggregate efficiency.

6. For the EU, no reliable data could be calculated for the year 1990, because the completion of the internal market in 1992 brought about substantial changes in trade statistics. Since 1993, the statistical coverage of intra-EU trade is much lower. Therefore, a comparison of intra-bloc shares of 1990 and 1996 would make no sense.

Bibliography

BAYOUMI, Tamin (forthcoming),
"Is There a World Capital Market?" in Horst Siebert (ed.), *Globalization and Labor*, Kiel Week Conference 1998. Tübingen.

BHAGWATI, Jagdish (1989),
Protectionism. Cambridge, MA.

CAIRNCROSS, Frances (1997),
The Death of Distance. Boston.

EUROSTAT (1997),
Erhebung über Arbeitskräfte. Ergebnisse 1996. Luxemburg.

FELDSTEIN, Martin and Charles HORIOKA (1980),
"Domestic Saving and International Capital Flows", *The Economic Journal*, Vol. 90, pp. 314-329.

GREIDER, William (1997),
One World, Ready or Not: The Manic Logic of Global Capitalism. New York.

GUNDLACH, Erich and Peter NUNNENKAMP (1997),
"Labor Markets in the Global Economy: How to Prevent Rising Wage Gaps and Unemployment". Kiel Discussion Papers, 305.

HABERLER, Gottfried (1955),
A *Survey of International Trade Theory*. Princeton.

INTERNATIONAL MONETAY FUND (current issues),
Balance of Payments Statistics, *Yearbook*, Part II, Washington DC.

KLODT, Henning (1998),
"Globalisierung – Phänomen und empirische Relevanz" in K.E. Schenk, D. Schmidtchen and M.E. Streit (eds.), *Globalisierung, Systemwettbewerb und nationalstaatliche Politik. Jahrbuch für Neue Politische Ökonomie*, 17. Band.

KLODT, Henning (1997),
"The Transition to the Service Society", Kiel Working Papers, 839.

KLODT, Henning (1988),
"International Trade, Direct Investment, and Regulations in Services", *World Competition*, Vol. 12 (2): 4967.

LORZ, Oliver (1997),
"A Bertrand Model of Wage Competition With Capital Mobility", *Economic Letters* 56: 339343.

MAURER, Rainer (1998)
Economic Growth and International Trade with Capital Goods: Theories and Empirical Evidence. Tübingen: Kieler Studien, 289.

MICHAELY, M., D. PAPAGEORGIOU and A.M. CHOSKI (1991),
Liberalizing Foreign Trade: Lessons of Experience in the Developing World. Cambridge, MA.

OECD (1996),
Employment Outlook. Paris.

OLSON, Mancur (1982),
The Rise and Decline of Nations. New Haven.

RODRIK, Dani (1997),
Has Globalization Gone Too Far? Washington DC.

SACHVERSTÄNDIGENRAT ZUR BEGUTACHTUNG DER GESAMTWIRTSCHAFTLICHEN ENTWICKLUNG (1998),
"Vor weitreichenden Entscheidungen", Jahresgutachten 1998/99.

SIEBERT, Horst (1999a),
The World Economy. London.

SIEBERT, Horst, ed. (1999b),
Globalization and Labor. Tübingen.

SIEBERT, Horst (1998a),
Arbeitslos ohne Ende? Strategien für mehr Beschäftigung. Wiesbaden.

SIEBERT, Horst (1998b),
Economics of the Environment: Theory and Policy. Fifth revised edition. Heidelberg.

SIEBERT, Horst (1997a),
"Labor Market Rigidities: At the Root of Unemployment in Europe", Journal of Economic Perspectives, Vol. 11(3): 37-54.

SIEBERT, Horst (1997b),
Weltwirtschaft, Stuttgart.

SPINANGER, Dean (1997),
"The WTO After the Singapore Ministerial: Much to Do About What?" Kiel Discussion Papers, 304.

STOECKEL, Andrew, David PEARCE and Gary BANKS (1990),
Western Trade Blocs: Game, Set or Match for Asia-Pacific and the World Economy. Canberra: Centre for International Economics.

TAYLOR, Alan M. (1996),
"International Capital Mobility in History: Purchasing Power Parity in the Long Run", NBER Working Papers, No. 5742, Cambridge, MA.

WORLD BANK (1995),
World Development Report. Washington DC.

WTO-WORLD TRADE ORGANISATION (1997, 1998),
Annual Report. Geneva.

5

Working for World Ecological Sustainability: Towards a "New Great Transformation"

by

Alain Lipietz
Centre d'Études Prospectives d'Économie Mathématique Appliquées
à la Planification
France

1. Introduction

The relationship of humankind to its environment, that is, the way one affects the other and the way the environment enables humankind to live, is the subject of human ecology, still called "political ecology" (humans being political animals). Demographics, followed by economics, are the main shaping forces in this relationship. Since the dawn of history, economic progress and the artificialisation of humankind's surroundings appeared to be the instruments which would irreversibly emancipate human beings from the constraints imposed by their environment's "load capacity". In the second half of the 20th century, after the long boom which followed the Second World War, the march towards emancipation reached its limits. Economic progress itself would seem to be a crisis factor in regard to sustainability. Does that mean that, where the long-term future is concerned, "environment" and "development" must be considered as opposites? This chapter is intended to supply a qualified answer to that question, which poses a formidable challenge to the OECD, whose "D" stands for "Development".

In fact, the creation of the OECD when the Second World War ended went in step with the institution of a new "model of development", one which was to bring North America, Western Europe, Japan, Australia and New Zealand thirty glorious years of economic growth.

The model marked the apogee of a "technological paradigm", namely the search for maximum work efficiency gains, thanks to the Scientific Organisation of Labour. Above all, it expressed a new way of viewing labour itself. Its cost (wages) was now seen primarily as the basic income of the mass consumer and hence as the key element in determining outlets for industrial production.[1] The regulation of these wages, and thereby of effective demand, changed the conditions governing how capitalism operated – a turning-point which the anthropologist Karl Polanyi (1957) called "the Great Transformation".

The "Great Transformation" of the 1930s and 1940s, according to Polanyi, expressed "the revolt of Society against the dogma of the market's self-regulating power", a power which during the Depression had shown its ability to destroy "the machine, the earth and labour". The solution could lie only in placing the laws of the market within a wider system of social constraints: habits, regulations, laws and conventions. Capitalism so reorganised would operate as much by "civic spirit" as by "self-interest".

Nobody these days disputes the reality of the "Golden Age", the boom that followed the Great Transformation, but nobody would dare presume to go back to it. Globalisation of the world economy has crippled the effectiveness of national regulations; and above all, the technological paradigm which attached top priority to raising labour productivity seems well and truly responsible for the particularly nature-fouling character of this model of development. It is as though, to quote Adam Smith's trinity formula, there had been a systematic attempt to economise labour by amassing capital and exhausting the Earth, and as though the Great Change of the mid-20th century, in failing to transcend a civic spirit anchored in the Nation-State, had (at least during the "thirty glorious years" 1945-1975) been able to save only the Machine and Labour – by intensifying the plunder of the Earth.

The argument defended in this chapter runs as follows:

– Any fresh "long boom" will be constrained principally by its "viability" or ecological "sustainability".

– It will therefore have to be grounded in a technological paradigm that husbands the "Earth" factor, *i.e.* the environment and more especially energy.

– This being so, it will be fuelled by research into and investment in energy-saving and, more broadly, environment-friendly techniques.

– It will hence be guided by new forms of regulation that add environmental to social protection.

Section 2 provides a very short review of the age-old history of the environment-development relation, up until the crisis of the economic model that saw the founding of the OECD. Economic globalisation, as is well known, played a decisive (though not exclusive) role in this crisis, and any way out of the crisis must deal with this problem. Section 3 distinguishes two concepts, "local ecological crisis" and "global economic crisis", along with the latter's diplomatic repercussions. Section 4 treats the contribution of economic thinking to the management of local ecological crises. The fifth section concerns the first lessons to be drawn from global crises. Section 6 explores the global crisis presenting the most danger for the 21st century, and currently the subject of internal divisions among OECD countries, namely the greenhouse effect. Section 7 forms the chapter's conclusion.

At the end of this journey we shall have gained some inkling of the new technological paradigm, the new civic sensibility, and the new modes of regulation that should enable the world to experience a new phase of prolonged growth compatible with environmental constraints: a "New Great Transformation" that will open the way towards "sustainable development".

2. A short history of human ecology

If we are to guess what the long-term future holds, our only guide is study of the long march of history.

Long ago, the "viability" of human groups depended almost entirely on the natural environment. Human ecology differed very little from that of other living species: a predator-prey system converging towards eco-demographic equilibrium, no doubt cyclical (Lokta-Voltera equations). The population grew as far as the load capacity of its hunting-grounds permitted, then ran into a *scarcity crisis*. The human difference lay almost certainly in an ability to see ahead and, by population displacements, to adjust to changes in the environment, whether they resulted from very slow climate fluctuations (like the glaciation cycle), or from human pressure itself.

With the Neolithic Revolution, begun 10 000 years ago and ending in our time, man learned how to "domesticate" nature by selecting seeds and raising animals. The subsequent artificial leap in the load capacity of the environment allowed, and indeed demanded, social specialisation distinguishing the leaders of what must already be called an "economy" from those who followed their orders.[2] The specialisation was itself expressed by the appearance of towns, writing and history. From then on, ecological crises of scarcity (the collision of demographics with environmental load capacity) were compounded by crises stemming from faulty proportions in the social distribution of the wealth produced.

The most spectacular (and instructive for us) example of this kind of crisis was the "great bi-secular fluctuation" at the end of the European Middle Ages (14th-16th centuries). The excessive pressure of the nobles and their wars on the peasantry produced an over-exploitation of communal property by the peasants, general penury, and vulnerability to the Great Plague, which exterminated over half of the European population. Europe recovered thanks to the agricultural revolution of mixing farming and husbandry – a revolution within the Neolithic Revolution – which entailed sweeping changes in technical productivity and in the legal system of land use. This agricultural revolution of the modern age in turn allowed the Industrial Revolution to gather strength.

From the start of the modern age (16th-17th centuries), ecological crises seemed completely subordinate to economics, and to the latter's dual aspect. As rational organisation of production, it embodied the promise of final deliverance from scarcity. But, as a politico-social system founded on private interest regulated by the market (spreading around the world with a raging force that makes today's "globalisation" look tame), it showed itself to be a scourge even more pitiless than climate. The major calamities that followed one another since the 16th century (the "destruction of the West Indies" by colonisation, the ravaging of Africa by the slave trade, the Irish famine, etc.) could no longer be blamed on the human overloading of ecosystems; the fault lay in the overloading of the mass of mankind by certain social groups.

The Great Slump of the 1930s marked the paroxysm of this "autonomisation" of the forces capable of devastating the market economy. The "Great Transformation" studied by K. Polanyi signalled the rebellion of world society against this power of destruction. The Second World War would lead to a "domestication" of economics, expressed in the creation of the OECD among other things, and the birth of the concept of "economic development".

Many economists dubbed this postwar development model "Fordism". It rested on three pillars:

– Scientific organisation of labour (Taylorism), designed by engineers, relying on automation and mass production, and characterised by impressive gains in apparent labour productivity.

– Distribution of productivity gains to the workers, granting them access to mass consumption and, via the sustaining of effective demand, guaranteeing full employment.

– A thicket of labour agreements and social legislation, combined with a strong welfare-state system, ensured that mass production and mass consumption would run in tandem. This mode of regulation, buttressed by the state, was given legitimacy by a new civic consciousness that paid attention to "social issues".

For thirty years, between 1945 and 1975, this model seemed to have banished not only economic crises but also the ecological crises arising from either insufficient land or labour productivity or from unsatisfactory product distribution. In the 1970s it ran into trouble, following a new spate of globalisation (which shook the third pillar) and the exhaustion of the Taylorist model of labour organisation (which eroded the first pillar). The OECD countries, faced with this twin crisis, have diverged for twenty years. Some prefer to look for a solution in the free play of market forces; others seek a degree of continuity with the "organised capitalism" of the postwar period and count on the "mobilisation of human resources" to renew labour and capital productivity (Lipietz, 1995). The divergence is reflected in stronger or weaker commitment where the new ecological problems are concerned.

Alongside the economic crisis, a quite novel form of ecological crisis – the *crisis of abundance* – was making itself felt. It was the tainted legacy of the postwar economic miracles. In the OECD area, technical progress had at last made it possible to feed mankind, but at the price of a dangerous impoverishment of biodiversity and landscape variety. Town-dwellers, crowded into megacities, discovered traffic jams and pollution as the cost of their mobility. Epidemiology was increasingly relating morbidity and mortality not to under-consumption, but to excessive consumption of certain items. More generally, the industrial model was threatened by a new scarcity of natural resources – not so much, as the Club of Rome had feared, in terms of raw materials as in terms of the planetary ecosystem's capacity to recycle wastes. The artificialisation of the living world was bringing dramatic "industrial illnesses" (blood contamination, mad cow disease) in its wake. The cutting-edge of artificialisation, the cyber world, developed its own pathologies (computer viruses, the "millennium bug"). In the Third World, which had never experienced Fordism but was familiar with uncontrolled industrialisation, all the historical forms of ecological crisis (scarcity, distribution, abundance) were superimposed.

At the approach of the 21st century, ecological crisis is thus detectable at the very core of the economic system. It is a hydra-headed crisis, similar in seriousness to the Great Plague but vastly more ramified. It is no wonder that it feeds irrational fantasies. Regaining control over the economy and mastering the parameters of a new "long boom", at a level which embraces not only market forces but also techno-science, are the crucial issues at stake in a "New Great Transformation".

3. Local crises and global crises

Ecological crises – in addition to their variety, as has just been seen – are characterised by human ability to deal with them. An initial distinction needs to be made between "local" and "global" crises.

Every modern ecological crisis is rooted in a malfunctioning of the socio-economic system or, more precisely, in an inability to keep the system in good running order given the inherited environment. ("Socio-economic system" here refers to the economic system adopted by a given society.) The governance of this society usually depends on compromises that have been institutionalised in a national framework, "diffracted" into local bodies. "World society" exists only as a myth, ethically useful but for the moment largely inoperative.

In concrete terms, there are ecological crises whose victims nearly all belong to the institutionally organised society whose operation is itself the source of the crises. These may be termed "local" crises. Then there are crises whose effects are felt round the world, even though they originate in malfunctioning that is located in particular societies whose members are rarely their main victims. These may be termed "global" crises.

In the case of a local crisis, the society concerned theoretically possesses the means for controlling, for "regulating" it. These means are a matter of morality, civic spirit, the law or market organisation. "Victim" groups have ways of exerting pressure on the "perpetrator" groups: demonstrations, press campaigns, the ballot-box. Examples are local pollution of a city's water supply or atmosphere by a particular factory, industrial epidemics induced by insufficient nation-wide policing and regulation (use of asbestos), and traffic snarls and pollution caused by an inadequate public transport network.

At the other extreme, the depletion of the ozone layer above territories in the Southern hemisphere, the drift of the greenhouse effect and its dramatic consequences for the Indian Ocean rim countries, for example, depend to a very large extent on the industrial economic model adopted decades ago by the OECD countries. There is no democratic mechanism by which potential victim societies can shield themselves. Only action followed by diplomatic agreements can oblige the perpetrator societies to alter their practices, if they are willing to do so.

The distinction is too crude, however. Some local crises are "trans-border" by nature. Closeness to the border means that the effects are felt in the neighbouring country, or the place of pollution is actually the border (pollution of the Rhine). Diplomatically negotiated methods of regulation had urgently to be devised. The Convention on Long-Range Transboundary Air Pollution (against acid rain) was a recent example – destined for ever-broader enlargement, as the Chernobyl "trans-boundary" accident makes clear.

Some kinds of local crises are so common that, by addition, they end up creating a global problem. Deforestation, for example, which is locally dangerous (it depletes soils and induces irreversible erosion) contributes globally to the greenhouse effect. The industrialisation of local agriculture leads to a breakdown of global biodiversity. In this case, international diplomacy can take advantage of local mobilisation to make the general interest prevail – providing that modes of economic regulation do not generate pernicious effects of the "everyone loses" kind.

It is in this field that the OECD countries bear a special responsibility. Further on, we shall examine their prime role in solving the most serious global problem threatening the 21st century, namely the greenhouse effect. Even now, however, their influence in international trade negotiations endows them with particular responsibilities concerning the ability of local societies to deal with their own crises. Ecological crises spread not only through air and water but also through traded goods.

There is, luckily, one border which economic liberalism has never dared to cross: the plant-health frontier. All sovereign states have stubbornly clung to their right to protect themselves against dangerous or spoiled goods. This legitimate protectionism is not contrary to the GATT or WTO principle of "national treatment". If it is forbidden to import an article, it is because the domestic production or consumption of that article would also be forbidden. The compartmentalisation of the world meat market in response to foot-and-mouth disease is one example.

Foot-and-mouth disease is a case of a naturally originating crisis affecting livestock farming. But modern ecological crises are born of technology. When a crisis occurs, "sacred" national self-interest becomes legitimate once more, as was seen in the European Union with the mad cow crisis. In order to prevent such crises, the "precautionary principle" was recently imposed, *i.e.* the obligation laid upon a state to prohibit or defer the introduction of a process whose harmlessness is dubious. Doubt not being certainty, the precautionary principle can give rise to situations of "questionable legitimacy" where production is authorised but may in the end be boycotted by the consumer population, on account of the risks it represents.[3] It is futile to retort that these risks are exaggerated. A society has a perfect right to accept death in war and at the same time refuse the slightest risk posed by the genetic or hormonal treatment of what it eats. Only the democratic process can decide, however enlightened it may be by independent investigations.

This means that no society should be able to force on another society articles produced by manufacturing processes that this society would not itself allow. It is the "Do not do unto others as they would not be done by" principle.

The OECD, were it to militate within international trade regulation forums for an enlargement of the "national treatment of products" principle into a "national treatment of products and production processes" principle, would be sending a strong message for preventing ecological crises at the most strictly local level and stopping their spread.

The "Do not do unto others as they would not be done by" principle should naturally be coupled with a "Do not do unto others as you would not be done by" rule. The author here refers to problems of "international environmental justice". In the most developed countries, a century and a half of citizen mobilisation has imposed social and environmental standards. There is a strong temptation for transnational firms to ignore these standards when they are operating (producing or selling) in emerging economies. True, the laxity of these countries' legislation often supplies the "comparative advantage" that enables them to industrialise. It would nonetheless be difficult to prove (and terribly damning for the OECD economic model if it were proved) that this "take-off" absolutely requires deviation from currently employed standards. Once techniques are the same and guarantee comparable productivity, standards should also be comparable.[4]

The OECD recently spurred an international citizen's movement against a draft Multilateral Agreement on Investment, which seemed to violate the first principle. Indeed, a multinational firm would have had the right to sue, before the International Court of Trade, and obtain compensation from a democracy that decided to introduce more effective regulations for protecting the environment. Such a compensation principle would systematically rule out any future environmental taxation. There was much less publicity surrounding the OECD's code of professional ethics for multinational enterprises, which is a good illustration of the second principle. It recommends that these firms, when they delocate, should at least observe the standards of their country of origin. The OECD, as an institution and as a group of countries, would greatly enhance its world legitimacy by promoting the code and having it incorporated in the WTO corpus.

4. On the regulation of local ecological crises

The most frequently cited "tools" for solving latent or declared ecological crises are divided into two families, the "regulatory" (laws, standards) and the "economic" (taxes, permit markets). There is a third type, consisting of self-restriction agreements, good conduct codes, etc.

This third type is, in fact, the first type in all forms of human conduct. Women and men (including economic agents), before observing laws, comply with implicit social norms (what is called "civic sense" or "civility") and together work out practical arrangements, including the place where they settle, in face-to-face negotiations. Combining the insights of Fernand Braudel and Pierre Bourdieu, it could be said that "society" exists on the one hand in its "habitat" – the material environment which it has already given itself – and on the other in a mentally integrated and sometimes institutionalised system of norms and habits. The "New Great Transformation", which will enable mankind to adopt an ecologically sustainable development model, first requires a cultural revolution in which certain former practices are "delegitimised", stigmatised by consumers, neighbours, the press, competitors and lastly by governments. Concurrently, better practices, codes of good behaviour, self-limitation agreements and negotiated standards will come into being in civil society well before the law makes them mandatory or price-signals make them attractive.[5]

Furthermore, the environment, the physical space in which economic activity takes place and which is constantly remodelled by it, has been the primary concern of policy since Neolithic times and Sumeria. Governance is above all the production of a collective good, the "habitat", and the regulation of access to it (beginning with the irrigation system). The spontaneous activity of civil society – merely choosing where to live – automatically creates a physical environment: urban aggregations, groupings of industries. The art of placing together industries, the wastes of some of which are the raw materials of the others (energy co-generation, use of water, etc.), is beginning to be called "industrial ecology". This could be said to form a new type of "Marshall-style industrial district" where the factors pleading for juxtaposition are not only the social division of labour but also the "social" division of by-products and related products. Local authorities will certainly be required to channel what are still groping attempts, by a new kind of town planning whose goal will no longer be to enlarge cities but to restructure them through the installation of diverse networks (public transport, telematics loops, etc.), and better-thought-out zoning schemes.

Alas, in real-life ecology, most private activities contribute to damaging the environment. This makes it necessary to introduce explicit forms of regulation, a responsibility that also falls to the political sphere. What are the justifying reasons?

In economic language, the local environment may be termed a "collective asset", at once freely accessible and "non-rival" in the sense that its use by certain agents does not hamper the ability of other agents to make use of it… at least up to a certain point, which is what ecologists correctly call its "load capacity". Public regulation of the environment always aims at obliging or persuading agents not to abuse this load capacity, and if possible to increase it. This indeed is the crucial element in the "New Great Transformation". Whereas the aim of the one described by Polanyi was better distribution of wildly increasing output, the "New Great Transformation" will be also have as its guiding thrust the redirection of technological progress so as to increase the sustainable load capacity of our environment. It will thereby have the effect of stimulating a "long boom" in the equipment of households and industry and in the generation of ecologically sustainable collective infrastructure.[6] This, according to the World Commission on Environment and Development (1995) (Brundtland), is the true definition of sustainable development: "development that meets the needs of the present and, as an over-riding priority, those of the world's poor, without compromising the ability of future generations to meet their own needs".

Why should the quest for private satisfaction run counter to such collective goals, in contradiction with the faith of the fathers of liberalism? It is largely a consequence of the properties of collective assets ("the tragedy of commons"). Each actor involved has a personal stake in accentuating pressure on the environment. But once, as a result of joint use, exploitation of the environment approaches the load capacity threshold, collective satisfaction – for the community of potential users – wanes. For each individual agent, on the other hand, the pressure they exercise on the unrestricted and cost-free environment represents a virtual rent, that is, a surplus of satisfaction and profit in comparison with what they would be prepared to pay if the environment stopped being unrestricted. This is the contradiction that it would be well to regulate.[7]

To this end, the public authorities have an arsenal of possible policies at their disposal. A first distinction may be made between:

- Regulatory instruments: bans (to prohibit uses that do too much damage to the environment) and norms (to ration legitimate uses within a sustainable "envelope").

- Economic instruments, which work by their "price-signal": environmental taxes (or rather, pollution taxes) and tradable quotas.

Another distinction may be added to the list, that between "goals policies" and "instrument policies". A goals policy regulates the impact of practices on the environment. After determining the lawful (sustainable) envelope for users, it:

- Either fixes an "intensity" limit for each potential user (norms policy). This technique is a powerful industrial policy tool when it generates economies of scale. However, through an agglomeration effect, a host of users can exceed the sustainable threshold, even though they all respect the permitted norms.

- Or it "allocates" the total volume allowed in the shape of quotas or permits granted to private users, which are then freely tradable, as after an agrarian reform. This method, the one chosen in Kyoto for dealing with the greenhouse effect, gives maximum power to the government authorities, who plan both overall use and (at least to begin with) each party's share.

Instrument policies, on the other hand, do no more than prohibit or set a direction. Prohibiting does not mean eliminating; everything depends on the severity of the penalty. A fine, after all, is only the extreme form of a pollution tax. While the effect of a pollution tax is to induce agents to adopt increasingly efficient practices, there is no saying in advance whether the tax is high enough.

From the user's standpoint, buying a quota and paying a pollution tax amount to the same thing. The user pays once in one case and continuously in the other. It is like the difference between buying land and renting it. The two instruments, which allow the user to choose their techniques and extent of use, are particularly appropriate where large numbers of different sorts of users threaten the environment.

But just what do they pay for? The OECD countries have adopted the Polluter-Pays Principle without dwelling too much on its signification. Is it a question of paying for:

- The cost of repairing the environment? This should be called a fee.

- Damage caused to third parties? This should be called compensation.

- The price which, by confiscating polluters' virtual rent, deters them from damaging the environment? This should properly be called a pollution tax.

In the realm of the standard general equilibrium theory, the three definitions would be interchangeable. In the real world, this is not at all so. Why? Precisely because the environment is a collective asset, sometimes international and always inter-generational (all the agents concerned are not simultaneously present on the market); it is, moreover, subjective (what is the price of noise, the pain of illnesses, the loss of beauty?). The guiding principle should therefore be the third definition (a deterrent tax) configured by an assessment derived from the second one (damage caused). Naturally, government revenues accruing from pollution taxes or the initial auctioning of quotas can be used for "repairing" the environment, but this is not always possible. Whatever the case, these revenues, apart from the "primary dividend" provided by the instruments (protecting the environment), offer the body collecting them a "secondary dividend" in the shape of funds for other policies, *e.g.* lowering the cost of labour as part of a jobs policy.

This leads to the social aspect of the "New Great Transformation". In the 21st century, a dense forest of ecological regulations will most probably develop. What will be its redistributive effect? It will surely not be neutral; and it will be fairly complex.

The least well off are hardly in a position to create pollution, and their satisfaction will come mainly from a healthy environment. They will be the chief beneficiaries of a general shift towards sustainable development. The wealthiest will have their virtual rent somewhat amputated but at a high income level where its marginal utility is smallest. The short-term losers could be the "middle poor", those for whom restrictions on an open and cost-free use of the environment will push the dream of the "Fordist" consumer model for all even further away – even though they may well be unaware of its unsustainable and health-endangering character.

This "U-curve" will require New Deal-style social reforms to be combined with the new ecological policies. If they are not, these policies will not seem justified. The same remark, as we shall see, applies to global crises and international relations.

5. Global crises: first lessons

The first international agreements – the Washington convention forbidding international trade in endangered species, and especially the Montreal protocol for protecting the ozone layer – are by now textbook examples. The scenario is always the same.

– Specialists, with a world view, ring the alarm bells on a subject that is at first disputed.

– Public opinion in a few developed countries becomes convinced and takes fright.

– Consensus, and sometimes an international agreement, is achieved among the OECD countries.

- At this stage, emerging economy governments realise that they will be prevented from doing what the countries preceding them in the dominant economic development model had been doing for over a century. They protest, and demand waivers and compensations, even if their own people would have been the first to benefit from the agreement.

To break this deadlock (because the emerging countries have the power of obstruction, suicidal though it be), there are three indispensable requirements:

- The agreement put forward by the OECD countries must clearly and effectively respond to the global threat, with the OECD countries assuming more than their fair share of the burden.

- The results of the agreement, in terms of protecting the planet, must be not only positive but popularised among the people in the least developed countries and the emerging economies; NGOs in the South have a vital role to play in this.

- The agreement must have a redistributive function that will hasten the transition towards sustainable development in both groups of countries.

Let us take the example of one of these agreements, that on biodiversity, which the United States rejected at the Rio Conference in 1992 but subsequently accepted.

Unknown genetic biodiversity is for the most part that of wild plants and traditional peasant varieties. It acts something like a planetary immune system reservoir, as distinct from the super-selected varieties of modern agriculture. It provides raw material for the pharmaceutical industry and biological engineering. By definition, this raw material is located essentially in the developing countries. The user industries, on the other hand, are located in the OECD area. It is the classic set-up for North-South disputes.

The OECD's snap reaction is to say that biodiversity is naturally free but that selection of useful genes must be covered by patents – a position which the South countries find unacceptable. The agreement negotiated in Rio provides therefore that the North must pay royalties to the biodiversity source countries and offer the results of its research to the South countries at favourable prices.

The agreement was crippled by the WTO framework on intellectual property rights which has stalled its implementation. Since then, private control over useful genes has grown. What is worse, the agro-food industry is marketing on a large scale genetically modified organisms whose effect on the human system, and on ecosystems, has not been tested over the time scale of even one generation, whereas natural biodiversity no longer presents any danger to mankind from the food angle. For hundreds of generations, human beings selected danger-free peasant varieties and did not feed on wild biodiversity.[8] Industry practice contravenes the precautionary principle which Europe, chastened by the completely unpredictable phenomenon of mad cow disease, holds particularly dear where food is concerned. Today's rules of international trade, by not allowing for any compartmentalising of risks variously accepted by different publics, breach the "Do not do unto others as they would not be done by" principle.

The present dynamics of unregulated technological progress therefore engender a serious crisis, among OECD countries and between Member countries and the peasant communities of the South. For the moment, luckily, the risks are still virtual, and to date there has not been a bad accident arising from a genetically modified variety imposed on the whole world by the agro-food industry.[9] It is to be hoped that OECD countries will be wise enough to propose and impose upon themselves sound rules before any such accident happens.

Their responsibility is on the line also in a global crisis whose imminence is now recognised: the greenhouse effect.

6.   The case of the greenhouse effect

Of all the global economic crises looming over the first half of the 21st century, the climatic disorder caused by the growth in the greenhouse effect is the one that poses the greatest challenge to the model of economic development. The beating heart of human activity is involved – agro-industry through the methane cycle, and energy through the carbon dioxide cycle.

a)   The situation

Since Arrhenius at the end of the 19th century, scientists have known that certain molecules imprison in the atmosphere the infra-red radiation emitted by the Earth (radiative forcing). Only in the late 20th century, however, was the concentration of these gases in the atmosphere, as a result of human activity, put in relation with an observed warming of the planet, first as a strong presumption [at the 1990 Conference of the International Panel on Climate Change (IPCC)], and then as a near-certainty (IPCC 1995).

The greenhouse gases (GHGs) are water vapour (whose radiative forcing does not vary significantly), CFCLs (already covered by the Montreal Protocol) and, especially, carbon dioxide (CO_2) and methane (CH_4).

Methane is associated particularly with paddy fields and grazing animals. Forty times more dangerous than carbon dioxide, it has only a short life-span in the atmosphere, which means that the methane problem can be settled at any time by energetic measures. The carbon dioxide emitted into the atmosphere, on the other hand, is up there for a century, which is to say practically forever. For this reason the different greenhouse gases are measured in "CO_2 equivalent".[10]

Carbon dioxide is for the most part produced by the burning of fossil fuel reserves (coal, oil and gas in descending order of CO_2 emitted by amount of energy produced) and, to a lesser extent, by the burning of wood for energy. The latter can be offset by a matching growth of the standing bio-mass, which acts as a "carbon sink". There are other reasons for deforestation, however – uncontrolled logging, clearing for farming purposes (suspended within the OECD area but widely practised in the Third World for lack of agrarian reform). Fossil energy may be replaced by nuclear energy, which entails ecological hazards of similar magnitude – to the point where major OECD countries have stopped developing it, in practice (the United States, Italy) or in law (Germany, Sweden, etc.).

It is for these reasons that the French General Commissariat for Planning (CGP, 1998) rightly concludes, "Economic growth is circumscribed by a triangle: climate risk, nuclear risk and land use conflicts".

To beat this challenge, mankind has two trump cards to play. First, the global ecosystem automatically fixes about half of the human carbon released into the atmosphere. This "sustainable envelope", matched against a human population that stabilises at 9 billion in the 21st century, would allow a flow of some 600 kg of carbon per person per annum. Attaining this "frontier of sustainability" (in flow) would mean halving the present production of greenhouse gases. Yet this would result only in stabilising CO_2 concentrations in the atmosphere (its stock) at the level they would then have reached. Temperatures would be markedly higher than they are today, and the reduction in flow would not produce a return to pre-industrial concentrations. Ideally, in order to reduce carbon dioxide concentrations to a level that would stabilise temperatures, a target of reduction in GHG production by a factor of three, and not by a factor of two, would have to be assigned rapidly. In any case, the flow must be reduced as quickly as possible, to prevent concentrations reaching too high a level before subsiding... in the 22nd century.

The second trump card is the reversal of the historic trend towards lower energy efficiency. The first agricultural and industrial revolutions had, by "lengthening the production detour", caused an ever faster decline in human labour per product unit, at the cost of a rise in the quantity of energy per unit. Then, in the 1960s, the ratio between GDP and consumed energy became stable. The oil price "shocks" triggered an unexpected turnabout – an "uncoupling" of the rise in the economic output of the industrialised countries and the rise in their energy consumption (which became much less steep or stopped altogether). With progress in technology, energy intensity (quantity of energy in national product) described an "inverted V" curve, first rising and then falling (at a present rate of 1 or 2% in Europe, according to the CGP's 1998 Report).

Man's technological hopes all rest on the gamble that this result can be generalised. If mankind can manage, at the level of production and especially of the structures of consumption, to achieve a boost in energy efficiency as spectacular as the rise in labour productivity, it has a hope of providing all future generations with an acceptable degree of material comfort without irremediably upsetting the world's climate.[11] But the risks are very great.

b) Consequences

Current IPCC mean estimates forecast, on the basis of the present rate of anthropogenically-generated GHG releases, a doubling in the 21st century of CO_2 concentrations, leading to an average temperature rise of 2° Celsius and a rise in sea-level (by surface dilatation) of 20-30 centimetres.

Experience with financial instability suggests that it is often a bad idea to make provision only for forecast averages. The IPCC does not predict the worst-case scenarios – melting of continental ice-sheets, escape of methane from the Siberian permafrost – for the next century. This does not mean that they are excluded. The consequences of even the mid-range (+2°) scenario are dramatic enough. Climate zones would be displaced by several hundreds of kilometres; the great overpopulated deltas and the low-lying islands would be submerged. The geophysical changes would affect ecosystems even more seriously, and have a crucial impact on human ecology. The climatic shifts would probably be too rapid to allow an organised transmigration of flora and the associated fauna. Above all, hostility to international mass migration would thwart the natural form of adjustment practised by early humans when faced with the slow climatic cycles of prehistoric times.

If no preventive remedy is found, this form of adjustment will be inevitable, and it will be the main cause of wars and crises in the 21st century. Preventive strategies themselves have geo-strategic and economic dimensions which lie and will continue to lie at the heart of negotiations on climate change.

c) The geo-strategic nexus

Not all countries are in the same boat, as regards either the costs of a prevention strategy or its benefits.

On the benefits side: countries are not all equally threatened by the greenhouse effect. Europe protects its deltas (Rhine-Meuse, Po); the Mississippi delta is sparsely populated. All the great unprotected and heavily populated deltas are located in the least developed countries (a typical example is Bangladesh) or the emerging economies. All the Small Island States (grouped in the AOSIS) are in this situation. These countries also have the largest proportions of rural inhabitants and the largest share of agriculture in their GNP.

The South countries are the first to be threatened by the drift of the greenhouse effect, and it is their populations which stand most to gain from a "precautionary policy". The OECD countries, on the other hand, have less to fear, at least according to the scenarios of 1990. Since then, the aggravation of temperate zone storms has awakened the attention of scientists… and insurers. The OECD area could be a major victim of "world tropicalisation". If a link were established between the intensification of the El Niño-La Niña phenomena and the observed warming of the surface waters of the Pacific (something which is not yet proven), the "cost" to the OECD area of the greenhouse effect could be very substantial indeed and the "benefit" would be to avoid it.

As to the costs of prevention policy, the dissymmetries are even more striking. Humanity cannot do without rice-fields or livestock, or even without some kind of land-clearing. "Basic needs" entail an incompressible production of anthropogenic GHGs, which in any case fits inside the "sustainable envelope" of 600 kg of carbon per head per annum (currently 60 kg in Bangladesh). The least developed countries have practically no leeway for reduction, except through agrarian reform and improvement in plant-energy efficiency. Conversely, industrial pollution is very largely concentrated in the OECD countries, which consequently all greatly exceed the sustainable envelope amounts – two metric tons per head in the United States, and two metric tons on average in the European Union and Japan (World Resources Institute, 1990).

It would be wrong, however, to think that greenhouse geopolitics are pitting a South interested in having a prevention policy at barely any cost to itself against a North deriving dubious benefits from preventing the greenhouse effect and having huge costs to pay out. Such a caricature applies only to a contest between the United States and, say, Bangladesh or the Fiji Islands.

For one thing, in the South, the emerging economies are coming close to the threshold of sustainability and consider it normal to cross it for as long as the industrialised countries which preceded them have done. For another, within the OECD group of countries, serious differences surfaced in 1990 between the Europeans – the most determined advocates of precautionary policies – and the United States – which was not so convinced – with the other countries wavering between the two extremes. The same divergence was apparent during the preparation of the fourth Conference of Parties (COP-4) in Buenos Aires, between the European Union and the other OECD countries (the JUSCANZ in COP-4 parlance: Japan, USA, Canada, Australia, New Zealand). There is a double explanation for this friction.

As regards benefits: Europe feels vulnerable, if not to its own greenhouse crisis, at least to that of its African and West and Central Asian neighbours. The JUSCANZ countries view themselves on the contrary as "large island States" having little to fear from a rise in sea-levels or migration pressures and (except for Japan) possessing plentiful amounts of space and natural resources.

As regards costs: Europe already has technical systems that are two to three times as energy- and GHG-efficient as those of the United States. Any restraints imposed on the whole OECD area would work in its favour. Furthermore, its model of social regulation accords considerable importance to compromise goals dictated by the general interest. America's faith in free enterprise has, on the contrary, resulted in an energy-voracious model, in terms of both production and consumption.

d) Negotiation: the state of play

Command over climate risk will involve decades of bickering and compromise. A "certain idea of the ultimate goal" already governs the first stepping-stones in all negotiations, however.

In 1990, the United States expressed scepticism as to the reality of the green-house effect; it took an optimistic view of any disadvantages it might have to endure, and was adamant about any effort it might have to make. The best the World Resources Institute would do was to suggest a "percentage" dividing of the burden – in other words, conservation of historically acquired shares of rights to pollute the atmosphere.

The Third World found this position unacceptable. A protest movement, launched in 1990 by Amil Agarwal and Sunita Narain of the Centre for Science and Environment (CSE) in New Delhi, soon joined by the Group of 77 and UNCTAD, retorted by postulating a principle of equality – each country would ultimately have a right to pollute which would be sustainable and proportionate to its popu-lation. At the same time, the theorists who were the artisans of this position, A. Agarwal and M. Grubb, proposed a flexibility mechanism: countries that did not use all of their quota could sell the remainder to those which exceeded it. A gen-eral pollution tax would be levied on all countries exceeding the sum of their quotas, allocated or purchased.

The New York Framework Convention, solemnly signed at the Rio UNCED in 1992, endorsed a compromise suggested by Europe: only the "Annex I Group" (in effect, the OECD countries and the industrialised ex-Socialist countries) would initially constrain themselves to make efforts at limitation, the others being ·invited to temper the increase in their GHGs. According to interpretation, it was possible to understand or refuse to understand a planned return by the year 2000 to the levels of 1990. As to instruments, Europe considered proposing a general environmental tax, but was incapable of imposing it on itself. A decade was wasted with little to show for it.[12]

Then the new certainties acquired by the IPCC and the intervening climatic accidents altered the "climate" of the negotiations. At the COP-3 (Kyoto, 1997), the American delegation let itself be persuaded by Europe to accept quantified reduction targets – unevenly distributed among Annex I Group countries accord-ing to considerations that were more diplomatic than scientific – for the time-frame 2010.[13] It set two conditions: commitment by the newly industrialising

Third World countries to make abatement efforts, and economic flexibility mechanisms, all based on the idea of purchasing abatements where their marginal cost was lowest: a QELRO (quantified emission limitation and reduction objectives) quotas market and "joint implementation" among Annex I parties, a "clean development mechanism" in the Third World.

At the time of writing, the Kyoto Protocol has been ratified by only the most typical of the AOSIS countries, the Fiji Islands. The COP-4 in Buenos Aires had no other ambition than to clarify this compromise. It could hardly be said to have succeeded in doing so.

Significant advances were nevertheless made in Buenos Aires. In the first place, it was decided not to specify the flexibility mechanisms until the compliance with commitments verification mechanisms had been elaborated. This was a wise decision which put the horse before the cart again. Second, thanks to an alliance between Europe and the Third World, the idea was introduced – an essential point, as will be seen – of making general convergence the goal where atmospheric rights are concerned.

e) Hopes for a world compromise

As things now stand, negotiations are stalemated. Europe refuses to accept flexibility for quantitative objectives that are already too low; the United States will not accept binding objectives unless the Third World agrees to commitments; the Third World will not agree to commitments if it is denied the same right to development as that enjoyed by the North.

The only thread on which to pull to unravel this tangle is a solemn recognition, prior to any negotiation, of the equal right that all human beings of all countries and all generations have over the atmosphere. A declaration of this kind would be in conformity with the values that oversaw the foundation of the OECD, after the end of the Second World War. In practical terms, it would mean that, in the final analysis, all the people in the world would have a roughly equal right to "the common envelope of sustainable use of the atmosphere", i.e. about 600 kg per person if the aim is to stabilise CO_2 concentrations, less if the aim is to reduce them.

Were this to happen, a compromise – founded on a principle of reduction objectives converging towards this final target allocation – between the Third World (including the emerging economies) and the OECD area (including the JUSCANZ countries) should be attainable. The compromise would have to take into account the energy intensity "inverted V" curve. While the industrialised countries, whose improvement in energy efficiency outstrips their growth, would immediately have to embark on a downward per capita pollution path towards the target, the emerging economies would be entitled to let their pollution mount slightly higher than the sustainability threshold (but well beyond their present emissions – an imaginable figure would be 1 000 kg per head of population per year); beyond that, quantified reduction objectives would become mandatory.

The first major compromise would therefore be to couple recognition of an egalitarian target level with mandatory entry into Annex I for all countries exceeding the target level by more than a certain amount.

At the same time, it would be understood that this threshold beyond which abatement is compulsory would act as a mid-course convergence target for Annex I countries, with 2030 as time-frame, for example. After this date and this threshold, all countries would be required to abate their per capita emission levels in parallel, at a rate to be set at about that time in accordance with the state of knowledge at that time.

A compromise along these lines reflects the spirit of the "historic" compromises that have marked the close of the century. The idea is to make commitments now for problems which will become apparent only in the long run, at a time when the benefits of action will appear more clearly than they do today.

What instruments should be associated with this goals policy? From the moment that these goals clearly set mankind on a path for overall quantified reductions in GHG emissions leading to an egalitarian right over the atmosphere, every economic "mechanism" inducing respect for this path becomes licit.

User responsibilisation, propagation of "best practices", self-restriction agreements by manufacturers, energy consumption norms for machines and appliances, will, as in the case of local crises, be the surest way of translating awareness into wise behaviour, shaped by a budding "planet-wide civic consciousness". The problem is that norms, agreements and even the sense of responsibility are inadequate. They determine intermediate goals without offering an incentive to go further. They thus create an impression of disappointment when a new, sterner norm has to be imposed. They do not, moreover, enable effort to be concentrated where it is the most effective.

Economic instruments, on the other hand, motivate a permanent quest for increased efficiency. It is true that they are ineffectual when they are not associated with trading practices, as in the case of slash-and-burn cultivation. But the great mass of atmospheric pollution comes from trade-related economic practices aiming for profit maximisation and virtual rents. Any rise in the costs weighing on a factor's use therefore encourages the search for techniques to husband it.

In the current negotiations, two traditions confront one another: environmental taxes (which should more properly be called pollution taxes) and tradable permits. The latter, after being introduced into the geo-strategic greenhouse effect debate in 1990 by A. Agarwal of the CSE, are today preferred by the United States, which sees them as genuine market mechanisms that can possibly remove the need for government-style agencies. The Europeans for their part regard trade in QELRO quotas as a ploy for dodging domestic efforts. What is worse, trades might concern fake reductions – either the "seller" might not implement the agreed abatement of emissions, or the abatement might owe more to an economic recession, which it is hoped will be short-lived, than to a sincere effort to increase energy efficiency. At the Kyoto Conference, for example, Russia was allotted a 0% reduction in its GHGs in 2010 compared with 1990. Its fearsome economic crisis has already caused a drop of 30% in its GHG emissions. Its QELRO quotas could therefore be offered on the market to the highest bidder. Yet they are not matched by any change in its productive system. Worse yet, indebted Third World countries might be tempted to sacrifice their chances of future development. This could create a sort of "atmospheric serfdom", over and above the servicing of high-interest debts. For this reason, the European Union is tempted to set quantitative caps on the use of "economic flexibilities", thereby giving priority to domestic efforts spurred on by a pollution tax on energy.[14]

Even granting the legitimacy of the European reservations (supported by international NGOs), their carrying power needs to be qualified. As has been said, once all countries agree to an overall scheme for reduction, there is nothing shocking about seeking reduction where it is least expensive, especially if it is associated with an increase in labour productivity. Funding efficient stoves in the Sahel, for example (whether by buying Sahel quotas, by "joint implementation" operations, or through "clean development" mechanisms[15]), would not only be friendly to the atmosphere, it would also ease the toil of the women whose forced wood-gathering chore is ruining the savannah.

Moreover, where the buyer is concerned, tradable permits are tantamount to a capitalised pollution tax. This is quite obvious if it is supposed that only one-year pollution permits may be sold; they would take exactly the same form as an annual tax matched to the amount of emissions produced. Of course, it is important to be sure that the quota is actually be paid for. This remark raises the question of the rules of competition on the quote market. Since a quota is merely a capitalised pollution tax, a state which handed out free quotas to its business firms would in effect be subsidising them. Such a practice would in all likelihood be contestable before the World Trade Organisation.

In fact, a quota market requires not less government than a pollution tax, but more. With a pollution tax, each state goes no farther than setting a direction and supplying a more or less powerful incentive to reduce emissions. But with quotas, an international states treaty must first determine each state's initial allocation – the reduction obligations "map". Then a supra-national agency must oversee the sincerity of transactions, *i.e.* the effective reduction. Lastly, this agency would probably have to regulate quota prices so as to prevent a buyer with unlimited credit from cornering the market and dispensing with domestic reduction, or an indebted seller from pawning away its future development potential. The quota price, like any market mechanism, serves only two purposes:

- To send a price signal to both buyer and seller, conferring "worth" for both parties on the economising effort associated with the object of their transaction – here, the interest they have in air pollution abatement, regardless of the degree of development already achieved.

- To transfer from buyer to seller the financial means for re-producing the object of the transaction – here, a more industrialised and polluting country would be financing the "clean development" of a less developed one.

In short, the international permit market supervisory agency should set a floor-price for transactions, in line with broadly established practice in the world's three dominant economic entities (United States, EU, Japan) once agriculture is involved. The reader will surely want to reflect upon the deeper reasons for this parallel.

If this were to happen, the difference between European demands and American preferences would dissipate. A floor-price is, after all, the mirror counterpart of a ceiling quantity. The agency could, for the four-year exercise 2008-2012, fix a floor-price so calculated that 80% of reduction efforts in the domestic space of countries already parties to Annex I would cost them less than the floor-price.[16] The most "prodigal" countries, those where the marginal cost per carbon tonne avoided is the lowest (United States), would centre their efforts on improving domestic technologies. The most expensive 20% of reduction efforts, involving more particularly countries that have reached the technological frontiers of clean development, could be sought in countries not having these technologies – and would be a way for those countries to acquire them.

7. Conclusion

At the Kyoto Conference, the world's people chose to give their preference to objectives quantified by country or group of countries (the EU). This primary strategy cannot now be altered. It can, however, be perfected:

- By setting it in a very long-term prospect of convergence in the allocation of pollution permits, respecting the equal rights of all human beings from generation to generation.

- By reserving the choice of instruments (regulations, pollution taxes or permit markets) for national or continental subsidiarity.

- By laying down rules for fair international competition in addition to the different national instruments.

- By stabilising price ratios in domestic and international flexibility mechanisms.

Over and above this example, the main lines of the "New Great Transformation" are coming into focus:

– A new "global civic consciousness" that recognises the egalitarian right of all humans of all generations to a healthy environment.

– International diplomatic arrangements that establish common rules (against global ecological crises) and limit, by rules on free trade, the pernicious effects of competition, so as to enable national (or continental) societies to handle their local crises.

These new methods of regulation (rules, pollution taxes, quotas) will raise the cost of using the environment in a way that will favour the technologies that economise this use.

– Applied research, spurred by corporate economic interest, stimulated by aid measures and encouraged by the pooling of best practices, will turn towards pollution abatement and energy consumption savings. A new investment boom will bring productive systems and infrastructure into line with the most environment-friendly technologies.

– Income from pollution taxes and quota auctions will enable the taxation weighing upon labour costs to be lightened, allowing use of this factor to be "de-intensified" (reduction in work-time, development of low-labour, productivity-gaining cultural or neighbourhood services), and setting in motion a return to full employment.

These economic instruments, framed by norms that are consonant with an ethic of human rights and responsibility towards future generations, can influence the trajectory of technological progress in accordance with a new paradigm – the search for maximum energy and environmental efficiency. From then on, the possibility will emerge of a new period of prolonged development, ecologically viable for the whole world: sustainable development.

Notes

1. Whence the name "Fordism", in honour of Henry Ford I's famous observation that the working-class was America's most populous class, and that it should become a well-off class if American industry wished to market its huge output. On Fordism and its crisis, see Lipietz (1995) and, for a more quantitative treatment, Glynn *et al.*, 1990.

2. E*c*onomics, *ec*ology and *dom*estication hark back to two linguistic roots (one Greek and the other Latin) that mean the same thing: the domain around the dwelling-place.

3. The concept of "questionable legitimacy" was proposed by Olivier Godard (1996).

4. The notion of comparability needs to be fairly flexible. It is not a question of fixing a worldwide pay standard for the same hour's work while overlooking differences in productivity. Such uniformity is not applied in either the social or environmental fields within the European Union, or even among regions of the same country. It is easy, however, to compare social legislation in the presently less productive countries with the social legislation obtaining in the past in the countries that are now the most highly productive. It has to be admitted that in the mid-20th century, many OECD countries tolerated schoolchild labour when there was heavy work to be done in the fields. It would be inadmissible in international trade, however, for countries that launch satellites and have computer industries to condone social standards that were already out of date in Europe before the invention of the electric motor!
What is all-important is the existence of a neutral supra-national referee (which could be the International Labour Office and the Commission on Sustainable Development working under the UN Secretary-General). The decisions handed down would then be applicable by the WTO.

5. Case studies do not invalidate the idea that the "first-mover", the economic agent who acts in advance of future norms, can thereby obtain a competitive advantage even though the corresponding equipment is very expensive at the beginning. An environment-friendly initiative of this kind usually goes hand in hand with a technical renewal that increases productivity. Secondly, the "civic-consciousness" of their production methods gives their product the advantage of respectability. Their location becomes more appealing to the population, in particular its skilled elements. Lastly, when the implied norm propagates and becomes law or an official standard, the accumulated experience acts as an entrance barrier. This consideration tempers the need for explicit binding rules – in any case, where social pressure is sufficiently strong (see OECD, 1997).

6. A distinction needs to be made here between the transition towards this new order and the new order itself. The transition, providing its financing is correctly organised, will induce a temporary boom similar to that of post-1945 reconstruction. The real problem lies in the sustainability of the new order ten or so years after the transition begins. P. Quirion (1999) goes through all the forecasting and calculable general equilibrium models that test the assumption of a pollution tax on energy recycled as a reduction in employers' social insurance contributions. The results predict variable but low impact on GDP growth (compared with a continuation of the present order), and a clearly favourable impact on employment (up to +1-2%). They confirm the instinctive idea of a Labour/Earth substitution, with the factor Capital changing more in form than in quantity. The findings are all the more remarkable in that Labour/Energy elasticity is greater in the model, and the model's degree of disintegration enables restructuring of consumption and production to be better apprehended (DIW, 1994; Barker, 1997). It should be noted that this research deals with local and not internationally co-ordinated policies. They confirm, incidentally, that a country does not run much competitive risk by being the first to take action.

   To be honest it must be emphasised that, according to these models, environmental regulations do little to accelerate traded GDP growth; by reducing pollution, they do, however, make it more sustainable – the "primary dividend" increases *net* domestic product. Such regulations are a necessary, but not sufficient, condition for a long boom. At best, they could be expected to produce quickened growth in employment. Sufficient conditions would involve regulation of supply and demand, and new work organisation paradigms. As to the extra-environmental conditions for the "New Great Transformation", see Lipietz, 1997.

7. For a more detailed analysis of "local" modes of environmental regulation, see Lipietz, 1998.

8. Land-clearing does, however, put the human race in contact with reservoirs of unknown germs, and this can be a cause of new epidemics such as Ebola-virus disease.

9. Let us again remember the precedent of bovine spongiform encephalopathy (mad cow disease), apparently due to the mutation of a prion, which was innocuous to humans for centuries as long as it remained in sheep, but which jumped the species barrier as the result of new livestock industry practices.

10. In France, CO_2 emissions are also measured by the mass of carbon atoms in the gas. In other countries, they are measured by the molecular mass (3.66 times greater) of CO_2. This chapter uses the French system.

11. At the height of Fordism, between 1950 and 1970, the quantity of direct labour per product unit was divided by three in France. Such a rate, kept up over forty years and applied to energy efficiency, would be more than enough to fall within the sustainable CO_2 envelope, without reliance on nuclear energy. See Goldemberg *et al.*, 1987.

12. From 1990 to 1996, world emissions grew by 17%, those of the United States by 9%, Japan's by 11%. The EU countries almost stabilised theirs (France +1.6%, Italy +3%, United Kingdom –0.4%, Germany –8%). The emerging economies posted spectacular increases (China +33%, India +44%, Korea +75%). Yet China and India, which together contain nearly half of the human race, still do not much influence the world total, which is growing at half their speed.

13. With 1990 as base year, the idea was to reduce emissions of six GHGs by 2010, on a four-yearly sliding average, by a CO_2 equivalent of –8% for the EU, –7% for the United States, –6% for Japan and –5.2% for the Annex I Group.

14. The European Commission proposes a pollution tax, joining together GHG deterrence and promotion of energy-saving, regardless of source.

15. As before, these are mechanisms by which one country finances the reduction of pollution in another country and "credits itself" with the reduction obtained.

16. The Commission of the European Union is considering a pollution tax of $10 per barrel of oil equivalent, which it feels is enough to return to a sustainable level in Europe. This being a ceiling price for QELRO quotas, the floor-price could be something like $8 per boe.

Bibliography

AGARWAL, A. and S. NARAIN (1991),
Global Warming in an Unequal World: A Case of Environmental Colonialism. New Delhi: Centre for Science and Environment.

BARKER, T. (1997),
"Taxing Pollution Instead of Taxing Jobs: Towards More Employment Without More Inflation Through Fiscal Reform in the UK" in T. O'Riordan (ed.), Ecotaxation. London: Earthscan.

COMMISSARIAT GÉNÉRAL DU PLAN (1998),
Energie 2010-2020. Paris: CGP.

DIW-DEUTSCHES INSTITUT FÜR WIRTSCHAFTFORSCHUNG (1994),
"The Economic Effect of Ecological Tax Reform", DIW Economic Bulletin No. 7, Bonn.

GLYNN et al. (1990),
"The Rise and Fall of the Golden Age: An Historical Analysis of Post-War Capitalism in the Developed Market Economies" in Marglin and Schor (eds.), The Golden Age of Capitalism: Reinterpreting the Post-War Experience. Oxford and New York: Clarendon Press.

GODARD, O. (1996),
"Stratégies industrielles et conventions d'environnement : de l'univers stabilisé aux univers controversés", Environnement-Economie, Proceedings of the Paris Colloquium, 15-16 February 1993, INSEE-Méthodes Nos. 39-40, pp. 145-174.

GOLDEMBERG, J. et al. (1987),
Energy for a Sustainable World. Washington DC: World Resources Institute.

LIPIETZ, A. (1995),
"Capital-Labour Relations at the Dawn of the 21st Century" in Schor and You (eds.), Capital, The State and Labour: A Global Perspective. London: Edward Elgar.

LIPIETZ, A. (1997),
"The Next Transformation" in Cangiani (ed.), The Milano Papers: Essays in Societal Alternatives. Montreal: Black Rose Book.

LIPIETZ, A. (1998),
"Economie politique et écotaxes", Report to the Prime Minister's Council for Economic Analysis, 16 April, Conseil d'Analyse Economique No. 8. Paris: La Documentation Française.

OECD (1997),
Environmental Policy and Employment. Paris: OECD.

POLANYI, K. (1957),
The Great Transformation. Boston: Beacon Press.

QUIRION, P. (1999),
"Les conséquences sur l'emploi de la protection de l'environnement", Doctoral thesis, Écoles des Mines de Paris.

WORLD COMMISSION ON ENVIRONMENT AND DEVELOPMENT (1995),
Our Common Future. United Nations.

WORLD RESOURCES INSTITUTE (1990),
World Resources 1990-1991: Guide to the Global Environment. Washington DC: World Resources Institute.

6

Policy Drivers for a Long Boom

by

DeAnne Julius
Monetary Policy Committee, Bank of England

The probability that the world economy will experience a sustained period of significantly higher growth – referred to throughout this volume as a long boom[1] – during the first quarter of the 21st century is low. The statistical odds, judging from past history, are against it. Over the past two centuries, with the exception of post-war spurts of rebuilding, world growth appears to have stayed within a narrow track of around 3% during most periods.[2] This is probably because economic growth is the by-product of such a complex web of technological, social, demographic and political developments that even if trends in one or two of them take a sudden surge, the overall result is held in check by the others. Recent history does not even suggest that growth is rising. Despite rapid technological change and the absence of major wars, the 1990s and 1980s have seen slower world growth than the 1970s and 1960s.

Against this backdrop it may seem fanciful to consider the policy requirements for a long boom. Yet to say that such a boom is improbable is not to say that it is impossible. Supportive policy – however defined – is likely to be a necessary though by no means sufficient condition for it to develop. Given the transformation that a sustained period of high growth could bring to the lives of a large share of the world's population, policies that could increase its probability deserve careful consideration. These may not be the same policies that deliver "growth as usual", because a long boom is clearly unusual. Just as a runner setting out to break records in the marathon may need a different training regime from one whose goal is to improve a bit over last season's average, so the policy drivers for a long boom may be more radical and arduous than the conventional prescriptions.

The type of policies needed will depend on the underlying dynamics of the boom itself. The first section below reviews the basic economic framework for decomposing growth into its constituent parts and suggests how each of these might drive a long boom over the next quarter-century, given the initial conditions of the late 1990s. The sections following develop three geographic scenarios for long booms with different dynamics that depend in part on the technological, social and demographic characteristics. None of these scenarios is a "base case", in the sense of a most likely forecast of world growth, since all are defined as outside the bounds of historical probability. But as a thought exercise it is useful to have a stretch target – say, 3.5 to 4% average annual world growth for 25 years – to sharpen the focus on growth-enhancing policies. By specifying the fundamental drivers of each scenario it is possible to identify which policies would be most important, and which policies should be avoided, if such a boom is to be created and sustained. The scenarios are not mutually exclusive, but they are driven by quite different dynamics in order to clarify the logic involved in different pathways and to trace the political and social strands that accompany different economic outcomes. They represent three different ways that a long boom could be created if the facilitating policies were put into place. The final section compares these policies, identifies overlaps and contrasts the degree of policy infrastructure required to drive the three boom scenarios.

1. An economic decomposition of growth

At the most general level, the growth of world output (or GDP) depends on the growth of world inputs of labour and capital and the growth in efficiency of the process of turning inputs into outputs. The last term, variously called the Solow residual, disembodied technical change or total factor productivity (TFP), is estimated as the residual of an aggregate production function, with labour and capital as its independent variables. It is generally interpreted to include technological change, in the broadest sense. As well as new technology, TFP sweeps up managerial innovations, improvements in the quality of labour, regulatory changes, etc. While many restrictive assumptions are necessary to apply this framework in a strictly numerical sense,[3] it is nonetheless useful in classifying the possible sources of a long boom into labour-led, capital-led and productivity-led. Combinations of these are used in the scenarios developed below, but at this stage it would be helpful to consider them separately.

a) Labour-led

A step-change in the labour input into the global production function over the next 25 years will not come from the OECD Member countries, which currently account for around 60% of world GDP. The labour force in most Member countries will peak during that period and the hours per worker are static or declining (OECD, 1998a). Japan is at the forefront of this trend. Its labour force may have already peaked (at 68.6 million in 1997) and the numbers are likely to fall rather rapidly as the population ages (Statistical Bureau, Government of Japan, 1998). In other OECD countries the trend towards earlier retirement, even if it merely stabilises at current levels, will bring labour force growth to an earlier end than has been predicted.

If there is to be a labour-led long boom, it will have to be strong enough in the developing countries to more than offset the fall in labour-based growth in OECD countries. This is certainly possible. There are three trends which could intertwine to create a huge increase in the economically productive labour force of developing countries. First, the demographic bulge from high reproductive rates over the past four decades will continue to increase the size of the working-age population for decades to come, despite declining population growth rates now in all regions. Second, the continuing shift of labour out of subsistence agriculture and into the market economy increases the effective size of the labour force for a given population profile. This process could be accelerated by advances in bio-technology and food production during the coming decades. Third, the long-term investment in primary and secondary education in developing countries is now delivering a rapidly rising share of skilled labour in the total workforce. The proportion of highly skilled is also rising, and in several Asian countries where education is highly valued, the share of the labour force with university-level qualifications has already overtaken that in several European countries. All three of these trends are well established and likely, over the next quarter-century, to bring about a step-change in the growth of the quality-adjusted, economically available labour force for the world economy. The scenario called "Growth Shift" is based partly on this labour-led dynamic.

b) Capital-led

Despite at least three decades of globalising capital markets, it is still the case that national investment rates are closely correlated with national savings rates.[4] Although the world's pool of savings is large and growing in absolute value, only a very small share crosses borders in search of the most productive investment. Since it is highly unlikely that risk-adjusted rates of return on investment are already equal across countries, this implies that there must be scope for a step-change in capital-led growth through better allocation of global capital.

In the 1970s and 80s the focus was on raising savings rates in the developing countries and expanding the cross-border flow of investment funds from the slower-growing capital-rich countries to the faster-growing capital-scarce ones. Both of these roads to raising economic growth through capital-deepening were succeeding, spectacularly so in Asia. However, the financial crises beginning in 1997 in Thailand and spreading to Korea, Indonesia and then beyond Asia during 1998 have led to a sobering reassessment of capital-led growth.

With hindsight it is clear that investment can be too high as well as too low, especially when domestic financial institutions and corporate boards are weak or lack external checks and transparent accounts. In some countries the situation was further aggravated by devoting monetary policy to an exchange rate target that was under upward pressure from large inflows of foreign investment. Asset prices rose precipitously, wasteful investment was undertaken because of the artificially low cost of capital and the perception of foreign exchange risk, and the countries' vulnerability to financial market turbulence – whether externally or domestically provoked – grew alarmingly. When the price bubbles burst and the exchange links broke, the shock and cross-country contagion was much greater than implied by pre-crisis risk premiums.[5]

Many of the policy lessons being drawn from the Asian crisis are not supportive of a long boom scenario. Tighter bank regulation, controls on short-term capital inflows, gradual debt workouts and larger stand-by arrangements by the international financial institutions may all be worthy, and in some cases even necessary, reactions to what has already occurred in the most affected countries. They may also help prevent similar crises in other countries in the future. But they are essentially damage-limitation devices rather than growth-enhancing ones. Two of the scenarios below, the aforementioned Growth Shift and another called "Growth Clusters", develop alternative policies to facilitate a capital-led stimulus for a long boom.

c) Productivity-led

A step-change in (total factor) productivity growth is most futurologists' favourite candidate for driving a long boom. This is logical, both because TFP growth has been the largest single contributor to overall economic growth in most countries in most periods in the past, and because the evidence is all around us of rapid innovation in fundamental fields such as those relating to information and communications technology (ICTs), biotechnology, new materials, nanotechnology, etc.[6] It is already clear that many of these have widespread applications across industrial sectors, and that some (particularly ICTs) are already changing the way businesses operate internally and the way they interact with their suppliers, employees and customers. As with the steam engine and the rise of the railroads, or the internal combustion engine and the spread of the automobile and road transport, such fundamental technologies can roll out over decades to transform organisational structures, industrial location, employment patterns and the social and environmental fabric of communities and cities.

The dynamics of such technology-led growth are so complex that broad-brush (but internally consistent) scenarios are one of the only tools available for their economic analysis.[7] Each of the following scenarios is based on technology-led growth. The first depends on *leading edge* developments in new technologies and new applications of existing technologies. One important driver in the "Growth Leader" scenario is that firms in those countries that are the key players in ICT, bio-technology, advanced automotive development and other large-scale research-intensive areas generate powerful growth spin-offs for the rest of their economies and reap the intellectual property rents from the rest of the world. Remaining at the leading edge of these technologies requires massive investment, which tends to mean that large firms in established markets reap the largest gains.

A second type of technology-led growth is through the application of *catch-up* technologies and transfer of best practice. In the Growth Shift scenario the main stimulus to growth comes from the transfer of new and existing technologies and their related organisational structures to production facilities outside the OECD Member countries. Coupled with the dynamic of rapidly expanding, well-educated but still relatively low-cost labour in the developing countries, and the shrinking workforce in the OECD countries, catch-up technology transfer creates a quick and powerful route to sustained higher growth in many developing countries.[8]

Third, the biggest technological impetus to growth in the first quarter of the 21st century may NOT come from any new breakthroughs that are made in the research labs of large companies and governments, but from an innovative explosion of *small-scale applications* of ICTs that transform supply and value chains in both the manufacturing and service sectors. The biggest beneficiaries of this would be small firms and highly skilled individuals who suddenly gain access to the same real-time information and global customer base that only large multinational firms had in the past. The optimal boundary between firm and market – between those activities that can most efficiently be carried out inside the firm and organised through hierarchies and those that are cheaper to outsource and organise through contracts (Williamson, 1975) – may already be shifting strongly towards markets. If technological and policy developments accelerate this shift, it could result in the scenario called Growth Clusters, in which communities of specialised firms and individuals congregate where their aggregate productivity is greater than the sum of their parts. The location of these clusters is partly serendipitous, partly influenced by history, geography and policy. But through their success in providing what the global consumer wants, they shape growth in their industries and link into each other for supplies and support, regardless of location.[9]

In addition to the organisational choice between firms and markets, the decentralising tendency of ICT will affect the relative efficiency of the public and private sectors. Much of the early rationale for public sector provision was based on economies of scale (telephones, transport, post offices, utilities) or informational externalities (healthcare, higher education). Innovations in communication such as mobile telephones and e-mail, along with the near-zero cost of making information available to household decision makers (potential patients, students and parents), will erode some of the advantages of state provision. Thus in Growth Clusters we finally see the long-heralded decline of the nation state.

2. Three geographic scenarios for a long boom

The focus of this book is on the possibility of a *global* long boom, for which there is no historical precedent. It is nonetheless the right focus, because the most striking initial condition of the 21st century is also without precedent: the degree of global interconnectedness. Not only (or even mostly) on the economic front, but also in scientific research, in popular fashion and music, in environmental concerns and in news and current events, the world scale is more relevant than the nation scale. There are no island economies left.

Yet there are island governments. And it is the geographic dimension of any long boom that will determine policy, because policies are made and enforced by geographic entities: states; regional and international organisations; international treaties signed by states; communities and sub-regions with delegated authorities; etc. Thus we need to map the forces that could create a long boom into geographic scenarios that can provide the basis for policy.

Each of the three scenarios below is self-contained and built upon its own internal logic. Each is thus a stylised version of how the world might develop. No probabilities are assigned to them; each represents a logically possible but statistically improbable future. If they are well-built scenarios, then the real future is likely to contain elements of each. In that sense they are not mutually exclusive, and within each there may be some countries, or some industries, that follow other routes. As with economic models, scenarios inevitably simplify the world they attempt to portray in order to illuminate the key causal relationships and keep their size down to a manageable level. But, as the quantification in the last section shows, there is no scope for diluting the policy requirements in any of these scenarios without jeopardising their growth prospects. None provides an easy or automatic route to a long boom.

a) Growth Leader

In this scenario the United States consolidates its position as the economic and political hegemon for at least the first quarter of the 21st century. Its economic leadership derives from a complex of technological, macroeconomic and institutional features that provide a favourable environment for leading-edge, technology-led growth. Information/communications technology and, later, biotechnology evolve into the "general purpose technologies" (Lipsey, in this volume) that drive the long boom. In ICT, many of the leading-edge advantages that come from setting industry standards have been appropriated by US companies such as Microsoft, Oracle, Netscape and PeopleSoft. One reason is that breakthroughs in digital technology often come from individual entrepreneurs and small, start-up companies, both of which flourish in the low-tax, flexible-labour-market, equity-driven environment of the United States. Another is that when large-scale resources are required for the marketing and development of new ICTs, the competitive US market in corporate control facilitates the partnership or, more often, the purchase of start-ups by established players with easy access to the deep domestic capital markets.

The application of ICT to wave after wave of industrial sectors (continual re-engineering) continues to happen first and fastest in the United States, driven by domestic competition and shareholder-value pressures. This strong demand response to falling ICT costs creates a positive externality for the rest of the economy. The cost-saving benefits of new ICT developments are broadly spread, enhancing the international competitiveness of US companies across a range of product and service sectors.

The social turbulence created by such Schumpeterian restructuring is aggravated by the wide and sudden differences in wealth created by equity-driven rewards. This degree of social disruption and income divergence is less politically tolerable in other OECD countries, yet it may be a necessary condition for generating a long boom through rapid, technology-induced change.

Biotechnologies are also likely to advance fastest in the United States due to scale economies and the importance of pre-commercial research in universities and government labs. The protection of intellectual property rights (IPR), upon which the diffusion of biotechnology depends, is also well-established in the US market.

The macroeconomic fundamentals of the US economy as it enters the 21st century are supportive of this Growth Leader scenario. A decade of political wrangling over the budget – including such memorable extremes as a shutdown of federal government spending and Congressional threats of default on the national debt – has finally resulted in a sustainable budgetary balance which turns into an ever-growing surplus (at current tax rates) under even modest assumptions of economic growth (US Congressional Budget Office, 1998). In the US political context, there can be little doubt that such emerging surpluses would result in tax cuts rather than spending increases. This tight fiscal position allows the monetary stance to be accommodating, which both economic theory and comparative history suggest is the optimal policy mix for sustainable (investment-led) high growth with low inflation. Despite low interest rates, the dollar is likely to rise against the euro in this scenario, reflecting the relative productivity improvement in the United States and acting as a brake on the international competitiveness of US firms.

US political leadership, derived initially from the collapse of the Soviet superpower in the late 1980s, was reinforced by the difficulty the European states had in agreeing common foreign and defence policies during the 1990s and by the long-running Japanese recession which weakened Japan's political influence both in Asia and beyond. With each crisis that arose – Iraq, Bosnia, Korea, Indonesia, Russia – it became increasingly clear that US leadership was required for international action to take place. Thus, in Growth Leader, policy initiatives in the early 21st century have to match the US agenda.

Europe and Japan also benefit from technology-led growth in some sectors and through their market integration with the United States. European companies continue to lead in chemicals and pharmaceuticals, and many of those in service sectors gain from the scale advantages and competitive spur provided by the introduction of the euro across most of the single market just after the millennium. Japanese companies retain their lead in consumer electronics, computer peripherals and advanced automotive engineering (including hybrid electric/gasoline models and car navigation systems). The commitment to research and the close integration of design and production in large Japanese companies help them to regain their competitive prowess in this scenario, where scale and efficiency are keys to remaining at the technological frontier.

Although their economic growth is strong, on the social and political front this is an uncomfortable world for Europe and Japan. The hyper-competitive pressures emanating from the United States, coupled with its undisputed political clout on the international stage, mean that there are continual commercial and policy pressures to converge toward the US socio-economic and legal models. In Europe the burden of high social overhead costs must be reduced, pension financing reform becomes an urgent budgetary priority, agricultural support payments are increasingly disciplined through the WTO, and European governments more generally are forced to scale back their activities for budgetary reasons. All of these changes are growth-enhancing in the long run, but they require wrenching political trade-offs.

In Japan the current economic crisis has already provoked a number of TV commentators and editorial writers to campaign for a complete redesign of the Japanese economic system based on "Anglo-American style capitalism" (Fukushima, 1998). The Japan Association of Business Executives, Keizai Doyukai, recently published a booklet entitled "Declaration of Market Ideology" which argues for corporate governance along American lines. A decade of further restructuring ensues – first in banking, then in the corporate sector – as Japan transforms itself yet again. By 2010 Japanese companies and banks are again leading many world rankings and the domestic service sector has been dramatically modernised by new investment.

For the developing countries too, there is economic gain coupled with some political pain in Growth Leader. Latin America gains from its proximity to the US market, but it chafes under the renewed influence of US banks and multinationals on its domestic politics, both directly and indirectly through the central role of the United States in shaping IMF and World Bank policies. East Asian countries, especially China, are also vulnerable to political strains with the United States but their ties with its West Coast, where much of the ICT development takes place, bring high economic rewards.

For this scenario to deliver the long boom on which it has been predicated, international policy initiatives have to reflect US priorities, and the domestic policy refrain outside the United States becomes (with apologies to Frank Sinatra), "We did it your way!" Most of the policy reform would be domestic, driven by the pervasive pressures of policy competition in this economically integrated world. In most European countries the focus would be on labour market reform to increase flexibility, fiscal consolidation to allow tax rates to fall, privatisation of state-owned industries, and the gradual scaling back of welfare support, probably through tighter eligibility criteria. This is an agenda scarcely likely to appeal to the eleven of fifteen EU countries currently led by socialist, or at least left-of-centre, governments. The pressures for change would come from the corporate sector, faced with the competitive need to restructure their businesses based on falling ICT costs, and from institutional shareholders managing internationally diversified investment portfolios. Profit performance by the "best in class" in each industry would rapidly become the yardstick by which other firms in that industry are judged. Individual share prices often exhibit winner-take-all behaviour in their overshoots and crashes as international investors reassess their company rankings. This would put strong pressure on corporate management to follow industry leaders (often headquartered in the United States) in downsizing or outsourcing.

At the international policy level, few initiatives would be required – or could be delivered – in this scenario. The basic thrust of postwar trade and investment liberalisation would be maintained. However, US attempts to focus new WTO rounds on IPR and sectoral negotiations in services (taking further the financial services and telecommunications agreements and adding new service sectors), rather than on the "old" areas of agriculture and textiles, would be resisted as unwelcome action to undermine the "grand bargain" tradition of past rounds. Those international institutions with a structure that allows a heavy US influence would grow in importance – *e.g.* the IMF, the World Bank, the OECD, NATO – while those that do not would decline, at least in relative importance – *e.g.* the UN, the WTO, the ILO. The United States would often take the route of bilateral negotiations in areas of particular interest such as intellectual property (as it has done with Korea, Chinese Taipei, Japan and others), which would tend to spread US standards directly and thereby reinforce the competitive position of its companies. The response to international crises, whether of political or financial origin, would become more *ad hoc* and based on personal diplomacy rather than formal institutional structures.

As long as the United States Government remains committed to international engagement and to building a new world order, albeit in their own image, then

Growth Leader can deliver a long boom, led by those countries that can converge most rapidly and successfully on the US economic model.[10] *Laissez-faire* capitalism provides a highly nourishing culture for growth by the strongest and most enterprising firms. And inside existing firms and government organisations there is still a huge potential for x-efficiency gains in productivity if downsizing and re-engineering were to be ruthlessly pursued. But this scenario has a fragile political base, particularly in Europe and in the larger developing countries where US influence is likely to be most resented. It is also vulnerable to swings of political opinion in the United States and it is difficult to see how global environmental problems could be tackled. It is not an attractive scenario for most of the world, and its political feasibility is its weakest link.

b) Growth Shift

In this scenario the economic centre of gravity of the world economy shifts decisively from the OECD countries to the emerging market economies[11] (EMEs) in Asia and Latin America. This shift is driven by an economic dynamic in the EMEs and by a coincident but independent social dynamic in North America, Europe and Japan.

In the richer countries of the OECD, the shift in consumer preferences towards services and away from goods, which began in the 1980s but slowed in the 1990s, gathers pace in the early decades of the 21st century. This is partly because many services, especially customised ones, are "luxury goods" for which demand grows more rapidly than income as income itself rises. Gourmet meals in fine restaurants are an example. As household income increases, expenditure on such meals rises from a once-a-year anniversary treat to a once-a-month outing with friends. Holidays abroad are another example; the statistical relationship between demand and income traces a classic S-curve shape. When an economy's average income level passes into the steep part of the curve, total demand tends to grow very rapidly for a decade or two. This provides a strong growth stimulus to those industries supplying such luxury goods. As the two examples above demonstrate, such industries may be domestic (because essentially non-tradable) or foreign. But when customising is involved, the domestic element tends to increase.

The ongoing shift in the OECD consumption basket towards (mostly non-traded) services (*e.g.* entertainment, leisure activities, gardening, education, health) and away from goods (*e.g.* food, clothing, appliances, automobiles) has a profound effect on employment creation, relative wage rates, and manufacturing industry's choice of location for expansion. Services tend to be more labour intensive than goods, and less susceptible to automation. Thus the demand for labour in the service industries rises by more than it falls in the OECD countries' manufacturing industries. At the same time, because of demographic change, the overall supply of labour is stagnant or shrinking in most of the Member countries. Average real wages are bid up despite low productivity growth in the service sectors. In some countries this leads to higher immigration, but in most it simply widens the gap between inflation in goods and services.[12]

Although at the millennium most manufacturers' largest markets are still in the OECD countries, demand growth there is stagnating while EME demand is accelerating. Coupled with the rise in wage costs in the OECD, and the increasingly well-educated workforce in the EMEs, it makes overwhelming sense to locate new production in the EMEs. As policy reforms lower the commercial and financial risks associated with investment in those countries, some existing capacity in Member country markets is also closed in favour of new capacity in the EMEs. By 2025 the share of manufacturing employment in the OECD countries is below 10%.[13]

Demographics and the prospect of medical advances from biotechnology provide additional drivers for Growth Shift. The rise in population share of retired people in OECD countries over the next decades will be dramatic. For the OECD area as a whole the dependency ratio[14] will rise from below 55% in 1990 to nearly 65% by 2030, with most of this increase in the retired end of the age range. In the most extreme case, Japan, the ratio will go from below 45% in 1990 to nearly 70% by 2030. The social welfare implications of this shift will put increasing strains on the tax and spending requirements of those countries – mostly in Continental Europe – whose pension systems are primarily state-financed. But while change may be difficult and protracted, these are wealthy countries whose retirees are increasingly among the most financially sophisticated and politically influential groups in society. Their long-term interests are unlikely to be neglected.

The young and well-educated have considerable bargaining power in the workplace. Their skills are in demand and many of them work in sectors that are sheltered from international competition. The scope for collusive behaviour is high, by the younger generation in the workplace and by the older generation with time to devote to special interest groups. OECD countries in Growth Shift are classic examples of Mancur Olson's "stable societies with unchanged boundaries" which "tend to accumulate more collusions and organisations for collective action over time... Special interest organisations and collusions reduce efficiency and aggregate income" (Olson, 1982). Yet many of these special interest groups also contribute to society through their work in the voluntary sector, improving the local environment and providing social services to those in need. Such charitable work is not counted in the GDP but it clearly contributes to the quality of life, both of those providing the services and of those who benefit from them.

Medical advances, both in drugs (Viagra) and in interactive treatment/prevention therapies (physiotherapy, massage, health clubs, spas) are of particular interest to the affluent retirees with time to spare. As knowledge expands and brings new drugs and treatments to the market-place, a growing share of expenditure (either private or public, depending on the healthcare delivery system) will be devoted to health and medical services. As with leisure services, a large share of these is non-tradable.

There are two key differences between the retirees of the 1970s and 1980s and those of 2000-25: the latter are healthier and wealthier. Medical technology and pharmaceuticals that are now under trial (e.g. for cancer detection, osteoporosis) will greatly improve the quality of life and extend the productive potential of the retirees. And they will have money, as well as time and energy, to spend. In the United States 80% of financial assets belong to people over 55. In Europe, because of the wars and hyperinflation of the 1914-44 period, the generation retiring over the next decade is the first to inherit significant housing wealth from their parents. In Japan, because of high savings rates, the average household already has net financial assets equivalent to 2.3 times its annual income. This is why "there is no sense of urgency from the ordinary Japanese citizen for demanding a higher growth rate" (Fukushima, 1998).

Savings and pension investment funds, whether publicly or privately funded, will become significant players in international asset allocation. The numbers involved are already enormous. In the United States the total assets of the mutual fund industry (many of which are held in 401k retirement accounts) are as large as those of the banking industry at around $5 trillion (Hale, 1998). The number of funds offering international equity investments expanded from 29 in 1984 to 543 in 1996, with assets of over $215 billion. American pension funds began diversifying earlier and had over $480 billion in foreign markets by the end of 1996. Most of these foreign assets are elsewhere in the OECD countries, but over the early decades of the next century, as OECD area growth rates slow, fund managers increasingly look to stock markets in EMEs to boost their portfolio returns.

The net result is that the OECD countries in Growth Shift become capital-rich *rentier* societies working fewer hours, spending more time on leisure and family-related pursuits, retiring earlier and specialising in end-user services such as art, fashion, sports, tourism, gardening and home improvements, health and education. Their rate of economic growth slows (to around 1% p.a.), while their labour force is shrinking. Thus the low average growth rate accommodates a faster growth in labour income for those in the workforce and a higher marginal propensity to consume (because of accumulated savings) of many of those no longer in the workforce.

Meanwhile in the developing countries, achieving high rates of economic growth and the rise in living standards it brings remains the top priority, pursued with renewed vigour and determination after the unexpected setback of the late 1990s "Asian crisis". The silver lining in that crisis was the cathartic effect it had in sweeping away the old corporate structures and bureaucratic powers in the most affected countries that had contributed to inefficient investment and poor risk management. With the vested interests gone or fatally weakened, exchange rates reset at hyper-competitive levels, domestic industries more open than ever to foreign direct investment (FDI) and macroeconomic stability regained, the area known as "developing Asia" enters the 21st century poised to be a huge engine for economic growth.

The critical policy requirements for a long boom in this scenario are mostly at the international level. They are the policies needed to support a major increase in cross-border trade and capital flows from OECD countries to the EMEs. On the trade front there must be a continuation of WTO-bound trade liberalisation, lowering tariffs further in those sectors where protection is still high and finally bringing textiles and agricultural products under the full WTO disciplines. China and Russia should be brought into the WTO by 2000. The resources available to the WTO Secretariat should be doubled to enable it to provide the intellectual leadership and negotiating support necessary to make rapid progress in these difficult areas.

FDI represents the quickest route to raising total factor productivity in the EMEs and to penetration of the OECD market-place by goods produced in developing countries. Both greenfield investment and mergers/acquisitions are means to these ends. Several Asian countries have already eliminated or raised their ceilings on the share of foreign ownership that is allowed, and there are signs of some companies in Member countries reviving their investment plans. With the collapse of the Multilateral Agreement on Investment (MAI) negotiations at the OECD in 1998, it is important that FDI be brought fully onto the WTO agenda (not just trade-related investment). The author has suggested elsewhere that the WTO dispute settlement procedures should be made available for disputes over FDI, and that the private companies involved in any such international disputes should be given full access as affected parties (Julius, 1994).

Restarting cross-border bank lending and stimulating portfolio investment by OECD country pension funds into the stock markets of the EMEs will require policy changes on both sides. The "Asian crisis" has dealt a severe blow to the appetite for cross-border financial flows by both lenders and recipients. Yet large increases in such flows are essential if demand and output in the EMEs are to recover promptly and lay the groundwork for the production shift that drives this long boom. The EMEs will need to increase transparency in their banking systems, inject new discipline into corporate sector governance and apply international accounting standards to corporate accounts. Such reforms will make it easier for Member country fund and bank managers to assess risk and compare returns with those available from similar companies in home markets. In Growth Shift it would rapidly become obvious that the highest returns were in the EMEs. International agreements are not necessary to achieve such reforms, but they could be encouraged by IMF and Bank for International Settlements (BIS) discussions with EME governments and central banks.

To allow the share of pension fund investment going into EMEs to increase, it will also be necessary to liberalise pension investment rules in some of the OECD countries. Member country pension reform more generally is needed in this scenario. With the exceptions of the United States, the United Kingdom, Switzerland and possibly Australia,[15] state-provided benefits will have to be reduced, tax incentives increased for private pension contributions, and restrictions on where pension funds can invest relaxed to allow asset diversification.

Cross-border investment of all kinds would be hugely facilitated if stable exchange rates could be established between the investing and recipient countries. There is no easy or low-risk way of achieving this in a world of deeply integrated and open capital markets. But the major historical period of large-scale long-term investment by Europeans in Latin American railway and other bonds took place during the gold standard era. The closest modern equivalent is the currency board.

In Growth Shift a system of regional currency boards gradually develops. Not all developing countries choose this route (or manage to stick to it once chosen), but many of the Latin American countries adopt the US dollar; the euro is favoured by eastern European countries, parts of Africa and the non-oil-exporters of the Middle East; and hybrid varieties including the dollar, euro and yen are adopted by many Asian countries and the oil-exporters. This requires some accommodation by the three anchor central banks in terms of money creation, which is co-ordinated through the IMF just after the millennium. Although exchange rate targets are not agreed, the heads of the three central banks pledge themselves to the same target range for inflation in order to stabilise expectations about exchange rate movements among the big three currencies.

Because this is a world where the economic interests of the OECD and EME countries are so clearly intertwined, it is easier to reach international agreement on global environmental protocols.[16] Industrial energy use shifts to the EMEs along with manufacturing capacity. A system of tradable permits for carbon emissions, with initial country allocations based partly on population and partly on current energy use, is agreed, with global patterns to be reviewed every five years. Trading (i.e. buying and selling) is freely permitted as long as trades are transparently registered with a central record-keeping authority. However, this system does not really start to bring about significant reductions in global carbon emissions until it is joined by a tax and regulatory drive, led by OECD countries, to raise the share of renewable energy in their own total energy consumption. The resulting increase in demand for solar panels, underpinned by rising government targets looking ten years ahead, brings the unit cost of solar energy down sharply through capturing economies of scale, which also makes it the economic choice for new generating capacity in many developing countries.

c) Growth Clusters

In both Growth Leader and Growth Shift, the policies that permit rapid growth are national policies, sometimes internationally agreed. By contrast, in Growth Clusters the critical geographic unit of growth is not the nation but the city or small geographic region.[17] Thus in different global industries the leading-edge companies are found in such places as Singapore, Silicon Valley, Shenzhen, the City of London and Canary Wharf, Route 128 around Boston, Bangalore, the Hsinchu Science Park outside Taipei, Paris and Milan.

In this scenario, the communications revolution built on the Internet during the 1990s creates a step-change in productivity growth in the 21st century like that of the Industrial Revolution in the 19th century. As with the development of mass production, the disappearance of communication costs transforms the economic supply chain that links suppliers to producers to customers. The difference is that cyberspace transfer of knowledge, co-ordination of production, and advertising/sale of product are almost instantaneous. The cities and regions that are home to the dynamic companies that develop new ways to produce, distribute and sell quickly rise above their neighbours and connect to each other like nodes on a global economic overlay.

The driving forces in this scenario are network competition and agglomeration economies. While competition between companies is fierce – made fiercer for being global – it has shifted onto a more complex plain that is also more difficult to regulate. Network competition is often about competing standards – e.g. operating systems or Internet browsers in computers, GSM *versus* CDMA in cellular telephony. The company or group of co-operating companies whose standard becomes the generally accepted one gains a huge advantage. But the consumer also gains from a generally accepted standard; indeed, without it, the gains from rapid diffusion of technology will not bring about the long wave of growth on which this scenario is predicated.

Agglomeration economies are the gains to one firm derived from locating itself close to other firms or to its key customers. Early work in economic geography used the idea to explain the location and growth of cities, where the gains were primarily in terms of savings in transport costs either of inputs from other firms or outputs to final consumers (e.g. cities with ports or at railway nodes). More recently the growth of industrial clusters has been studied by Rosabeth Moss Kanter (1995) and Michael Porter (1998) as a basis to advise cities and regions on enhancing their attractiveness for inward investment and job creation.

Clustering is particularly evident in rapidly changing industries that are intensive in highly skilled or highly specialised people, such as software development, financial services, leading-edge medical care and cinematography. New firms are formed in the cluster, new people are hired or poached from other firms already there, independent contractors or consultants set up locally to provide specialist skills particularly to new firms, and the entire cluster grows in its attractiveness to both customers and competitors. The initial location of such private sector growth is often serendipitous, but when it is supported by public sector investment in infrastructure (e.g., modern airport development), speedy processes for planning permission and reasonable tax policies, then a powerful dynamic for regional growth is created.

While local politics is probably the biggest obstacle to the creation of a growth cluster, there are also intrinsic geographic elements that come into play. Being "too close" to an already successful cluster can be a severe limitation. The hopeful newcomer faces almost insurmountable competition from the established rival, both for resources and in terms of the choice and depth of what can be offered to the customer. For example, in the airline industry a carrier whose hub is at a large established airport with frequent flights (some by rivals) to the most popular locations and short transfer times for connecting passengers can command higher prices than a new competitor operating from a smaller city nearby or a less established airport. The customer clearly benefits from (and therefore is willing to pay for) the concentration of flights at a single source that permits greater frequency and ease of rescheduling. Another example is the difficulty of establishing local theatre companies in suburban towns close to a major theatre centre such as London. The best actors and directors can always earn more in London where the theatres and audiences are larger, while the suburban theatre-goers are reluctant to pay London prices for a local performance, however professional.

For global financial centres the time zone is a critical geographic limitation. As dealers in a firm with offices around the world pass the trading book from one centre to another in 24-hour markets such as foreign exchange, it makes economic sense to concentrate trading activity in just three or four cities where 8-hour/day markets can touch. With New York and London long established in two of those zones, it would be difficult for Boston or Frankfurt to take over their lead roles in foreign exchange dealing. In East Asia, by contrast, exchange markets are newer and there is less difference in the volume of business done in Tokyo, Hong Kong and Singapore; regional dominance is not yet established.

In a world of relatively free trade, capital and information flows, the hard-to-shift advantages conferred by history and geography may be the key determinants of high-growth industrial location. The long-term effects of this on social patterns and income distribution are difficult to predict. Agglomeration economies have their own self-correcting mechanism built in. A cluster becomes more and more attractive for a certain industry and its relations for a time, but at some point the cost of fixed assets such as land and well-located buildings starts to rise and congestion externalities begin to erode productivity growth. This puts limits on the attraction of capital and highly skilled people into existing clusters. New ones will form around entrepreneurs or investors who choose unspoilt, low-cost locations for those reasons. There are also some new service industries, such as call centres, where ICT has allowed the jobs to move to the available workers rather than vice versa. Call centres have been a major source of new employment in the north of England, Ireland, parts of India and Jamaica. There are also two ubiquitous industries – agriculture and tourism – which are unlikely to be subject to job clustering.

For all these reasons, clusters are likely to prove more significant for output (GDP) than for employment, and if overall economic growth is high then new cluster creation is rapid. The social risk in Growth Clusters is that regional disparities in per capita income within countries may increase. However, there are also at least two offsetting socio-economic benefits created by Growth Clusters. First, ICT, including the Internet, enables many otherwise isolated entrepreneurs and small firms with specialised skills or new products to access the global marketplace. This helps them overcome whatever national, ethnic or locational disadvantages that might otherwise hold them back. ICT also brings cross-border educational opportunities through distance learning courses to people who could never afford to travel to attend such courses in person. And second, beyond the economic benefits, ICT enables people to stay in touch with their relatives and friends more easily, cheaply and directly than ever before. It is hard to place a value on these largely free gains in social inclusion, but the rise in cyber cafés for youth around the world and the growing use of Internet e-mail by the elderly attest to the ability of ICT to benefit socially vulnerable groups.

The "winners and losers" table of countries is also more difficult to predict in this scenario than in the others. ICT has levelled the playing field for firms and communities regardless of their country affiliation. Countries with a tradition of small-scale enterprises (India, Taiwan, Italy) might be expected to thrive. Those with highly educated, English-speaking business classes would have an advantage (India again, Korea, the Philippines, South Africa). City-states such as Singapore and Hong Kong, China and successful small countries such as the Netherlands have always thought in terms of clusters, hubs and networking in their policy design. Japan might have particular difficulty adapting in this scenario because of its distinctive language, hierarchical culture and high local costs relative to the rest of Asia.[18]

Many of the policy requirements for economic success in Growth Clusters relate to the cluster itself. To promote and sustain a cluster it will be necessary to have high-quality inputs in the form of educated people and efficient infrastructure. But the real gains in productivity, at least according to Michael Porter (1998), come from complementary investments and policies by the public and private sectors:

> Leaders of businesses, government, and institutions all have a stake – and a role to play – in the new economics of competition. Clusters reveal the mutual dependence and collective responsibility of all these entities for creating the conditions for productive competition. [...] The lines between public and private investment blur. Companies, no less than governments and universities, have a stake in education. Universities have a stake in the competitiveness of local businesses. By revealing the process by which wealth is actually created in an economy, clusters open new public-private avenues for constructive action.

Such partnerships between firms and local governments would also be an effective way to tackle pollution, congestion and other local environmental problems. It is possible that this model could be scaled up to the international level, where there is already substantial advisory participation by business leaders (*e.g.* at the Rio and Kyoto conferences). But it is difficult to see how the private sector could take the initiative on an issue such as global warming where the trade-offs between countries are central to its solution.

Growth Clusters are more likely to develop if global standards and global networks are allowed to evolve in response to competitive pressures and customer choice. Thus beyond productivity-enhancing local policies and partnerships, a global long boom will require international advances in competition policy, intellectual property protection, and the relatively untracked field of policies relating to electronic commerce.

Competition policy may be the most difficult. To allow market-driven development of global standards, governments will have to redefine some of their traditional tests for monopoly power, contestability and anti-competitive behaviour. The current US Government case against Microsoft illustrates how complex the issues are. The triple-jeopardy faced by American Airlines and British Airways in their battle with regulators in Washington, London and Brussels for approval of their airline alliance demonstrates another flaw in the current approach. When the relevant market is worldwide, the need for consultation and then mutual recognition of regulatory approval is urgent. International jurisdiction is probably an impossible dream.

The Internet makes intellectual property protection and the policing of IPR violations more difficult. Yet without it the gains in information exchange and market penetration by small companies are unlikely to be sustainable. Because information is global, the appropriate policy forum for most IPR discussions is the WTO. Its mandate should be extended beyond trade-related intellectual property and its dispute settlement procedures made more open and transparent to the companies concerned.

Finally, electronic commerce, upon which the high growth of this scenario depends, will need to be nurtured by supportive regulation. A substantive start towards defining regulatory principles was made at the October 1998 OECD Ministerial Conference.[19] The basic thrust is that tax treatment should be neutral between electronic and conventional commerce; that business and governments should work together to protect and enforce IPR in cyberspace without imposing burdens on intermediaries; that government policies should facilitate market-driven standards that are interoperable; and that mutual recognition of regulatory schemes for privacy or consumer protection is crucial. Much thinking remains to be done, however, in jurisdiction, choice of law agreement, and enforcement issues.

This scenario also has implications for the evolution of government policies. As e-commerce comes to represent a large share of total consumption, its taxation will become more complex, especially for countries with VAT systems. The current trend of moving from direct (income and profits) taxation to indirect (sales and value-added) taxation is likely to be reversed. The domicile of people and firms is easier to track than their transactions.

Common standards of all types facilitate e-commerce as long as they are market-driven, voluntary and (thus) open to competitive challenge. English would become even more widely used as the language of business. Generally Accepted Accounting Principles (GAAP) would be voluntarily adopted by companies across the clusters to attract equity investors. Two or possibly three currencies – the dollar, the Euro and the yuan – would come to dominate world commerce with most prices quoted in them. The choice of currency would generally be determined by what the customer uses, not the producer. Banks would offer special international charge cards to facilitate e-commerce purchases with minimal transaction costs and liability coverage for fraud. Such shifts in the burden of consumer protection from regulators to private firms would be a central feature of Growth Clusters.

3. Policy overview for a long boom

This chapter has presented three scenarios, each of which could deliver a quarter-century of above-average world economic growth. Growth Leader does this through productivity gains by big firms and governments based on large-scale, leading-edge technology in information/communications and biotechnology, driven by economic and policy competition emanating mostly from the United States. In Growth Shift global productivity gains come from the transfer of production and technology to emerging market countries where the skilled labour force is rapidly expanding. OECD countries become low-growth, but high-income, *rentier* societies where employment and spending are increasingly focused on services. Growth Clusters is truly a new world order where the role of national governments withers and private/public partnerships at the local level are the deciding factor for competitiveness. Productivity growth is driven by the reshaping of global distribution (supply and value chains) by the rise of electronic commerce and the new opportunities it brings to individuals and small firms, regardless of location.

GDP growth rates consistent with these scenarios are shown in Table 1. The OECD countries would continue at roughly their present growth rates in Growth Clusters, with higher productivity growth offsetting the fall in labour force growth. In Growth Leader the whole OECD area would achieve the high growth performance of the United States during its 1990s upswing. This would require total factor productivity growth approaching 2.5% per year for 25 years, which is outside the historical bounds derived from a growth accounting framework. It would require serious corporate and public sector restructuring to capture x-efficiency gains as well as technology-led growth. The OECD countries' slowdown in Growth Shift reflects the structural shift of their economies towards services, with their lower productivity growth, as well as the preference shift from labour to leisure, especially by older people.

For the developing world, all of the scenarios show higher growth than that experienced over the past two decades.[20] This is consistent with the optimistic intent of long boom scenarios that are not constrained by including a maximum likelihood case. Indeed, it is not possible to create a global long boom unless developing countries do better than they have recently. Their performance in Growth Leader is only slightly better than the recent average, since little of the leading-edge technology development takes place outside OECD countries, and the international policy climate is only marginally better for the developing world in this scenario than at present. In Growth Clusters there is a rapid transformation of growth potential around key cities and enterprise zones in the developing world, which pulls them into the global (electronic) market-place

Table 1. **GDP growth 2000-2025**

Average annual percentage

	Growth Leader	Growth Shift	Growth Clusters
OECD countries	3.0	1.0	2.5
Non-OECD	4.5	6.0	5.0
World	3.7	3.7	3.7

Source: Author.

much faster than was possible in the past. And in Growth Shift emerging market economies show very strong growth as catch-up technology and skilled workers enable them to leapfrog in some sectors to the levels of productivity seen in industrial countries today. The prices of manufactured goods fall, their production shifts to the developing world, and trade volumes grow at double-digit rates for more than a decade.

These divergent growth rates in the OECD and developing countries create strikingly different distributions of world GDP by 2025 in the three cases, as shown in Table 2. In Global Leader world output is evenly split between developed and developing countries, compared to the roughly 60/40 split at present. However, in Growth Shift today's balance has been decidedly reversed in favour of the developing world.[21]

Table 2. **World GDP shares**

	2000	Growth Leader 2025	Growth Shift 2025	Growth Clusters 2025
OECD	60	51	31	45
Non-OECD	40	49	69	55
World	100	100	100	100

Source: Author.

From the discussion above it is possible to identify three common international policy requirements for a long boom and the key additional policy areas for developed and developing countries in each scenario. Before listing these, however, there are three more general comparisons that can be made about the policy intensity and focus of the different scenarios.

First, all three scenarios require major policy reform or new initiatives in some parts of the world in order to deliver a long boom. Even with optimistic assumptions about technology drivers, sustained high growth depends on policy change.

Second, the focus for policy action is at different levels in the three scenarios. In Growth Leader it is predominantly national governments that need to reform their labour and welfare policies (in the OECD countries) and restructure corporate control and foreign ownership laws (in the developing countries). In Growth Shift the major policy action is at the international level through the WTO and IMF; this enables the acceleration of trade and capital flows that drive world growth. Growth Shift is also the scenario that has the best chance of tackling global environmental problems. In Growth Clusters the private sector takes the lead, both at local/regional and at international levels, often working in partnership with the public sector to develop growth-enhancing infrastructure and to define the principles for self-regulation and broadly compatible standards in electronic commerce.

Third, while all scenarios require policy action to deliver high growth, the degree of policy change – what one might call the "policy intensity" – differs among the three. Growth Shift has the highest policy intensity, but it also has a higher upside to growth than the other two[22] and is the only scenario likely to address global warming concerns. Growth Clusters needs less actual policy change, but it rests upon private/public mechanisms that are still in their infancy and deals with the virgin area of electronic commerce with few policy signposts to guide it. Growth Leader has the lowest policy intensity; it requires few changes in the United States or at the international level, and its internal competitive pressures would produce strong domestic forces for political change in Europe, Japan and beyond the OECD area. However, many of these changes would be politically difficult to achieve, and the scenario is vulnerable to opinion shifts in the United States as well as to global environmental threats.

At the international level there are three policy priorities that are common to all scenarios:

– *Trade liberalisation* – As a minimum (in Growth Leader and Growth Clusters) the current international undertakings through the WTO must be maintained, anti-dumping complaints resisted and rulings by the WTO's dispute settlement panels complied with. There are worrying indications, from steel to bananas, that the current economic slowdown, the price effects of recent devaluations in East Asia and the looming US election season may combine to increase trade frictions. Backsliding on openness to trade would swiftly kill any hopes of a long boom in the new millennium.

  In Growth Shift the WTO process for liberalisation and expansion needs to be accelerated. Textiles and agriculture need finally to be brought under full WTO disciplines. China and Russia need to be brought quickly into membership. To do this, as well as handling the broader agenda of issues below, the resources available to the WTO Secretariat would need to be substantially increased.

– *Intellectual property protection* – All three scenarios rely on the rapid transfer of new information/communications and other technologies between OECD countries and the emerging market economies (in Growth Leader and Growth Shift) or high-growth clusters (in Growth Clusters) in other parts of the world. Unless intellectual property rights are protected and enforced, this transfer will not take place. With growth increasingly dependent on these technologies, concerns about IPR could lead to new technological access barriers against those countries where lack of enforcement is suspected.

The start made in the Uruguay Round on trade-related intellectual property needs to be broadened to all IPR, and a special focus should be given to the problems of copyright and related protection needed for electronic commerce.

 – *Foreign direct investment* – Both greenfield investment and substantial equity investments (up to and including 100% ownership) will need to be accelerated to generate the higher growth rates in developing countries that all three scenarios postulate. One of the painful lessons of the 1997/98 Asian crisis is that short-term portfolio flows and cross-border bank lending do not provide a sound basis for long-term development. They can be helpful at the margin, but they also carry high risks for small economies with thin financial markets and vulnerable exchange rates.

Since the collapse of the MAI negotiations at the OECD, it is even more important that FDI (not just trade-related investment) be brought fully onto the WTO agenda. Its dispute settlement procedures should be opened to companies and governments where they are the directly affected parties.

In addition to these common international policy priorities, it may be helpful to highlight the single most important enabling policy focus for OECD and developing countries in each scenario. These are shown in Table 3.

Table 3.   **Key enabling policies**

	Growth Leader	Growth Shift	Growth Clusters
OECD countries	Domestic economic restructuring to improve flexibility in the EU and openness in Japan/Asia	Pension reform, both in financing and to remove investment restrictions	Competition policy reform to better accommodate ICT and other network industry growth
Non-OECD countries	US-style corporate governance and accounting transparency	Open trade and FDI-friendly policies, especially in manufacturing	Physical and policy infrastructure for linking into e-commerce

Source: Author.

Even with fair geopolitical and technological tailwinds, the extent of policy change required to reach a higher global growth path is sobering. None of these scenarios is easy to achieve, and only one may be capable of early action on global environmental concerns. Yet taken together, they suggest a set of policy priorities that can significantly raise the chances of a global long boom. It is worth remembering that such scenarios are not mutually exclusive. In this case, the policies conducive to the success of one are not detrimental to the others. Predicting the future developments that differentiate the three scenarios – both in technology and in politics – is a hazardous game. Proceeding on all three policy fronts is the best bet for the new millennium.

Notes

1. In this chapter the term refers specifically to a period in which both productive potential and aggregate world demand are growing at higher than historical rates, so that the real GDP growth rate increases while world inflation remains stable.

2. See the Introduction to this volume.

3. In particular, neoclassical growth accounting assumes constant returns to scale. OECD estimates of ten Member countries' growth during the 1970s and 1980s showed that the 2.9% average annual GDP increase was composed of 0.6% growth in the labour force, 1.1% growth in capital and 1.2% TFP growth (Sakurai *et al.*, 1997).

4. This was first brought to widespread attention by Feldstein and Horioka (1980), and has since been corroborated by many others.

5. Among the many analyses of the causes of the Asian crisis, one of the best is Miller and Luangaram (1998).

6. See Lipsey's chapter in this volume.

7. Wack (1985), McRae (1994).

8. Evidence on the strength of this catch-up route is found in Proudman *et al.* (1998).

9. An even more extreme version of this technology-driven organisational change is Malone and Laubacher's depiction of the "e-lance economy" run by electronically linked freelancers, as described elsewhere in this volume by Lipsey.

10. In a speech earlier this year, Alan Greenspan, Chairman of the Federal Reserve Board, seemed to suggest this is the way the world is heading when he said: "My sense is that one consequence of this Asian crisis is an increasing awareness in the region that market capitalism, as practised in the west, especially in the US, is the superior model; that it provides greater promise of rising standards of living and continuous growth." The affected countries in Asia are "endeavouring to move their economies much more rapidly toward the type of economic system that we have in the US" (FED home page, 1998).

11. The author uses this term loosely to refer to all low- and middle-income countries with relatively stable political conditions. In practice, for this scenario, most of Africa and the Russian Federation would probably be excluded. The term "developing countries" is here synonymous with non-OECD.

12. This assumes that countries have an explicit or implicit overall inflation target. If it were, say, 2% and wages and service prices were growing by 3%, then assuming a

50-50 split of consumption between goods and services, goods prices could only be growing by 1%. This simple arithmetic is complicated by the traded/non-traded character of goods/services and by the important share of consumption out of wealth rather than wage income in this scenario.

13. See Brown and Julius (1993) for another route to this figure based on an analogy with the shrinking share of agricultural employment in five OECD countries during the earlier part of this century.

14. Defined as the population below 14 years of age and over 65, divided by the total population.

15. The first three countries already have low state-provided pensions and large pension trust funds in either public or private sectors. Australia has recently implemented pension reforms.

16. See Lipietz's chapter in this volume for a description of the difficulties encountered at Rio and Kyoto.

17. Michael Porter has recently published an article in the Harvard Business Review (Nov./Dec. 1998) in which he also uses the term cluster to describe a "geographic concentration of interconnected companies and institutions in a particular field" that affects competition by "increasing the productivity of companies based in the area... driving the direction and pace of innovation... and stimulating the formation of new businesses, which expands and strengthens the cluster itself." Although some of his links to productivity growth go beyond what could be expected and he does not focus on the importance of interconnected clusters, the ideas are sufficiently similar that the author has retained the same term.

18. Japan is currently 21st in the number of Internet domain names registered per capita, partly because it requires those wanting a jp identification in their Internet address to use a Japanese service provider whose prices are among the highest in the world (Fortune, 1999).

19. See the OECD.org site for the background papers and documents resulting from "A Borderless World: Realising the Potential of Global Electronic Commerce".

20. For the period since 1974, the average annual real GDP growth of developing countries excluding the former Soviet Union and Eastern Europe was 3.5% (World Bank, 1997).

21. The calculations behind Table 2 do not take into account possible shifts in exchange rates between OECD and non-OECD countries. Over such a long period, and with much higher economic growth in the non-Member countries, their currencies could be expected to appreciate against those of the OECD, a possibility explored in Brown and Julius (1993). Such exchange rate trends would increase the share of the developing countries in world GDP, but it would be an exaggeration to assume that they would reach full purchasing power parity by 2025 or that they could do so without a significant effect on export growth. Thus the figures in Table 2 are closer to a lower bound estimate for the non-OECD share based on the other assumptions of each scenario.

22. It is possible to imagine the OECD countries growing somewhat faster in this scenario. The social preferences story that drives their accelerated shift to services and the tilt in their labour/leisure choice is an internally consistent but not logically necessary counterpart to the high growth in the developing countries.

Bibliography

BROWN, Richard and DeAnne JULIUS (1993),
"Is Manufacturing Still Special in the New World Order?" in Richard O'Brien (ed.), *Finance and the International Economy: 7, The Amex Bank Review Prize Essays*. Oxford University Press.

FELDSTEIN, M. and C. HORIOKA (1980),
"Domestic Savings and International Capital Flows", *Economic Journal* 358, June.

Fortune magazine (1999),
"Wrapping the Web in Red Tape", 1 February, p. 24.

FUKUSHIMA, Kiyohiko (1998),
"Asia Shift, High Tech Shift, and Reform Shift: Silver Lining Behind Japan's Stagnant Economy". Paper presented to the 12th Asia Pacific Roundtable, June.

HALE, David (1998),
"Has America's Equity Market Boom Just Begun or How the Rise of Pension Funds Will Change the Global Economy in the 21st Century". Unpublished paper.

JULIUS, DeAnne (1994),
"International Direct Investment: Strengthening the Policy Regime" in Peter Kenen (ed.), *Managing the World Economy: Fifty Years after Bretton Woods*. Washington DC: Institute for International Economics.

McRAE, Hamish (1994),
The World in 2020. London: HarperCollins Publishers.

MILLER, Marcus and Pongsak LUANGARAM (1998),
"Financial Crisis in East Asia: Bank Runs, Asset Bubbles and Antidotes". CSGR Working Paper No. 11/099, University of Warwick, July.

MOSS KANTER, Rosabeth (1995),
World Class: Thriving Locally in the Global Economy. Boston: Harvard Business School Press.

OECD (1998*a*),
Maintaining Prosperity in an Ageing Society. Paris: OECD.

OECD (1998*b*),
"A Global Action Plan for Electronic Commerce Prepared by Business with Recommendations from Governments", SG/EC(98)11/REV2, October.

OLSON, Mancur (1982),
The Rise and Decline of Nations. London: Yale University Press.

PORTER, Michael E. (1998),
"Clusters and the New Economics of Competition", *Harvard Business Review*, November/December.

PROUDMAN, James, Stephen REDDING and Marco BIANCHI, eds. (1998),
Openness and Growth. London: Bank of England.

SAKURAI, N., G. PAPACONSTANTINOW and E. IOANNIDIS (1997),
"Impact of R&D and Technology Diffusion on Productivity Growth: Empirical Evidence for Ten OECD Countries", *Economic Systems Research*, Vol. 9, No. 1, pp. 81-109.

STATISTICAL BUREAU, GOVERNMENT OF JAPAN (1998),
Monthly Report on the Labour Force Survey, August.

US CONGRESSIONAL BUDGET OFFICE (1998),
"The Economic and Budget Outlook: An Update", August.

WACK, Pierre (1985),
"Scenarios: Uncharted Waters Ahead", *Harvard Business Review*, September/October.

WILLIAMSON, O.E. (1975),
Markets and Hierarchies: Analysis and Antitrust Implications. New York: Free Press.

WORLD BANK (1997),
Global Economic Prospects and the Developing Countries. Washington DC.

Annex

List of Participants

CHAIRMAN

Donald JOHNSTON
Secretary-General
OECD

PARTICIPANTS

Fernando ALVAREZ
Director of Economic Studies
CEMEX
Mexico

Walter BRINKMANN
Senior Vice-President
Coca-Cola Greater Europe
Belgium

Paul A. DAVID
Professor of Economics
Stanford University
United States

Frederik von DEWALL
General Manager and Chief Economist
ING Group
The Netherlands

Emilio FONTELA
Professor of Economics
University of Madrid
Spain

Robert GOEBBELS
Ministre de l'Économie,
des Travaux Publics
et des Transports
Luxemburg

Orhan GÜVENEN
Under-Secretary
State Planning Organisation
Prime Minister's Office
Turkey

David HALE
Global Chief Economist
Zürich Insurance Group
United States

Martin HUEFNER
Executive Vice-President
Hypo Vereinsbank
Germany

David HUMPHREYS
Chief Economist
RIO TINTO plc
United Kingdom

DeAnne JULIUS
Member of the Monetary Policy
Committee
Bank of England
United Kingdom

Alain LIPIETZ
Professeur
Centre d'Études Prospectives
d'Économie Mathématique
Appliquées à la Planification
(C.E.P.R.E.M.A.P.)
France

Richard LIPSEY
Professor of Economics
Simon Fraser University
Canada

Maria LIVANOS CATTAUI
Secretary-General
International Chamber of Commerce

Wolfgang MICHALSKI
Director, Advisory Unit
to the Secretary-General
OECD

Herbert OBERHÄNSLI
Vice-President, Economic Studies
and International Relations
Nestlé
Switzerland

William PFAFF
Writer on Contemporary History
and Politics
The International Herald Tribune
The Los Angeles Times Syndicate
France

Christopher PLEISTER
Member of the Board
DG BANK Deutsche
Genossenschaftsbank AG
Germany

Peter SCHWARTZ
President
Global Business Network
United States

Robert J. SHAPIRO
Under-Secretary for Economic Affairs
Department of Commerce
United States

Horst SIEBERT
President
Kiel Institute of World Economics
Germany

Friedrich-Leopold von STECHOW
Member of the Board
DG BANK Deutsche
Genossenschaftsbank AG
Germany

Kari TAPIOLA
Deputy Director-General
International Labour Organisation

Jitsuro TERASHIMA
General Manager
Mitsui & Co., Ltd.
Japan

Bernd THIEMANN
Chairman of the Managing Board
DG BANK Deutsche
Genossenschaftsbank AG
Germany

Heiko THIEME
Chairman
American Heritage Management Corp.
United States

Ignazio VISCO
Head of the Economics Department
OECD

Martin WOLF
Associate Editor
Financial Times
United Kingdom

OECD SECRETARIAT

Barrie STEVENS
Deputy Head, Advisory Unit
to the Secretary-General

Riel MILLER
Principal Administrator, Advisory Unit
to the Secretary-General

Pierre-Alain SCHIEB
Principal Administrator, Advisory Unit
to the Secretary-General

Also Available

21st Century Technologies: Promises and Perils of a Dynamic Future
(03 98 03 1 P), ISBN 92-64-16052-3   140 FF   US$23

Energy: The Next Fifty Years
(03 99 01 1 P), ISBN 92-64-17016-2   160 FF   US$29

China in the 21st Century: Long-term Global Implications
(03 96 05 1 P), ISBN 92-64-14924-4   120 FF   US$33

The Economic and Social Impact of Electronic Commerce
(93 99 01 1 P), ISBN 92-64-16972-5   135 FF   US$22

Open Markets Matter: The Benefits of Trade and Investment Liberalisation
(22 98 01 1 P), ISBN 92-64-16100-7   120 FF   US$20

Trade, Investment and Development: Reaping the Full Benefits of Open Markets
(22 99 01 1 P), ISBN 92-64-17111-8   120 FF   US$21

Trade, Investment and Development: Policy Coherence Matters
(22 99 02 1 P), ISBN 92-64-17112-6   120 FF   US$21

For a complete listing of OECD publications, see the OECD Online Bookshop at:
www.oecd.org/bookshop.

How to contact us:

OECD Paris Centre
2, rue André-Pascal – 75775 Paris Cedex 16 – France
Tel.: (33.1) 45.24.81.67 (sales enquiries)
Fax: (33.1) 45.24.19.50 (sales enquiries)
E-mail: *sales@oecd.org*

Online orders: *www.oecd.org/bookshop* (secure payment with credit card)
Orders by fax: (33.1) 49.10.42.76

OECD PUBLICATIONS, 2, rue André-Pascal, 75775 PARIS CEDEX
PRINTED IN FRANCE
(03 1999 02 1 P) ISBN 92-64-17029-4 – No. 50791 1999